Change Your Life with

Self Hypnosis

Change Your Life With

Self Hypnosis

Unlock your healing power and discover the magic of your mind

Michael Hadfield

ISBN-13: 978-1-491-08529-5

ISBN-10: 1-491-08529-0

For my wonderfully, kind, thoughtful, generous, and loving daughters,

Vicki & Jenny.

I love you both.

"If you always do what you've always done, you'll always get what you've always got."

Henry Ford (1863-1947)

American founder of the Ford Motor Company

Contents

Acknowledgements

I would just like to thank my LCCH tutor, Jane Bannister, who, many years ago, ignited in me a fascination for the things that I never imagined hypnosis could accomplish. I am especially thankful to Jane for introducing me to that marvellous subject - PsychoNeuroImmunology (PNI). PNI is at the heart of most of the content in the Body section of this book.

The Journey

One day Alice came to a fork in the road
and saw a Cheshire cat in a tree.
"Which road do I take?" she asked.
"Where do you want to go?" was his response.
"I don't know," Alice answered.
"Then," said the cat, "it doesn't matter."

Lewis Carroll

The Journey

**"Let others lead small lives, but not you.
Let others argue over small things, but not you.
Let others cry over small hurts, but not you.
Let others leave their future in some-
one else's hands, but not you."**

Jim Rohn

This book has the power to change your life.

Many people suffer unnecessarily. Anxiety, stress and worry affect millions. Introverts live uncomfortably in an extroverted world. People suffering from chronic shyness end up lonely and isolated. Physical problems, for which there is no medical treatment, are endured when it is possible to ease the discomfort and improve life quality. There are people who feel lost, without direction, and have no idea that help is available because they themselves are unable to *label* the problem.

The real problem, of course, is what to do.

Medical experts either prescribe drugs that ease the symptoms but do not cure, or offer nothing more than ineffective counselling.

What is wanted is a solution.

But no one is providing it.

The mistake is to look for the solution outside of you. The answer lies within. I am sure that you have come across this idea before, and maybe even tried self-healing and had no success, but that can only be because the approach you tried was not structured appropriately.

The world is changing rapidly. In the past the medics were in charge; drugs actually seemed to cure; hospitals were magical places where you went in sick and came out well; but people are now realising the truth. The truth is that much of what doctors

prescribe is just making money for incredibly wealthy pharmaceutical companies. These companies abuse their power by playing on the fears and hopes of the ignorant.

People are looking for new solutions. People are realising that
there is an intimate connection between mind and body. This
intimate connection makes it possible for you to use the power
of your mind to control and direct your destiny. But with that
power comes a new freedom – the freedom to impact your own
mental, physical, and spiritual health. When you learn how to
use this connection, at the very least, it could mean the difference
between suffering and peace.

Along with this realisation that you can control your own destiny
comes a freedom like no other. The difficulty is recognising that
this possibility exists and then acting upon it in order to make it
your new reality. You see, what you are about to encounter in this
book are ideas that many would dismiss out of hand – simply
because they still believe in the old world where the power of
life, death, and medication lies in the hands of a few specialists.

The new world is one of personal power and the freedom to be
who you want to be. So what I am providing here is an opportunity for you to discover how easy it is to use your own mind to
impact your mood states, your relationships, your confidence and
comfort, as well as your body's natural processes. All it requires
of you is that you follow a simple process, learn some new skills,
and make a commitment to take action, because without action
nothing changes.

I know that these things are true because I have been helping to
bring about positive change in people's lives for around 15 years
now. But in my own past I suffered for many, many years from
chronic anxiety, I was also severely agoraphobic - a shy introvert
who never seemed to quite find his place in the world.

I was someone who never seemed to fit in. My solution was to
withdraw. I did this so well that I experienced intense anxiety at
the mere thought of a social encounter.

I have seen doctors, psychiatrists, psychologists, been addicted to tranquillisers, and even spent 6 months in a psychiatric hospital. None of that did anything at all until I realised that the only cure was going to come from me. So the drugs only stopped when I decided to stop taking them. And I started to find answers and solutions when I started looking.

But it seemed that, as soon as I took personal responsibility, doors magically started to open and I was eventually led to hypnosis as a way to speed up the whole process of healing. I quickly realised just how powerful this technique was to solve problems like stress and lack of confidence. I was also very surprised to discover that hypnosis was equally powerful with physical symptoms too.

I have a reasonable expectation that if I can move from where I was to a place of professional respect and social ease, then you can too. The only thing I had going for me, eventually, was the realisation that I deserved better and that I was going to keep looking until I found it. If it is possible for me to find peace, enjoyment, and satisfaction in life, then it is possible for you to do the same.

What I am about to teach you in this book is what I have learned myself over the years. I am not only sharing with you my insights and knowledge, but also a way to learn how to do this for yourself – a way that is simple and easy. If you can close your eyes and daydream, then you can do this.

But understand also that *just* reading this book will not fix you. You are actually going to have to do something. You are going to have to follow my simple instructions if you want to achieve the results you are hoping for. This book is theory and practice. I know that you really wanted just reading the book to fix you without you actually having to do anything, but don't give up on yourself just yet.

This book can help you to improve your life, your health, and your enjoyment, just by following my advice. Once you have learned the basic skills, you can make progress quickly and easily.

Habits require no effort, so once you make this a habit then you will find that it becomes a normal and natural part of your day. From that moment on you will notice your life becoming richer as you realise that you have a valuable contribution to make to this world.

I would suggest that you read this book from front to back and resist any temptation to go straight to the chapter relating to the main difficulty in your life. This book is structured so that you build your way up to health and well-being. Even if a chapter appears to have no relevance to you right now, there are valuable insights to be gained in each one. Once you have been through it once then you can jump in anywhere you like.

The book is split into four main parts. The first part, *The Journey*, teaches you the skills you need. The remaining three parts, *Mind, Body, & Spirit*, teach you how to make the changes you wish to make.

The first thing you do in carpentry class is learn how to use the tools you need before you attempt to make a piece of furniture. Shaping wood can be easy or difficult. Cutting off a two foot length of timber is easier with a saw than with a chisel. Using a power saw is less effort than a hand saw.

When you learn to knit you start with simple tasks, then, as skill and neatness develop, you move on to more complicated and intricate patterns. It is no use attempting a sweater with cable stitch running down the front if you have not yet learnt how to maintain an even tension in your knitwear.

It is the same with self hypnosis. You need to learn the basic skills and then, as you develop competence, you can move on to the more difficult tasks. This book is structured to facilitate this. The skills are in the first section which tells you what you need to know about hypnosis; then self-hypnosis; what visualisation skills you need and how to develop them; how to formulate suggestions and why this is especially important. Then finally I introduce the idea of the value of goals and goal setting. Now before you start to think this isn't for you (goals always used to frighten the life out of me), *goals* is a shorthand term that just means *what you want*. A *goal* is just something you *want*. But when you make it a goal it suddenly has more power. It is almost as if, by making it a goal, you are inviting success and satisfaction into your life.

The remaining three sections of the book are about how to make changes. Your mind is the source of your problems so we need to effect change there first. Once we bring peace here, then the door is opened to move forward and really start making the changes that will allow you to live that life you want rather than the life you have. Body will teach you techniques you can use to effect physical changes in your body – even if that is just some symptom alleviation. Once you succeed with a small change, the fact that you feel you have some control will dramatically change the way you feel about yourself. Finally we come to Spirit. This section is purely about that in you which is inspirational – *inspired* is really *in-spirit-ed*. This is how we connect with purpose and meaning in life.

Under each of these three sections I will be dealing with specific problems, like agoraphobia, stress, depression, weight loss, money, confidence, and other problem areas. The individual chapters are arranged in the order that I believe is most beneficial to you.

Before you move on and take the first steps towards mastery of self and life, I need you to know my intention for you with this book. In my experience self hypnosis books tend to be recipe books with a list of solutions for each life-problem you may be struggling with. The idea being that you turn immediately to the appropriate chapter; do what it says; then, hopefully, experience some change.

I have taken a different approach here because I believe the recipe book solution is outdated and ineffective. My intention here is to arm you with the skills you need to become a Master of your own mind and, with my help, learn some new skills and approaches to the life-problems you encounter. Yes, you will find chapters on anxiety and self-esteem as well as weight loss and stopping smoking, but here they are part of a structured step-by-step approach so that by the time you finish the book you will understand your own mind more deeply. You will also be able to apply the skills I have taught you to any situation in your life where you wish to change either your responses or your circumstances. So if you want a quick fix there are better solutions than mine, for a permanent change, read on.

I can help you to take control of your life and make it work for you. The techniques I teach are transferable and as your skills at self hypnosis develop you will realise how easy it is to adapt what you have learned to any new situation in your life. My intention is to teach you how to attain control over your mental and physical world so that your life becomes more pleasurable and is filled with more of what you want and less of what you don't want.

A complete recipe book would be impossible anyway because the list of ills is endless. My intention, therefore, is not to provide you with a book upon which you can develop a dependency. Rather it is to equip you with the skills and knowledge you need. By the time you have completed the exercises within these pages, you will know exactly what you need to do in order to create a solution to any challenge that you encounter in the future.

My aim is to help you become a Master of your own mind. This book will guide you on that journey.

One last thing before we get started.

Some of the treatments need you to do a little preparatory work in order for you to gain the maximum benefit. This occasionally means you need to get a pad and pen.

This symbol...

...lets you know when you need to reach for your pad and pen.

So keep them handy while you read.

...and this one...

...lets you know when it is time to do some trance work.

What's Wrong and How to Make it Right

*"Don't let life discourage you; everyone who got
where he is had to begin where he was."*

Richard L. Evans

If someone has a psychological problem that they need help with, they usually go to their doctor. Depending on the severity of the problem, the doctor will refer to a higher authority (psychiatrist or psychologist), a lower authority (counsellor), and/or prescribe medication. The only medication available is either anti-depressant, with SSRIs like Prozac being the favourite, or tranquilliser. Anti-depressants tend to win, even when the patient has no symptoms of depression, because anxiolytics have a bit of a bad press due to the addictive nature of the benzodiazepines usually prescribed. If it can't be medicated then either a referral or a "come back in two weeks if it is no better" will be the consequence of the visit.

One of the things I noticed from my own experience many years ago, and more recently, the experience of my patients, is that medication doesn't actually fix anything. Psychiatrists and pharmaceutical companies gave up, a long time ago, seeking to find cures. So all they seek to do with their drugs is to alleviate symptoms. Quite apart from anything else, insurance companies will not pay for long periods of treatment for psychological problems. They require a quick fix. If you can suppress symptoms so that a person can at least function again then that is good enough for the insurers even though it falls far short of honouring their customer. They are happy to take your money, but reluctant to give anything of real and lasting value in return. The movie the Rainmaker, starring Matt Damon and Danny DeVito, is a very moving and entertaining exploration of this aspect of health care.

Nowadays it is all about money. In the UK at least, a counsellor costs a lot less than a psychologist, so even if you need a psychologist, you have to endure six weeks of pointless counselling, and that is after waiting anything from weeks to months to be seen. Then you have to wait another two weeks for another doctor's appointment, then ask for another referral which places you on another waiting list which is probably several months long and then the psychologist gets six sessions to fix you. If that doesn't work then you go back to the beginning and start all over again. It is a bit like Monopoly where every time you pass go and collect your $200 you immediately land on Income Tax and have to give your $200 back to the bank. So you just go round in circles forever.

I was in this system in one way or another for around 22 years.

If you have a psychological problem that prevents you from living your life fully, then I hope you can see that the bad news is that you are not going to get any useful help from the medics. *Please note that I am not advocating that you avoid seeking medical help.* Just be aware of getting up your hopes that they will provide a cure. What they can do is provide medication that allows you to stabilise your emotional state and move yourself into a mind state where self-help becomes a real possibility. Certainly if you have a physical problem then it is most important that you seek medical help, even if this is only for a diagnosis so that you know what you are dealing with. From that point on you are free to choose whether or not to take medical advice, but at least find out what the options are.

I am not against doctors. There are wonderful doctors around. There are also excellent doctors who are aware of MindBody approaches to health and will happily share the available options with you – only one of which will be medication. If this is your doctor, then you have an ally in your search for well-being. If they aren't then I suggest you go and find one like this. It is just that for me a doctor is my last port of call. Only when my own knowledge and skills fail to bring about any change will I seek medical advice, but then I have a good doctor who does not push pills. I have only visited a doctor once in the last 13 years, and I came out reassured and without a prescription.

Please note I am **not** suggesting that you treat serious or life-threatening illnesses with self hypnosis. If this is the case, then get your physician's support and use self hypnosis for symptom relief as an addition to your medical care. Hypnosis is very useful for reducing the uncomfortable side effects from things like chemotherapy.

The medical world has gone off somewhere and become totally lost when it comes to mental health and well being. The problem is of course, that they see us humans as bits of bio-mechanical machinery with plumbing, wiring, and a load of internal scaffolding to keep everything in place. They see mind as a function of brain, and physical processes as totally separate from thought processes despite a ton of evidence that suggests otherwise.

The truth is that not only are mind and body intimately connected, but also that the body clearly demonstrates intelligent action independent of brain. It is a well-known fact that stress weakens the immune system. Stressed individuals suffer more frequent minor illnesses because stress, that is negative thoughts about life, has an impact on the health of the immune system and your body's ability to fight disease. Minor illnesses also give a legitimate excuse to avoid engaging with the source of the stress, for a few days.

Unfortunately, the traditional medical model is not geared to cure your problem. The medical model only allows for the alleviation of symptoms, and/or teaching you methods of coping with your difficulties.

I have solutions that will work for you because I am not locked into the short-sighted medical world view, nor am I constrained by budgetary requirements, nor controlled by insurance companies, nor groomed by pharmaceutical companies to prescribe their products. I once had a friend who worked for a pharmaceutical company and whose job was to *entertain* doctors and encourage them to use her company's products, so I have some inside knowledge of what goes on here.

I have been using hypnosis to change people's lives for around 15 years now, so I know that what I do works and that what I am suggesting to you is sound advice borne of years of personal experience treating patients.

A New Approach Is Needed

Clearly a new approach is needed, one that isn't tied to the profitability of drug manufacturing companies and isn't dependent on how much money is available to treat you. Not that there's anything wrong with profit. I hope to make some money from this book. But I believe I have integrity, and that is something I have not noticed with drug manufacturers and insurance companies. Mind you, you only have my word for that, but I hope that by the time you finish this book you will realise that I only want to assist you in having what you want in life. I suffered too much myself in the past to want anyone else to go through that unnecessarily. I have knowledge to share that has the potential to help you find peace. So I am sharing it. I just hope you take advantage of it.

Prozac, one of over 30 available anti-depressants, is taken by 11% of the US adult population. Its manufacturer, Eli Lilly, reported revenue of over $24,000,000,000 in 2011. Anti-anxiety medication (anxiolytics), frequently accompany anti-depressants on prescriptions. Xanax, related to tranquillisers like Valium, generates more revenue than sales of Tide detergent.

The US generates over 60% of the world's revenue for medication for psychological problems.

None of this would be a problem if these things did any good. If they cured the problems they were prescribed for I would have no problem with any of them. I took, for many years, various benzodiazepines, like Valium & Ativan, and anti-depressants, including SSRIs like Prozac, so I know about the effect they have. They numb you for a while, then you need more to maintain the level of numbness. They flatten your emotional responses so joy, happiness, and love are unavailable to you. But there comes a point, as happened with me and many others, where you find you are addicted to the medication. So your visit to your physician not only failed to fix the problem you went to get help for, but you also are left with an additional problem to battle with – your addiction to the medication and the hell you experience breaking that.

Of the 30 or so currently available antidepressants, there is not one that hasn't had to defend a lawsuit against it within 5 years of its approval. You don't hear much about these because settlement is almost always out of court with a very large payment made and a punitive contract signed preventing any mention of the harm the drug is alleged to have caused.

Two psychiatrists received $1.6million each from drug companies for recommending and promoting anti-psychotic drugs for children. Of course once you have a drug you want to popularise, and doctors willing to promote it, you have the stage set for the appropriate diagnosis to be made in order to use the drug, whether or not the symptoms fit.

This is why I mentioned integrity.

You go for help. Then because of profit and convenience you are given something that fails to help in any useful way. Then, when you eventually stop taking it, you find you still have the problem you wanted fixing in the first place.

The approach that the medical world is using to deal with treatable psychological problems is failing the people who need help.

It needs to change.

One of the ways it can change is when you decide to take responsibility for your own health and well being. From this point onwards you are empowered. Once you realise that it is up to you. Once you realise that it is possible for you to change. Once you realise that you can be free of a problem that seems to be part of your very nature. Then all you have to do is to learn the techniques that you need to use to bring this about. And you can bring it about with the comfort of knowing that it is all under your control and you can proceed at the perfect pace for you.

Now is the Time for Change

You can see now that it is time for change. It is time for a huge shift in personal responsibility. It is time for each of us to become responsible for our own health and our own well being. Without this, profit and convenience will win out every time and individuals will continue to suffer when easy and effective help is available.

Taking responsibility for your own health is a serious business, but then it is the BodyMind that you inhabit for the whole of this lifetime, so it makes sense to take care of it. Clearly you want to maximise your enjoyment of this lifetime. However, I need to make perfectly clear that when I advocate personal responsibility I don't mean doing your own surgery. Doctors are wonderful people to have around in health emergencies. They *can* fix some problems with the body, and we continue to require their knowledge and expertise.

What I mean when I recommend taking responsibility is that you become the decision maker. Either do the research yourself, or employ a medical expert to advise you. But ensure that you know that your doctor's input is just one source of information and one set of options and opinions. Get input from other experts. See what all the options are, and in non-emergency situations, my personal recommendation would be to use the least invasive, least potentially damaging, options first. If they work, great, if they don't, then move up a level. This way cutting you open and throwing bits of you away becomes last on the list; drugs with severe side effects, almost last; and all the way up to the least potentially damaging – but still effective.

You see that is one of the reasons I love using hypnosis. It has absolutely no side-effects (other than to make you feel good). It leaves no unsightly scars. Yet, it can be incredibly powerful. Now I know I am a little biased, but you are reading a book on self hypnosis, so I guess you want what I am offering here.

Hypnosis is a good place to start to discover how easy it is to make powerful changes that will reap rewards in a much improved quality of life.

The people who are going to be the winners are those who embrace the idea of being responsible for making the choices about their health. The losers are those who continue to swallow the pills that their overworked physicians prescribe because they don't have any other options. The winners will embrace tools like self hypnosis and discover how to maximise the benefits that this offers to them, but mostly they will be the ones enjoying their lives, achieving their dreams and overcoming any challenges that may come their way.

The disappointment that led to enlightenment

My first clue that all was not as it seemed in the world of medicine was when I had about six sessions with a psychologist *and nothing changed*. My second clue came when I was discharged after six months in the psychiatric unit at Withington Hospital and I still wasn't better. Up to that point I had this insane idea that if only I could get into a hospital where they knew what they were doing then they would 'sort me out' and I could live my life happily ever after.

I left unhappier than when I entered.

That was the point at which I realised that if I was ever to be okay then I would have to do the process of *okaying* myself.

So I started to look for answers.

I found books that helped a little, but it was very much two steps forward and one step back, though sometimes it seemed like three steps back. This was in the days long before the internet, so good and relevant information wasn't that easy to come by. My local library and bookshops were my only sources of information.

I tried out different things, including meditation, and gradually began to get a feel for the direction I needed to move. Then I was referred to a psychologist who was quite different in his approach. He actually used a meditative technique, along with group therapy, as the basis for change.

This was when things really started to come together and I felt some movement towards normality. It was during this period that I discovered that I had a talent for helping and guiding people along the path to wellness. That was when I got interested in hypnosis and subsequently trained and qualified as a hypnotherapist.

Then as I saw more and more people and heard more and more stories, I began to see patterns. I also noticed the power that hypnosis had to bring about huge changes. I remember in the early days one of my patients, at the end of the last session I had with her, said to me about the success of the treatment "it's like when you are a child and you come down on Christmas morning, and when you open your present it is the thing you wanted most in the world."

What I, and hypnosis, had done was to give her what she most wanted. And what she most wanted was her life back after undergoing a traumatic experience that left her in a constant state of fear.

Then as the years went by I realised that the medics had it wrong with regard to mental well being. The standard treatment for things like anxiety, stress, and phobias was medication. More recently counselling is being promoted, but counselling doesn't do what is needed and medication just exposes the patient to unpleasant side-effects without any hope of a cure. I have lost count of the number of patients who come to me, after the drugs have not changed anything, after the counselling hasn't changed anything, always as a last resort. They invariably leave assuring me that if they'd only known about what was possible with hypnosis they would have come to see me first.

Hypnosis is invariably last on anyone's list.

It needs to be first for this sort of problem.

This is why I decided to write this book so I could get the message out that what people see as a last resort needs to be first. It is safe, has no adverse side-effects, and I personally have experienced it producing such powerful results that even the patient has a tough time believing they are real.

Being Different

"The most beautiful people we have known are those who have known defeat, known suffering, known struggle, known loss, and have found their way out of the depths. These persons have an appreciation, a sensitivity, and an understanding of life that fills them with compassion, gentleness, and a deep loving concern. Beautiful people do not just happen."

Elisabeth Kubler Ross

From as early as I can remember I have felt that I was different from others. I have no idea whether that is normal or not, but I certainly had evidence to support the idea. I have a particularly sensitive gag reflex and I remember the excruciating embarrassment of annual school dental checks where, in full view of every child in my year, a dentist would stick things in my mouth.

Fairgrounds highlighted my sensitivity to motion sickness, so where all my friends would come off a ride glowing with pleasure and excitement I'd be feeling seasick. This alone separated me from others because the only thing I could join in with was the dodgem cars.

It seemed to me that the things that everyone else enjoyed were painful to me, and so the process of separation and isolation began. When I was fifteen we were given the opportunity to take a new English exam – the Certificate of Secondary Education or CSE. Part of this exam was to give a five-minute speech. Naturally I declined because the very thought of performing in front of an audience brought on intense anxiety and more isolation.

Then, one day, the deputy head asked our English teacher to send him a couple of lads with good voices. He chose me and my friend Kevin. We had no idea what this was about and when we got to the Head's office we were each asked to read a short piece from the New Testament. It seemed there was no contest between us, I was the winner and my prize was to read a passage from the Bible to the school during morning assembly.

That would mean performing in front of 600 people plus the teachers - but mostly my own class.

I remember waiting backstage. They gave me a chair to sit on while the Head did his usual morning prayers and stuff. I thought I was going to throw up. I thought I wouldn't be able to open my mouth or that I would embarrass myself in some way that I could never live down. That waiting was, I think, the most excruciating anxiety I had ever experienced in my life at that point.

I was introduced and found myself terrified and staring into 600 faces. I knew everyone would hear the fear in my voice as I was reading. Then it was mercifully over. As I was walking off backstage the deputy head came over and although I can't remember his exact words it was something along the lines of *that was brilliant, I'd like you to do it again next week.*

I nearly died.

That was a week from hell. I spent the whole week worrying about my three minute performance. The ten minutes of waiting back stage was even worse this time, and it seems I did just as good a job, but by now Deputy Head was over the novelty of getting pupils to perform and life at school reverted to normal.

This was my first real taste of intense anxiety.

Things rolled along for a while and then my Dad died suddenly when I was 20. Because of this I missed the Easter term of my second year of degree studies and stayed home. I was at the cinema watching a film when suddenly my heart went crazy. Just sitting down relaxed, my pulse shot up. I could not concentrate on the rest of the film and was worried sick all the way home. Over the next few days this kept happening and I discovered that my pulse could go from around 60 to 200 in the space of a couple of minutes. I ended up at the doctors'. He didn't label it just gave me some pills. But once more, here I was being different from everyone else.

When I eventually went back to college I started having panic attacks, but neither of the doctors I saw identified them as such. One pretty much told me to push off and leave him to deal with more serious cases and the other gave me some stomach medicine.

Then my tutorial groups required me to talk and comment and I found this well-nigh impossible so I just avoided those, and life started to go downhill from that point onwards. Interviews were horrendously difficult so how I managed to eventually get a job I am not really sure.

I started my first job at the Met Office in Plymouth and for the first year suffered frequent panic attacks and would often find myself throwing up on the way to the start of my shift. After a couple of years of that I moved to another Civil Service Department, but that entailed a move to London and an unpleasant flat in Hackney. This was followed rapidly by my first *nervous breakdown*. I resigned and came back up north, where I spent the next several years living off tranquillisers, anti-depressants and other odds and ends that my doctor would try me with from time to time. Each drug change produced a return of the intense anxiety, resulting in a dread of my weekly doctor visits for fear of a change of medication.

After two years of this and with my doctor's encouragement I trained as a computer programmer and managed to get a job. Again I experienced much anxiety and frequent vomiting in the mornings and on the way to work. This would be the pattern for many years. There would be intense anxiety, usually around periods of change and then a settling down for a while, before the whole cycle would start again.

Two weeks after starting this new job, I was off sick for two weeks with anxiety. And within five years I was off sick for a whole year; six months of that as a patient in a psychiatric unit where they were attempting to wean me off my tranquilliser addiction.

I only discovered later that part of the problem was agoraphobia, but no one was treating me for that.

Eventually, on my fifth or sixth breakdown and another 10 months away from work my company very kindly allowed me to take the offer of voluntary severance.

The Beginning of the End

So I was once more at home, terrified of going out – not, I hasten to add because being outside frightened me – but because I was terrified of having to talk to anyone.

This went on for a while and at some point I realised, though I am not sure where the realisation came from, that I could stay 'sick' for the rest of my life or I could look for solutions. What drove this was a deep feeling that I was worth more than my current experiences were suggesting. I have always loved reading and when I have a problem my first port of call for solutions is books. Now at this point in my life I had no experience with self-help in any form, so I really didn't know where to look and this was where I had my first experience of that intuitive guidance that, once we have made a definite decision, starts to guide us outside of our awareness.

I felt I was guided towards a book written by an Australian doctor. The book was called Peace from Nervous Suffering. It began to open doors for me. I discovered physiologically what was going on and it gave me a strategy to apply. It wasn't an easy strategy by any means (from what I remember it was pretty much a 'Face the Fear' sort of solution), but it was a strategy and from that moment on things started to get better. The improvement was painfully slow and probably only noticeable to me, but I was soon ready for Dr Weekes Self Help for your Nerves.

Then my doctor referred me for psychiatric help at the local hospital. I met with a psychiatrist, really nice guy, and went through an emotionally very difficult interview with him. At the end of it I was thinking, thank god that is over but I like this guy, I think he might be able to help me. Then, as a parting gift, he said that he was leaving the hospital and my next appointment would be with someone else. So I had to go through the night-mare all over again a month later. After five sessions my new psychiatrist admitted he was making absolutely no progress with me and referred me to a psychologist. My new psychologist, Dr Robin Hensman was brilliant and I warmed to him immediately but after just two sessions he brought me into full confrontation with my worst nightmare – a group session where everyone sits in a circle and talks about their problems.

But before he did that he gave me an interesting document.

It was called Cognitive Relaxation. It was quite a thick photo-copied document that talked about Robin's approach to good mental health, but disguised within its pages was a meditation. When I came for my second visit I mentioned to Robin that his program looked like meditation, he agreed and said that calling it Cognitive Relaxation was more acceptable to the NHS than Meditation. Practising Cognitive Relaxation (CR) had a pro-found effect on my life. CR has similarities to self hypnosis.

The group therapy was the worst and the best thing that ever happened to me. You see one of Robin's *rules* was that no one need do anything that they felt uncomfortable with. I felt intensely uncomfortable talking within a group – so I didn't. But what I did do was use that experience to truly learn how to listen.

As time went on, and the group sessions were three hours long once a week, I became more comfortable and slowly learned that it was okay for me to be feeling whatever I am feeling and doing whatever I was doing. But my intense listening during those early days had an interesting side effect.

I could hear what people were not saying.

What I mean by that is that I discovered that I had an unusual insight into the problems people were discussing. Not only that, but I discovered I had an intuitive insight into the solu-tions too. Robin soon spotted my talent and recruited me to an inner circle he was forming of people with greater insight who could help guide others through the difficult process of becoming well when they believed that their world was falling apart. Later, under Robin's supervision, I started to teach people this meditation technique and to work with them on my own. Their transformation and healing was generally quite rapid.

It seemed I had a talent for therapy.

Then I was in the library one day and the spine of a book caught my eye. It was one of those moments that, when you look back on them, you realise you were being guided. Anyway I picked it up. Its title was Mind-Body Therapy, by Ernest Rossi & David Cheek. I didn't know it was about hypnosis, but by the time I'd finished it I knew that I wanted to learn how to do what they could do. Two things stuck very powerfully in my mind - one was that bleeding could be controlled by hypnosis (this was in a road traffic accident), without a formal trance induction, until medical assistance arrived on the scene. The other was the use of finger signals (ideo-motor responses or IMR) to communicate directly with the subconscious mind and bring about change totally outside of the awareness of the patient (this is the magical aspect of hypnosis).

So I signed up for the best training programme I could find, invested most of my savings, eventually qualified as a clinical hypnotherapist, and in the process discovered lots of interesting things about the Mind. I even discovered how to do impossible things - well things that a doctor or two had said were impossible, though I have long since discovered that the medical profession are not the experts on change and how to achieve it.

Early Success

I was still working with Robin while I did my hypnosis training and so I started to use some of the hypnosis techniques I was learning with my patients – with their permission naturally. One of my hypnosis tutors, Jane Bannister, seemed very much more tuned in to an alternative approach to healing than any of the others and she encouraged me to attend a Masterclass she was giving on a topic with a really weird name – PsychoNeuroImmunology, or PNI. It seemed that PNI was the way to use the mind to heal the body. It is an absolutely fascinating subject and Jane taught it so brilliantly that I couldn't wait to try it out. Masterclasses were normally restricted to fully qualified students, but an exception was made and even though I was only about three months into the course I was permitted to attend.

Then I had a session with one of Robin's patients. I'd seen her a few times before but this time when she arrived she looked really troubled. It seemed she'd had a persistent headache for some time. Painkillers were having no effect. The doctor said it was nothing critical. So I saw a golden opportunity to try out my new PNI techniques. The first time is always really scary because I have no idea whether or not it will work. So I asked if she would like to try something. She did. I did my PNI stuff and ten minutes later the headache was completely gone. She was amazed and I was amazed. This stuff not only sounded good it really worked.

On another occasion I got a phone call from a friend who suffered from arthritis. She had been helping me by allowing me to do some session practise with her to help me with my course work. She was in a great deal of pain, but she had a leg that was locked and she couldn't straighten it out. I spent a few minutes working with her, the pain magically disappeared, and full movement returned. I was amazed that I could even use this stuff over the phone.

Then I passed my exams, qualified as a hypnotherapist, and started to work on my own. I rapidly discovered that I could do with anxiety in six weeks what it had taken me over twenty years to achieve. Agoraphobia was the most difficult anxiety problem I treated, but I usually make significant progress within twelve weeks. I have had people who were afraid to go outside their front door alone who now go shopping in supermarkets. If you aren't aware, supermarkets, along with cinemas, are one of the most difficult places for an agoraphobe to visit alone. In fact I occasionally bump into one of my ex-patients at our local supermarket and she always tells me how well she is doing and how much she has to thank me for.

One day a patient came to see me for help with a problem she called fibromyalgia. I knew nothing about it so she described her symptoms. They were constant pain that involved most of the body. No more than two hours continuous sleep without being woken by the pain. No job, no life. It had taken doctors four years to diagnose and when they did my patient was told there was nothing they could do since it was a genetic problem.

I asked her to score the pain on a scale of 0-10 where 10 is excruciating agony and 0 is no pain. She said it was between 8 and 9.

I induced a trance, did my PNI stuff, and brought her back to full awareness - a process lasting around 30 minutes.

She scored the pain a 3.

When she came back the following week the pain had remained at 3 since leaving me the week previously. She had enjoyed 8 hours sleep every single night since that first session. She would have been happy to leave it at that, but I encouraged her to do some more work. When she left after that second session the pain was scoring 0. She came back the following week and she had remained pain free.

I heard about her again when she sent her husband to see me. She had a good job and was enjoying working again. I had truly given her a life worth living. I improved her husband's quality of life considerably too. I bump into them now and again and they are both happy and contented now.

Here's what another patient had to say when he came to see me for some help with his confidence:

> **"After a single session I noticed a significant improvement and by my 4th session my outlook had completely changed... I am more positive and self confident about any challenges I may face. Michael was patient and genuinely interested**

in my problem and in how to resolve it. I owe Michael a great debt and would wholeheartedly recommend him."

On another occasion I had a visit from a lady who'd recently had a mastectomy. She was past the point where the doctors had any concerns, but she was in constant pain from the operation. Nothing she was taking was helping. Again 30 minutes work and she was completely free of pain, but there was a side effect. On the side of the breast removal she had been unable to lift her arm above shoulder height. She hadn't mentioned this to me, but as soon as I brought her out of trance she lifted her arm right up in the air. She seemed more pleased with the return of full movement in her arm than with the pain removal – but that was because she expected me to remove the pain, she hadn't expected her arm to improve.

Then there was the time when I was seeing a young lady for help with self-confidence. She came one week in early summer and asked if I could do anything about her hay fever. I said I hadn't worked with allergies before but I was happy to give it a try. When she left she was free of symptoms. When she returned for the next session she had remained free of symptoms.

As I continued to work with patients I discovered that moderate anxiety states can be helped in a few sessions, severe anxiety states in more. Pain, if it goes, goes quickly. Phobias usually leave with little trouble but occasionally hang on tenaciously. People come to see me and then they fly fearlessly. I have helped golfers, rugby players, and basketballers improve their game, even though I know nothing about sport. I have helped motorcycle racers conquer their fears and enjoy their hobby once more. I have watched people as their confidence improves with each session and I have seen self-esteem climb higher and higher.

Hypnosis helps.

It helps people achieve what they want to achieve.

Hypnosis not only removes the chains holding you back, it removes the barriers to success so that you can have what you want.

However, it isn't magic and sometimes you have to work at it for a while before you reap the rewards.

But I have a problem. I can only physically see a limited number of people for one to one sessions when there are so many people out there who could benefit from my knowledge and unique perspective. I have lived through many of the problems that hypnosis can help with. I have insights into those problems that non-sufferers will never have. I didn't read about how to fix anxiety and agoraphobia, lack of confidence and low self-esteem in a book – as many therapists do.

I lived it.

I solved it.

I can teach you how to make your life better.

How to Make it Work for You

"Whether you think you can or you think you can't, you're right."

Henry Ford

I have not written this book in the way that most self hypnosis books are written. They are usually arranged so that you can open the book to the chapter on your problem, find the right affirmations to use in trance, and then solve that problem.

There is a very good reason why I have not done it that way.

No problem exists in isolation. When you look at solving just one specific problem, a phobia, or self-confidence perhaps, you are treating symptoms. Symptom treatment isn't healing and it isn't a cure. Symptom treatment doesn't solve the problem, nor does it get to the heart of the issue.

What you really want is freedom, though you may choose to call it happiness or confidence or a relationship or more money, and if you follow all the steps in my solution you will find that freedom comes as symptoms ease. However, if anxiety is your problem, it is perfectly alright for you to pay particular attention to the chapter that deals with that, but you need to learn some new skills first.

My approach is very straightforward.

First you need to learn a few new skills and understand what hypnosis is and what it can do. Then you can explore the process of change. New skills first, then look at making changes.

Just two things:

1. New Skills & Knowledge

- Discover what hypnosis is
- Understand self hypnosis
- Visualisation
- Formulating suggestions
- Goals & goal setting

2. Change

- Mind
- Body
- Spirit

New Skills

Before you can use hypnosis effectively you need to know what it is you are doing. Obviously I do not know about you, but I hate being told what to do. I also do not think that saying 'do this', or 'do that' is a very effective way of teaching. As soon as someone tells me to do something I feel an inner resistance that immediately wants me to not do what they want me to do. So you would probably find that if I jumped straight into how to cure anxiety with self hypnosis and told you what to do and what affirmations to use you would probably try it out (after all you have bought the book) but you would not do it for long because that inner resistance would kick in.

What I do find though is that when someone takes the trouble to explain the reasons they would like me to take certain actions I find it much easier to comply. This is because I now understand why I am doing whatever I am doing.

So before we start using self hypnosis to improve your life it is a really good idea to understand a little about hypnosis in general.

But do not worry, this is not complicated stuff. It is just basics that you will find helpful because when you understand, you can relax and let go and that is exactly what we need for success.

After that we will have a look at *self* hypnosis. There is a world of difference between the processes of being hypnotised by a therapist and of doing it yourself. It is important to understand these differences so that the time you invest in this process pays dividends for you.

Then I will take you through the process of what visualisation is and how to use it to maximise the benefits of self hypnosis. Some people believe they cannot visualise. In this chapter I explain how you can use visualisation whether or not you believe you are any good at it. I am rubbish at what most people think visualisation is, so if you are like me then that is not a problem as I will explain everything.

In the more traditional use of self hypnosis you need to make suggestions to yourself, in trance. The wording of these suggestions is the key to your success. In this chapter I will teach you the skills you need to formulate suggestions that will work for you and help to bring about the changes you desire.

Finally, before we get on to the actual process of bringing about change, we need to look at goals and goal setting. Goals used to frighten me, but I have discovered that Goals are nothing to fear. You see, quite often, people who struggle with life have a deep rooted fear of success. They might be unaware of this and just see themselves as unlucky, unfortunate, or maybe even a failure. If this is there, then Goals are indeed scary because they bring you face to face with your deepest fears. They do this because you know that once a Goal is set then if you want to achieve it, you will have to do stuff you don't really want to do. Even worse, if you don't achieve it you will have to admit failure, rather than just carry on pretending that you really are making progress.

So in Goals & Goal Setting I'll walk you through how to make goals work for you and how you can use them to your benefit regardless of the level of fear they invoke in you.

Making Changes

Now we get to the really good bit. This is where you discover how to make the changes you desire so that you can live the life you deserve. I know that there will be chapters in here that you feel do not apply to you – not everyone who suffers from anxiety is agoraphobic for instance. But I strongly suggest you read them anyway in the order I suggest.

In order to make changes we need to deal with aspects of Mind, Body, and Spirit. The mind is the prime source of all the problems we have in life. If you think the source of all your problems is your boss, or your partner, or your difficult financial circumstances, then go ahead and believe that but be prepared to discover that you are mistaken. The thoughts that you think about your world are the source of your anxieties, worries and stress. The thoughts that you think about you are where your lack of confidence and low self-esteem are born.

Mind deals with the thoughts; or rather it deals with where the thoughts come from – beliefs. If you change what you believe then your thinking will follow – effortlessly. The problem, of course, is that you believe what you believe and think it is true. Otherwise you would not believe it.

It is your view of the world and your beliefs about your reality that are the source of all of your problems. I show you how to begin the process of change by looking at belief and then showing you how to apply self hypnosis to change your anxiety state, or improve your self esteem and confidence. We begin with confidence because this will help you to feel confident about this whole process of change. This is followed by self-esteem so that your inner world becomes more congruent with your increasing confidence.

After self esteem comes anxiety/stress/worry. Each of these builds on the others so do them in sequence at first. It may take a little longer to get to where you want to be, but it means the change will be a lasting one. However, these three items are all intimately linked and I would encourage you to work on all three equally even if you believe that you only have a problem in one of these areas. So work on confidence until you feel a shift. Then self-esteem again until you feel a shift, and then anxiety/stress/worry. Then go back to the beginning and repeat. The shift will be a deep knowing that something has changed. Look for small changes, not big ones and be gentle with yourself always.

After the success you experience at making Mind changes you will be ready to move on to something more challenging. This is where we will look at the physical difficulties we have to face with addictions to food and cigarettes and other body-based changes we wish to make. Read through these chapters even though you don't have that particular problem, it will give you many more insights into the way the mind works and allow you, as your self hypnosis skills develop, to see how you can apply or adapt some of these techniques for use in those problems you have that I may not cover in detail.

Finally we come to the section on Spirit. With what we've already covered you have the tools and skills to make effective and lasting changes to your thoughts and behaviour – changes that are already allowing you to begin to get a sense of yourself freed from anxiety and worry. But this truly is just the first step. I have called this section Spirit because it usually follows after Mind & Body, but don't be fooled into thinking that you can ignore this because it is going to get a bit weird. Spirit is about finding yourself and freeing your mind from the chains that have held it captive for so long. This is where you find out about happiness and freedom. The previous sections have been about making changes that allow you to function more effectively in whatever circumstances you had been finding challenging. Spirit is about moving forward and ensuring that your future continues to get better and better. There may even be a tiny little bit of weird stuff, but you don't have to buy into it, and anyway, we all like to believe that there is a little bit of magic out there somewhere. This is the section that teaches you how to tap into that magic.

So you can see how easy it will be for you to make progress by following this structured system for learning and practicing self-hypnosis.

To begin with it is simply a case of familiarisation with the nature of hypnosis; understanding exactly what visualisation is and how you can benefit from it; mastering the art of formulating suggestions; and making peace with goals and goal setting.

With these safely under your belt we move on to the practical application of these techniques to solve your real life problems. This application begins with starting to see the world differently so that you are more peaceful within it. Then we move just a little away from the mind and discover how to apply these techniques to change our body's responses. Then we finish up with methods of opening up your world so that life becomes a much more pleasurable experience for you.

Concerns

I make it sound easy don't I?

Well you will find it just as easy as you allow it to be.

Of course you may have been the way you are for a very long time. The longer you suffer from difficulties, whether they be physical, emotional, or mental, the more you believe that they are you. You reach the point where you think that this is the way you are and because nothing you have ever tried before has produced lasting change then it must be your nature and although you are willing to give this a go you know it will end in failure. In fact you are only really trying this because you are hurting so badly and it wounds so deeply to see everyone else apparently enjoying what you would love to enjoy.

But I am reminded of the words of the Jedi Master, Yoda, in one of the original Star Wars movies

"Do or do not, there is no try".

If you fail you fail. So what? The minute you accept failure as something that happens, you open the door to success. The mistake is seeing failure as saying something about you and your worth.

I've failed at loads of things. I'm really good at failing. But I don't think it says anything of value about me. All it means is that I didn't reach a goal I set. Again – so what? If it's really important to me then I'll see what I can learn from the failure and approach the subject again. But mostly what I learn from failure is that I just didn't want it enough, or, more often than you might think, that it was really just what I thought was expected of me. For those things I want badly enough, I usually end up with a success under my belt.

Now, I'm not denying talent and natural ability here. If you insist on comparing yourself to others you will always find those who can perform with a greater level of skill and expertise than you can. Among my talents away from therapy I can unashamedly claim that I am a skilled and knowledgeable photographer - sufficiently talented that I could teach it if I wanted to. But I've been taking pictures since I was 14 years old and photography has always been a huge love of mine. So I've had a good few years to accumulate this knowledge. But when I look back at some of the early pictures I attempted to sell – they are truly dreadful. My images improve because I look at them with a critical eye and ask myself how could I make that better? With photography, and with any other subject that fascinates me, I am a perpetual student. I never think I have all the answers. I never believe there is no one better than me. I look to learn from those whose skills I admire, and I look to teach those who are less skilled than myself. What I don't do is give up because I take a couple of blurred pictures or because some new technique didn't produce the results I desired the very first time I used it.

Be this way with self hypnosis. See this as a process. Know that you will not be brilliant when you begin, but know also that the more you practice the better you will become. I chose to become a hypnotherapist. You only need to learn enough to solve your current problems and equip you for a much easier and more enjoyable journey through life. I needed to learn a lot. In comparison, you need to learn a little. So decide, right now, that you will succeed at this. But define success not as becoming a master, though that may happen, but just being good enough.

Can't be hypnotised

Another major concern is about ability to be hypnotised. The only people who have difficulty entering a hypnotic state are those who are convinced they can't and those who *think* they know how to identify it. Those who think they know how to identify it have, of course, never been hypnotised. The problem this group has is that they have a mistaken idea about what they think hypnosis is going to feel like and they are so desperate to experience this that all the time they are distracted with looking for something that does not exist. The others allow their belief to win out and because they expect failure that is exactly what they experience.

The trick to being hypnotised every time is amazingly simple and it uses something that everyone possesses – curiosity. Beginning with the very first time you take yourself into a self hypnotic trance, just be curious. Be curious about what it is going to feel like. Be curious about the sensations you are going to experience. Be curious about what exactly you will be most aware of. Be curious about the effect on mind and body that your silent words will have. In fact, all you need to do to be successful at taking yourself into trance is to follow my instructions, suspend any prior expectations about the magic you are hoping to experience, and just be curious about the whole experience.

Then do the same the next time and the next and be curious about those things that remain the same each time and those things that change. Remembering of course, to curiously notice how your skill improves each time you follow my instructions.

It might work for others but it won't work for me.

Of course you might be one of those people who believe that this will never work for you. You believe the process is effective for others, but it will never work for you because you are different and nothing ever does work for you. In fact you only have to look back at your life, at all the things you have tried, in order to be able to prove that nothing works for you.

If this is you then you have two choices.

1. Stop reading and go and do something more useful instead.

2. Entertain the possibility – not believe, just entertain – that you may be mistaken.

If you are still reading then I assume you have chosen option two.

I have had quite a few patients over the years who come to me and tell me how they went to another hypnotherapist and it just didn't work, but they are here with me just to give it another go. This is usually because nothing else they have tried worked either and they are becoming desperate.

I have never failed with any of these patients. In fact most are totally surprised when I return them to normal waking reality.

So why does it work with me when it didn't with another hypnotherapist. The reason is that I explain exactly what they will experience and use an induction that allows them to experience everything I talked about. So they are convinced into trance because of the preparation I gave them.

If you go through this book step by step then by the time you reach the point where you are going to take yourself into a self hypnotic trance for the very first time I will have prepared you so that nothing but success is possible. And I even have a back-up plan that makes the first time even easier if you are still doubtful about your ability.

Skills

"If you hear a voice within you say 'you cannot paint,' then by all means paint and that voice will be silenced."

Vincent Van Gogh

Skills

"I am always doing that which I cannot do,
in order that I may learn how to do it."

Pablo Picasso

In this section on skills you will learn about hypnosis, how it might not be quite what you think it is, and how easy it is to hypnotise yourself. Once you discover how easy it is to take yourself into trance then it is time to find out how to maximize the personal benefits of this wonderfully healing process.

Learning how to take yourself into trance is, perhaps, the easiest aspect of using your own mind to create a new world for you to enjoy. Three other areas need your close attention.

The first of these is visualisation. Many people misunderstand what is required when they are asked to visualise. This chapter will clear things up and remove any concerns you may have about your ability to visualise effectively.

Once you understand what is required we move on to the requirements for formulating self-suggestions. These may also be considered direct suggestions, or affirmations. In this book I do not focus on the use of direct suggestions because I see it as less effective than the other techniques that I use. However, many people like, and are responsive to, suggestions. So for completeness I include this chapter on how to get the best out of them if you enjoy this form of behaviour-change. Where I think it is appropriate I also include some suggestions for your use at the end of each of the chapters dealing with specific problem areas. Though I have to emphasise that it is always better to create affirmations yourself because you are the only one fully aware of what you need right now.

Finally I explore the importance of goals, or targets. Goals are things to aim for. The trick, to avoid failure, is to set up goals that are easy to reach. That way you achieve early success. This builds your confidence so you can move on to achieve ever greater successes.

What is Hypnosis

"If you can dream it, you can do it. Always remember that
this whole thing was started with a dream and a mouse"

Walt Disney

I would love to be able to tell you that hypnosis is the magical, mystical, watch-dangling, cure-all conjuring trick that the media portray it as. I would love to be able to tell you that hypnosis is going to solve all of your problems easily and effortlessly. But most of all I would love to be able to tell you that hypnosis will allow you to drift into unconsciousness for a while and that when you return your life will be the magical experience you always knew it was supposed to be - but somehow you must have got off the bus at the wrong stop and been struggling to find your way ever since.

I am afraid I cannot tell you any of that - at least not if I am being honest with you. Though I have to say that I have had a few patients who have experienced those things, but for the majority change takes just a little longer than magic.

Ok, so I hope I have got rid of the idea that this is magic. I have, however, sown the seed that you might have to put in a little time and effort to bring about the results you want. If you are still with me then you may well be about to discover how to make the magic work in your own life.

I have made it clear what hypnosis is not. So maybe it would be fair at this point to tell you what it is - and what you can expect when you learn how to use it effectively to bring about desired change in your own life. But, as you read on, I would like you to begin this journey of self-discovery about the amazing power of your own mind by allowing a part of your mind to begin to drift and dream about how you would like your life to be.

Imagine you could create your life anew:

- What would you remove and what would you keep?
- What would you bring in?

- What adventures would you give yourself?

- What experiences and training would you have already placed in your past?

Allow your mind to drift and wonder about these questions while I tell you a little about hypnosis.

Hypnosis is a tool. It is a tool that you can use to bring about desirable change in your life. Now even though I earn my living from hypnotising people, I am going to share with you some of my secrets so that you can do the same things yourself. Though I have to say, effecting change through hypnosis is much easier when you visit a trained and experienced hypnotherapist than when you do it yourself. But as long as you recognise that self hypnosis does not produce the same depth of trance as a session with a hypnotherapist, and does not work as quickly as when an expert is guiding you, then you can proceed knowing that you will have to put a little effort in, but you can still achieve amazing results on your own. As long as your desire is there and you are determined to succeed at this then you will.

Hypnosis is relaxation with suggestions added. Those suggestions can be in the form of affirmations or they can be in the form of pictures, sounds, feelings, sensations, tastes and smells.

The word Hypnosis sounds much more important than relaxation, but relaxation is pretty much what hypnosis is. There is one difference though. The majority of my patients, when I return them to their waking world, express that the level of relaxation they enjoyed under hypnosis was so much deeper than anything they had previously experienced. So much so that they wanted to stay there rather than wake up because they were enjoying it so much. The relaxation is a tool to remove the critical/analytical aspect of normal consciousness. It is designed to induce daydreaming. That way any suggestions slip into the subconscious without challenge. And that is pretty much all there is to it.

Now I have explained what hypnosis is in a very short paragraph. It took me over four years of study, and a significant investment, to finally qualify fully as a hypnotherapist, so I am sure you realise there's a lot more to it than I have mentioned in the paragraph above. That said though, the paragraph contains the essence of what you need to know in order to bring about effective change in your life through self hypnosis.

'Can I be hypnotised?' is a question I am asked frequently when potential patients phone for an appointment. It stands to reason it would be a concern when visiting a hypnotherapist. In fact I had a lovely gentleman come to me for help with stopping smoking, just a week ago. He told me about his concerns relating to a time he and his girlfriend watched a stage hypnotist. The stage hypnotist did the usual hand-clasp test. This is where they ask members of the audience to interlace their fingers and grip their hands together really tightly. At the same time the audience is told that when the hypnotist asks them to separate their hands they will be unable to do so. This is a suggestibility test. My patient reported that his girlfriend's hands were stuck together, while he separated his hands as easily as you would expect.

Obviously this caused some concern in my patient about his ability to be hypnotised.

I talked to him about what I do, and about what trance is, and what it is not. I told him what I expected of him during hypnosis, and how it was impossible for him to fail. He experienced a deep trance on his first session with me and a very deep trance on his second session with me a week later - so much so that the 50 minute trance time seemed to him like 5 minutes.

Suggestibility is only a part of trance work. Expectations and beliefs are equally important in controlling the experience of hypnosis.

One of those common expectations is that hypnosis is like a general anaesthetic. Patients expect me to pull out my watch on a chain (only joking) - they expect me to do something magical that renders them unconscious, do something even more magical to their mind (a bit like an operation), and then wake them up with everything sorted. I'd love to be able to do it like that, but I can't and I have never met a hypnotherapist who does. However, change happens. But the most interesting thing is that change still happens even on the rare occasion when I have a patient who does not think they have been hypnotised - because they 'heard everything I said'.

Think of it like this. It is a day, like Sunday used to be, when you do not have to get up and you are all warm and cosy in bed. You feel happy and contented. You are in a drifty, dreamy world where chunks of time just disappear. Yet, if someone you love came in with a cup of tea, coffee, or, even better, breakfast then you would be instantly alert and ready to enjoy it. Hypnosis is like that. Warm and cosy; relaxed; yet with a part of your mind fully aware of what is going on, while at the same time paying it absolutely no attention because the dreamy stuff is much more fun.

Now, for most people that is an easy state to get into when you have someone like me to guide you, and watch you, and alter the process dynamically in response to your resistance or acquiescence. It is not quite as easy when you do it on your own. But doing it on your own has many advantages so it is worth putting in just a little practise so that you become proficient - and all it takes is a little practise on a regular basis.

In the next chapter I am going to tell you how you can hypnotise yourself. In the subsequent chapters I will look at a range of common life-challenges. For each one I will explain simply and easily how you can use your new skill, at putting yourself into a hypnotic trance, to bring about positive change in your life.

Self Hypnosis

"It takes only one person to change your life: You"

Ruth Casey

In the previous chapter I gave you a brief overview of what hypnosis is. What I did not do is to explain how I bring about that state in a patient, or how I know when a patient has *arrived* in that state.

How I bring that state about is very simple.

I use words.

I am afraid that is all there is to it.

I use words.

Let me give you an example (the ... indicates a pause. *Italicised* words are not spoken. The vocal delivery is slow and unhurried).

"Make yourself just as comfortable as you can... and gently allow your eyelids to close... Now... notice the sounds around you... the music...(*playing softly in the background*) the ticking of the clocks... the sound of my voice... Now... allow yourself to become aware of your breathing... just notice the gentle rising... and falling... of your chest (*timed with the rise and fall of the breath*)... (*allow for several breaths in silence*) now just notice any sensations that you are noticing..."

Now... what did you notice about the above? Take a few moments to re-read it and imagine being on the receiving end. Imagine what effect it would have on you. Imagine what changes it would bring about within you.

The first thing I would like you to pay attention to is the gentleness of it. In fact gentle/gently is used twice to reinforce this idea. When you were reading it, did you become aware of any sound that you weren't paying attention to? Did you become

1

aware of the rhythm of your breathing? If you didn't, that is ok, if you did that is ok too.

Now look again and notice how many times I told you what to do. I did not actually *tell* you to do anything. I simply offered invitations that you were free to accept or decline. I invited you to become more comfortable than you were. I invited you to notice the sounds around you. I invited you to notice your breathing, and then I invited you to notice whatever you were noticing.

Try and just *not* notice what you are noticing.

That is one of the ways I get people to begin to relax and feel completely comfortable. I make it okay for them to be doing whatever it is they are doing. I make it okay to be experiencing whatever they are experiencing. This is the way I show my patients that failure is impossible because they only ever have to do what they are doing. However, by offering invitations I encourage them to do exactly what I want them to do – which is to place their attention where I want it.

But what I want them to do most is to have an enjoyable experience which results in the change they desire.

Now in my example above there was just one 'invitation' that was actually a hidden command. '…and gently allow your eyelids to close.' If the invitation is not accepted (and I wait for the eyelids to close before continuing) then I will modify the suggestion to "…and just as soon as you are ready to stop smoking, then gently allow your eyelids to close" and I will replace 'stop smoking' with whatever problem they have come to me for help with. This command allows me to assess subconscious resistance to change.

So, with a few gentle words spoken in an unhurried and easy fashion, I have someone: feeling more comfortable; having closed their eyes; more aware of what they can hear *i.e. my voice*; and focused on internal sensations rather than external distractions.

After that I work on deepening the relaxation until I am ready to begin therapy.

Self Hypnosis

And it is just words.

But it is carefully selected words and expressions designed to direct attention to where it is required. So, the question is, how do you get to do that to yourself?

There are two methods. The first is to make a voice recording that does what I would do in a session to induce the hypnotic trance state. I have included a sample script for you to use for this purpose if that appeals to you. You will find this in Appendix 1. I have also created a sample voice recording which, if you wish, you can download for less than the price of a good cup of coffee. Full details in Appendix 1.

The other method is to do something that doesn't require the use of language but is easy to remember and that is a physical relaxation method. Reading through the script will give you the basic idea, but I'll show you how to do that without listening to a recording.

Step 1.

Make sure that anyone living with you will not disturb you until you have finished. Turn off your phone. If you think it would help, play some gentle relaxation music - nothing with vocals, just music.

Step 2.

Make yourself as physically comfortable as you can. Sitting up in a comfortable chair that supports your neck is preferable to lying down. Lying down it is just too easy to drift off to sleep. With self hypnosis you need to maintain a higher state of alertness than when you are with a hypnotherapist because you are the one who is going to be making the change suggestions once you are nicely relaxed.

51

Step 3.

Make an agreement with yourself that whatever you experience this time is perfect for you this time. Hypnosis, like many things, is a skill and you get better at it the more you practise.

Step 4.

Deepen your breathing just a touch and ensure that at least some breath is moving into the deeper part of your lungs. This helps calm mind and body and that calming is an automatic response to just breathing a little bit more deeply. Most people only breathe into the upper chest area so their breath is quite shallow. Shallow breathing triggers fight/flight reactions and is associated with stress.

Step 5.

Move your attention in turn to each of these areas: scalp, forehead, eyes and eyelids, cheeks, mouth, neck, shoulders, arms & hands, chest, abdomen, thighs, calves, ankles & feet. In other words your body from top to bottom. Stop at each location and invite yourself to allow all of the muscle tension you can feel to soften and relax. Each time you do this the relaxation will increase. There is no rush with this. Take as much time as you need. The more thoroughly you relax at this stage the easier everything is for you later on in the process. You can see a detailed example of this process here in the Chapter on Sleep.

Step 6.

Imagine yourself at the top of a grand sweeping staircase; it can have 10 or 20 steps depending on your preference. Then imagine you are walking down the staircase and counting the steps - starting at 10 or 20 and counting down for each step you take. Imagine that with each step you take/number you count that you are relaxing a little bit more.

Step 7.

When you reach the bottom you will see/imagine a door. Walk through the door and find yourself in your Favourite Place. Your Favourite Place is any place you would love to be that is peaceful & safe. No one else is present. Places in nature, like beaches, woodlands in spring, meadows, or wilderness are good to use. Find yourself somewhere comfortable to settle down in this imaginary place. I usually imagine a strong oak tree growing on a small grassy mound. I sit on the mound with my back against the trunk. I feel the roughness of the bark through my shirt and sense the strength and security of this tree. I imagine its roots reaching deep into the soil and anchoring it firmly despite the storms that toss its branches around.

Step 8.

If you want to explore this place for a while that is fine, but then move on to the self-suggestions, or the visualisation, that you intend to use to bring about the desired change. The other chapters will cover this in detail. But if you want to practice without the suggestions then that will be beneficial and give you a feel for the process. My tree is in a meadow with a stream and I watch a kingfisher and wander along the banks maybe even remembering that lovely childhood activity of daisy-chain making.

Step 9.

When you have finished just count yourself up from 1 to 5, knowing that you will open your eyes on the count of 4 and be fully wide awake on the count of 5.

It is as simple as that.

The trick is to utilise step 8 to make the suggestions that you previously planned in order to bring about change in your life.

The self hypnosis part is easy and you can develop skill very quickly. What takes a little longer is knowing how best to use that trance state to bring about your desired change.

If all of this sounds a little complicated, or you try this and believe it is not working for you, then I have a shortcut you may enjoy.

I told you there was no way to fail at this.

On my Hypnosis website I sell a Self Hypnosis training MP3 download. This is a full hypnosis session, but it trains you, under hypnosis, how to take yourself into a trance. In other words it installs a post-hypnotic suggestion so that whenever you count down from 10 to 1 for the purposes of self hypnosis you will experience a deeper trance than you did before.

How much easier can I make it for you to succeed? However, there is a price to pay. But I am making an exclusive offer to readers of this book and making this recording available for around 50% off the normal price – as long as you buy it through this link:

http://www.self-hypnosis-mastery.com/html/readers-offer-mp3.htm

If you want to check out the full details go to:

http://www.hypnosisiseasy.com/selfhypnosis.htm

but don't buy it from that page or you will pay the full price.

The three options for inducing self hypnosis:

1. Make your own voice recording, using the script in Appendix 1
2. Use the 9-step process described above.
3. Purchase my self-hypnosis training MP3 recording.

Now, before I get on to the process of bringing about desired change we need to look at something that puts a lot of people off - and that is visualisation.

Visualisation

"The power of imagination makes us infinite."

John Muir

Hypnotherapists use the term *visualise* quite often. When I first started my practise I used to ask my patients to visualise… and then I'd go on to describe what it was I wanted them to visualise.

That was when I ran into a problem. I knew what I meant by visualise, but it seemed my patients did not. They thought I needed them to see things in their minds just as clearly as they could see with their eyes open. All I wanted them to do was to use their imagination or fantasise and we can all do that. Nowadays what I ask of my patients is something along the lines of… remember when you were little and you used to use your imagination, or maybe when you were a little older and enjoyed a fantasy or a daydream… well we all know how to daydream, and we all know how to fantasise, so I'd just like you to let the part of you that knows how to daydream to imagine that you are… and then I'd fill in some details or paint a word picture.

Sometimes I would just demonstrate by asking a few questions. Do you know what a beach ball is? Have you ever played with one? What did it look like? Where did you play with it? Show me how big it was? What colour was it? Where are you getting that information from about the beach ball?

The last question is key, because in order to answer the questions you have to have some sort of a 'mental image' of a beach ball, probably also accompanied by happy childhood memories. Visualisation is just accessing the place that is able to create or remember an image in your mind's eye.

I remember when I used to be a regular attendee at my local yoga class. The end of the session was always a guided visualisation where Val, our teacher, would paint a wonderful word picture of some place we were supposed to imagine ourselves at. When the class finished other students would express how real it was and how it seemed just like they were there - and I used to get very frustrated because all I ever got was the darkness of the back of my eyelids.

It was only years later that I came to realise that although some people can create mental images that seem as clear to them as if they had their eyes open; for many the experience is one of darkness and frustration. Eventually I realised that we are all different, and nice as it sounds to be able to conjure up real images in your mind I couldn't do it - no matter how hard I tried. The worst of it was a lot of the mental training and disciplines I was involved in at the time required that mental ability and insisted that all it took was practice. Well I disagree. I believe it is something that some people are good at and others do not have the capacity for.

So where does that leave you when something you want requires that you visualise that something and you can't do it? Well I realised something else too. I realised that I was well able to fantasise and imagine and daydream and when I did those things I could describe in visual terms exactly what it was my imagination was creating, but there was never an image in the sense that I see when my eyes are open. What was there was something that I can't describe but I know you'll understand. And it is that something that you need to access when you engage in self hypnosis.

So when pictures are needed to help you to make the changes you want to make, all you need to do is to do whatever you do when you pretend, or imagine, or fantasise, or daydream.

And now I will tell you why that information is so hugely important.

But, I also need you to understand that what I am about to tell you falls slightly more into mysticism than into science. If you have an interest in the Law of Attraction, Creating your Own Reality, or any thoughts of manifesting what you want then this is where the real world meets a more spiritual one. You do not have to believe in that stuff though and if you just follow my advice, you will change your life for the better no matter what you believe.

Tradition Misses the Point

The more traditional format for the therapeutic part of self hypnosis - the bit where you re-program your mind with the changes you want to make - relies largely on pre-formatted affirmations and suggestions. The following chapter explores this in more detail so I will not go into it here. What I want to draw your attention to is why that on its own wastes a huge opportunity for you to increase the power of your suggestions and make amazing changes in your life. When you make the maximum use of this opportunity you have within your grasp the ability to improve your sense of well-being and happiness, improve your financial status, improve the quality of all your relationships, and even modify your own physical health.

Let me introduce you to an idea. The idea is that your mind is the most powerful thing on the planet. Please note I am not saying that your mind is *more* powerful than other minds, nor am I saying that other minds are *more* powerful than yours. But in your own experience your mind is the most powerful thing that you will ever encounter. Just play with that idea for a few seconds right now; let your imagination run with it for a moment or two. Fantasise about what life would be like for you if that were the truth. Enjoy the idea for a little while.

I hope that was enjoyable. It is fun to play and, as adults, we can forget to play sometimes.

Have you ever been watching food on tv, especially acid stuff like slicing lemons, or watched someone squeeze lemon juice onto their tongue? Have you noticed that your salivary glands start moistening your mouth when you observe this? Is just reading these words and seeing those images in your mind's eye causing any salivary activation? That is your mind being powerful. It is using its imagination and your body believes what your mind imagines to the extent that it reacts as if the food were real.

Have you ever noticed, a little while after you have seen an ad for a food item, that you suddenly want to eat something, or eat some of that particular food? This again is the power of your mind responding to images and creating urges that did not exist prior to seeing the ad. Advertisements are purposely hypnotic, powerfully suggestive, and keyed to activate basic urges like sex, status, and eating.

That is why we use visualisation (I am going to use that term from now on, but remember that I actually mean imagination, fantasisation, or daydreamation) in self hypnosis. We use it because mental images have a huge amount of power, even to the extent that they cause your body to ignore your reality and behave as if the images were real.

So we carefully craft those images into stories that we play to ourselves. The more real we can make them, the more believable they are, the more your body will respond and react as if those stories were true. Let me give you an example. One of the most universal fears that people experience is about performance. Usually it is in the form of anxiety about giving a speech, a presentation, or even performing as an actor, musician, or other entertainer. I have helped a significant number of people with this type of problem. The basis of that help is getting them to see themselves, in trance, doing what they fear and enjoying it. It is not quite as simple as that and usually takes at least four sessions to achieve the desired shift in perception, but in essence that is exactly what happens. I get my patient to play with the idea in their own mind and see themselves having fun. And the first time they come to see me after they have successfully performed is always accompanied by a huge shift in confidence, happiness and well-being because they realise now that they can do anything they want to.

Your body does not know when your mind is lying to it. Your body believes whatever your mind tells it. This is why we get fear reactions to all sorts of things that are just not life-threatening. Getting us out of life-threatening situations is why fear was 'invented'.

So we make use of this in hypnosis to re-program responses to situations. That way the body gets used to responding in a new way so that by the time you are exposed to the situation in real life, your responses will be those you want, not those you have always suffered from.

All of that is all very well but I did promise you a touch of the mystical. So first realise that what I have just described makes sense just the way it is, from a practical and psychological perspective. So you can leave it at that if you want and skip ahead to the next chapter if you like to keep your feet grounded and your beliefs quite secure in a solid, physical reality.

You see 'reality' is not as solid or as real as you imagine it to be. Atoms, as you probably know, are full of empty space. So what we feel as solid is actually just the electromagnetic force fields that hold *stuff* together. At the quantum level matter changes depending on whether or not it is observed. Electrons blink in and out of existence and no one knows where they go while they are not in *our* Universe.

Let me give you a more personal example: take your sight for instance. In very basic terms (I am not a biologist or a quantum physicist, so I need to keep it simple so I can understand it) what happens when you see is that light hits your eye; your cornea and lens focus that light so it appears sharply on your retina; the light stimulates a bio-electrical change that moves along your optic nerves; switches brain hemispheres at something like a complicated railway junction; and finally stimulates some neurons in the optical cortex at the back of your head.

Some interesting things you might want to take note of. The image arrives on your retina upside down, because your eye-lens is a simple convex lens - like a magnifying glass. You may have done the experiment in school where you use a magnifying glass to project an upside down image of the world onto a piece of paper. At no point in time does your brain ever see an actual image. There is no projector in your head projecting an image inside your skull. All your brain gets is a bunch of chemicals, and a few sparks of electrical activity that *represent* the upside down image. When this is received by your brain your brain then makes up a story about those chemicals and creates the illusion of a right-way-up world outside of you.

Your brain makes it all up.

Granted it is given some information on which to base its making up, but it still constructs an image from something that is not actually an image.

Now, let me be clear, I am not saying that the world outside of you does not exist. Nor am I saying the world outside of you is any different from the world you think you see. What I am saying is that there is *no way for you to tell* one way or the other because you are making it all up - and you do the same with every one of your senses. All you can say for certain is that you are making up a reality inside of you and then projecting it outside of you.

If you just entertain the possibility that you might be making everything up - think of the film The Matrix - then you might also want to entertain the possibility that it might just be possible to influence what you are making up. The difficulty is knowing just how to go about doing that.

One of the easiest ways that I have found is using either meditation or self-hypnosis. It works like this... as I mentioned earlier, your body behaves as if what you imagine is real. Now that makes sense in terms of purely physical responses like saliva. But let us stretch that a little. I was listening to a recording yesterday (about using your mind to change your world) where the narrator told of a bit of surprising research. A bunch of students were separated into two groups. Both groups were selected so that at the start of the experiment their skills at getting a basketball in the net were equal. Their scoring ability was measured; then they separated for two weeks. One group practised on the basket ball court. The other group practised in their minds just visualising making perfect baskets. At the end of the two weeks the improvement, on the court, of both groups was comparable. For the mental visualisation group their skills and abilities improved to the same degree that real world practise produces.

Now, have you ever found yourself thinking about someone and then the phone rang and it was them? Have you ever found yourself thinking about someone and then bumped into them unexpectedly? Think about those odd occasions, occasions that most people dismiss as coincidence, and others like them. Were you were aware of something before it happened? Have you ever had an idle thought or a daydream about something you would like and then moments later it happened. I remember one day, just a couple of years ago, sitting here at my computer and wondering what it would be like to make a TV program. Just hours later I got a phone call inviting me to go and have a chat at a TV production company about a new series they were thinking of making.

Life is full of experiences like that. It is just that most people do not even notice them or make the connection between their thoughts and how they seem to make things happen that involve other people. I believe that using self hypnosis allows you to tap into this connectedness deliberately rather than just waiting for happy accidents. What I think happens is that when you use your imagination to create a desired future - whether that future is one free from anxiety, a future filled with confidence, a slimmer you, or you holidaying on your yacht in the Mediterranean, does not really matter - your subconscious mind sets about creating that reality for you because your subconscious mind *is* the reality you are creating. This is why if you entertain the possibility that you are making everything up anyway, you may as well make up something fun.

If you prefer a more rational explanation that does not depend on the connectedness of everything and does not make you in any way responsible for what you experience; then you might consider that if you, on a daily basis, spend some time focusing on a desired reality then it will be in the forefront of your mind and so when you make choices you will make choices that reference your longer term desires. For instance - if you become interested in a particular model of car (perhaps you are thinking of purchasing one) then you may suddenly start noticing them all over the place. This happens because you have started to pay attention to that model and so your subconscious mind picks up on this increased interest and draws your attention to cars that were otherwise ignored. Nothing changed on the roads, but your mind became selectively focused. So if you want to be slimmer you might start paying more attention to healthier recipes, if you imagine yourself more confident, you may notice safe opportunities where you can practise being confident, or you may notice times when you are naturally confident that you previously dismissed as unimportant.

Whichever explanation you prefer, focusing on a desired outcome tends to create circumstances that move you towards that outcome. The mystical explanation fits the details of these kind of occurrences in my own life much better than the rational one, and so that is what I am going to promote here. It requires nothing in the way of belief in order to work. All it requires is that you put in the time on a daily basis with self hypnosis until you achieve your desire.

It will come - you just have to want it enough.

Formulating Suggestions

"Once you become consciously aware of just how powerful your thoughts are, you will realise everything in your life is exactly how you allow it to be."

Melanie Moushigian Koulouris

Two things are required in order to perform self-hypnosis.

1. A method for inducing deep relaxation i.e. trance.
2. Something you want to change.

I have already covered step 1.

So now it is time to look at the things you might want to change and how to make that change happen.

There are two methods for making change happen.

Visualisation, which I discussed in the previous chapter, is the most powerful.

Suggestion is much more in line with traditional uses of hypnosis and you can regard it as another way of reprogramming your subconscious mind.

You may want - more confidence; the ability to talk comfortably to someone you find attractive; more money; better health; to feel better about yourself; to be more successful; to stop putting things off; to achieve a goal – it doesn't really matter what it is as long as it is achievable for you. Walking on the moon is, for most of us, an unrealistic expectation no matter how much we want to do it. So be realistic, but at the same time release your limitations. Begin to consider that you are capable of achieving very much more than you think you can.

Then you need to sit down with a pen and paper before you do any trance work.

Write down a statement that encapsulates what you want. It needs to state what you want as if you have it already. You will know you have the right statement when you get a pleasurable emotional reaction when you read it. The emotional reaction is important. Emotions are powerful mediators for change. You will find that the 'magical' stuff happens much more quickly when powerful, positive emotions are accessed during self-hypnosis.

Now the really important bit.

What you do with self hypnosis is to re-programme your subconscious mind.

Your subconscious mind has three key attributes:

1. It believes whatever you tell it

2. It doesn't understand negatives

3. If you keep on telling it something that isn't true, it will make it true for you.

Your subconscious mind has no critical abilities. That is the realm of consciousness, and that is why your subconscious takes at face value whatever you tell it. You can tell it in words. You can tell it in pictures. But the most powerful way to activate your subconscious is to tell it with emotions. Beware though, because your subconscious has no critical abilities you must always phrase words and images in the positive.

For example:

I am no longer poor.

I am not shy.

I am no longer a failure.

…all maintain the current situation.

The reason they maintain the current situation is that your subconscious mind looks for the words it can create pictures and emotions from. The only words in the above affirmations that your subconscious can create pictures and emotions from are *poor, shy, and failure*. Consequently poverty is maintained, confidence is as elusive as ever, and failure is the only thing you succeed at.

Phrase everything in a positive way:

I am enjoying paying all my bills on time and I have money left over to go out for a meal once a week and a wonderful holiday twice a year.

Accompany this with images of you looking forward to the bills, happily writing out cheques and putting them in the mail, or having fun on your holiday.

I am relaxed and comfortable in all circumstances and situations.

Accompany this with images of you having fun playing Frisbee in the boardroom with your managing director.

I am so successful that I am now a success guru.

Accompany this with images of you sitting cross-legged on your yacht with a group of admirers eager for your every word.

These are just suggestions. Please note the importance of the fun element. What works best are the images and words that emerge from within you, rather than just using my thoughts and ideas which say much more about my mind than they do about your mind and your needs.

The next step is to take yourself into trance in the way I described earlier, either with a physical relaxation or by listening to a trance-inducing recording. Now start to repeat your affirmation – the phrase that you chose to re-program your subconscious mind. Then, while you continue to repeat the phrase, bring into your mind the fantasy you created. Make it as real as you can.

Utilise all of your senses. Hear the sounds, see the colours, touch the textures, as best you can and feel the wonderfully positive emotion that you will experience when you achieve what you want to achieve. When you have fully experienced this allow the image to fade. Allow the mantra to fade, and start to count yourself back up to waking awareness. Remind yourself that when you reach five you will feel fully alert, refreshed and ready to enjoy the rest of the day/evening.

It is time now for the final part of the first section – Goals. Once you understand the power of Goals you will be fully equipped to start making some changes.

Goal Setting

"Nobody ever wrote down a plan to be broke,
fat, lazy, or stupid. Those things are what
happen when you don't have a plan."

Larry Winget

Now you have a good idea of the technique, and what is required from you in order to succeed at using self hypnosis to make positive changes in your life. The next step is to decide exactly what it is that you do want to achieve. In other words, give yourself a goal - something to aim for.

Talk of goal setting always used to scare me because it seemed like all I was doing was setting myself up for failure. If I did not have a goal, then I could not fail and that is so much easier to live with - so I ended up wandering aimlessly through life until I eventually discovered things that fascinated me so much I could not leave them alone. Out of that fascination about minds and how powerful they truly are, I discovered something interesting about goals. They do not have to be huge life-changing events that take years to achieve. They do not have to be things that require difficult skills or perseverance to attain.

Goals can be small. Goals can be medium sized. Goals can be huge. All that is really necessary is that it is something that you want and something that you believe is possible for you. It is not that *impossible* goals are actually impossible, but if you believe it is impossible for you then your subconscious will engage in self-sabotage so that you do not experience any inconsistency between your beliefs and your reality.

If you have a written goal you are much more likely to achieve it.

I would imagine that before purchasing this book you had some idea of the area or areas of your life that you wanted to change. Perhaps some life event overtook you and is forcing you to take action and you are reading this in the hope of discovering an anxiety-free way to do whatever it is that life is forcing you to do. Or maybe you just felt that it was time for change and that if only you knew an easier way to bring it about you would start the process immediately.

Whatever your reason for reading this, whatever you hope to gain, it is really important that you have a clear idea of what it is you want to achieve with my help. Without knowing what it is that you want, you will never know whether or not you have achieved it. Once you have achieved one small thing you are ready to move on to the next greater thing that you desire. We all need to make progress. Growth is normal. Learning new skills and overcoming challenges is normal.

The best and easiest way to make sure you know what you are aiming for is to write it down.

I HAVE A VERY POWERFULL IMMUNE SYSTEM ⅃

I would like to enjoy giving a presentation to 20 people.

IHAM A VERY POWERFUL MEDIAM 4

My goal is to lose 10lbs of weight.

I NOW HAVE ALL MY ABILITES THAT I HAVE NOW 3

I want to fit comfortably into a size 12 dress.

I CAN HYPNOSIS MY SELF WITH THE WORD PETER 2

I would like to feel relaxed and comfortable standing in a supermarket queue.

I CAN MATEYLISF ANYTHING I DESIRE NOW

My blood pressure is going to be 120/80. 2

I HAVE A PERFCT YOUNG HEALTH BODY

I am going to become a non-smoker.

IC AN NOW WALK & RUN

I will sleep undisturbed for at least 7 hours each night and

I AM VERY RICH awaken refreshed and alert.

I WIN LOTS OF LOTTERY

The living room will be completely redecorated by 15th July, 20nn.

I HAVE MILLIONS OF POUNDS

You get the idea.

ALL MY DESIRE WILL HAAPEN

One thing you will notice about all of those statements is that they have something to measure within them. A presentation to 19 people hasn't achieved the goal. Losing 8lbs isn't quite there. Only two of those statements don't have numbers in them: the one about smoking and the one about the supermarket. But you either smoke or you don't. You may argue, and I would agree with you, that there are levels of relaxation and comfort, but if this were your problem then you would know whether or not you were ok in a supermarket queue.

The beauty of something to measure is that it is easy to tell whether or not you have arrived. Of course, if you like to avoid success (and this is quite common) then the very idea of putting numbers in a written goal will be a little anxiety provoking. But remember this, the numbers will be yours not mine, so make it easy on yourself. If you want to lose weight, say, plan your goal to lose 8lbs rather than 30. You can always lose another 8, and another, and another. There's no limit to the number of goals you can use to get where you want to go. If you create easily achievable goals then this will encourage you and you will find that your work with self hypnosis is enjoyable and motivating.

There is one other thing.

The goals I have written above are all set in the future.

Written goals need to be set in the present - as if you have already achieved them. You can use the form *I allow* or *I am* depending on whatever you feel most comfortable with.

I allow myself to enjoy giving a presentation to 20 people.

I allow myself to weigh (whatever your weight is minus 10lb).

I allow myself to fit comfortably into a size 12 dress.

I feel relaxed and comfortable standing in a supermarket queue.

My blood pressure is 120/80.

I am a non-smoker.

I sleep undisturbed for at least 7 hours each night and awaken refreshed and alert.

Because the last statement has a deadline built in you can either leave it the way it is or rewrite without the deadline.

The living room is now completely redecorated.

If you present your subconscious mind with a goal that is set in the future then that is what your subconscious will help you create - something that is always in the future.

If you state it as a present moment achieved event then your subconscious recognises that there is disharmony between external reality and internal reality and so it sets about re-arranging external reality to remove the disharmony - but only if you believe this to be true. So *I am a non-smoker* will work the moment you stop smoking, but if you induce self-hypnosis, and make the affirmation 'I am a non-smoker' with every intention of lighting another cigarette as soon as you wake yourself up - then it will not.

Using the form 'I allow myself' gives you a little wiggle room. It is present tense, but doesn't deny that you aren't there yet. *I allow myself to fit comfortably into a size 12 dress* - accompanied by an image of you wearing a size 12 and looking and feeling fantastic - works even if you are doing the self hypnosis dressed in size 16. Allowing is just giving permission for your subconscious to create what you allow. There is no disharmony as long as you fully accept that size 12 is realistic for you and that you will achieve the necessary weight loss to wear size 12 comfortably.

I remember when I first came across the idea of using affirmations to reprogram me. The books always worded them as if they had already happened.

I feel great.

I am now wealthy.

My health is perfect and I am free from pain.

70

The problem I had with this was that I always felt as if I was lying to myself. I would repeat these statements in the way whatever book I was reading had suggested and just know that they were not true. I could never reconcile this and pretty much abandoned affirmations. Whenever I used affirmations I could feel the disharmony in my body between my statements and my words. I knew it was wrong, but way back then I had no idea how to fix it.

'I allow' is one way to fix it, but there is another way that allows you to use present tense suggestion during self-hypnosis.

Consider this:

Time is an illusion.

You know that this is true because the only time that ever exists is now. The only time you are ever aware of is right now. Anything that you remember, and that includes your memory of reading the word 'reading', is in the past. Anything in the past *is* just a memory. Anything you anticipate or fantasise about *is* in the future. Even your planned appointment at the dentist next week is a fantasy at the moment. It only becomes present when you are sitting in the chair, and there is no guarantee that that will happen - only an expectation born out of your memories of similar experiences in the past. This expectation is that you plan something and then it happens. But the planning is not the happening. You plan a present moment in time and at some other present moment in time, a moment that for now is an imagined future, you do what you planned. Then, having done what you planned, you experience the memory of the event in some future now.

I hope you followed that.

So there is no time, therefore, phrasing affirmations in future tense is meaningless. This is why your subconscious cannot create it for you. But when you imagine something, and in your imagination engage yourself as fully as possible with your imagined experience your subconscious sets about bringing your reality in line with your mental pictures, thoughts, and feelings.

Pretend that you are terrified of public speaking, and because of your job, you are going to have to give a presentation to a group of visitors. The mental pictures you are currently creating are probably of failure, humiliation, and being seen to be nervous. These images are filled with fear and anxiety. So what message does the subconscious get from these pictures thoughts and feelings? Subconscious gets pictures of humiliation and obvious nervousness - maybe shaking hands, or a squeaky voice - accompanied by feelings of dread and physical discomfort. The Subconscious is stupid. If you keep on telling it something, then it *assumes* that that is what you want and creates it for you. So it helps you to have what you want and what you clearly want is an experience of nervousness, humiliation and anxiety - because that is what you are thinking about for most of the day in this particular circumstance.

Now imagine, as best you can, that you feel totally confident. This is difficult to do, when you lack confidence. So do your best to remember a time in your life when you felt good about yourself and relive that moment. This will bring those good feelings from the past into the present. Hang on to those feelings and take them with you into an imagined room with an audience of two people. Imagine yourself enjoying social conversation and then getting up and sharing your knowledge. Create that audience of two interested listeners who ask intelligent questions that you answer comfortably and when you finish see them getting up and shaking your hand and praising you for your knowledge and wisdom.

When you get comfortable with that imagined scene then increase the size of the audience and of the room in small steps - always connecting with feelings of comfort and ease at the beginning. If at any time you feel uncomfortable then take a step back, reconnect with your comfort and feelings of confidence and then continue. Continue with this until you can feel the power of the positive emotion as you hear the applause at the end of your presentation.

This is not lying to yourself. This is just an exercise in imagination. It is your fantasy so you can be as amazing as you choose to be.

But what your subconscious gets is you being amazing and enjoying yourself in front of an audience. So when you eventually step into that situation in a future *now* moment your simple-minded subconscious recognises the situation and says to itself "aha! I know what happens next," and then proceeds to re-create those positive feelings and that compelling performance.

This is the most powerful way to utilise self hypnosis to assist you in making any of your dreams turn into your reality. The Power of this technique comes from the emotions you connect with during the self-hypnosis. Emotional power is creative, and with that knowledge it is time to move on.

You now have an appreciation and understanding of the basic skills that you need in order to bring about your desired change. The next step is to discover how to use these new skills.

That brings us on to the next section of this book, Mind. Here I show you how your thinking style is your only real problem and demonstrate how to use these skills to bring about a new way of looking at your world that leaves you much more peaceful and relaxed.

We begin with how to build confidence.

Mind

"If you are depressed you are living in the past.
If you are anxious you are living in the future.
If you are at peace you are living in the present."

Lao Tzu

Mind

"What the mind of man can conceive
and believe, it can achieve."

Napoleon Hill

This section is the place where I introduce you to some specific techniques that will start the process of change for you. Here I concentrate on three key areas of personal development: confidence, self-esteem, and anxiety. I also add in here details of how to free yourself from the cripplingly isolating problems of agoraphobia and social phobia. I also teach you the technique that I use to help people release themselves from phobias of things like spiders and snakes.

In my experience little progress is made in any area of self-help unless and until there is some improvement in levels of confidence and self-esteem. These areas are the key that opens the door to everything you want in life. So after reading the book through, come back to these two chapters and work at them until you feel a shift and then move on to other areas where you would like to experience change.

Anxiety stress and worry affect all of us from time to time, but there are those who, through no fault of their own, feel powerless and unable to enjoy life because of circumstances they believe they have no control over. Following my guidance once more, you will start to experience freedom from the burdens of worry and stress.

Although many people are unaware of the quite serious nature of agoraphobia, the fact that around 1 in 20 adults suffer from it was sufficient to cause me to include it in this book. In the US there are around 3.2 million sufferers and the figure for the UK is around three-quarters of a million. Unfortunately it is frequently undiagnosed or hidden behind chronic anxiety. Many of the symptoms also exist in milder forms that just make life and social situations uncomfortable. So even if you don't think this applies to you, have a read of it, there is much in this chapter that will be of benefit to you.

Simple phobias are also included because many people experience them and they can, on those occasions you are unable to escape, be quite upsetting.

The final chapter in this section is about relationships. Relationships are very much about the mind and if your relationship could be better then you can achieve much greater harmony with your partner using nothing more than your mind – not to control them, but to change how you interact with them. As you change the way you think about them, they cannot help but change the way they respond to you. This is your first introduction to the magic of self hypnosis whereby you can change another's behaviour by doing nothing more than working on yourself.

This section on mind is designed for you to familiarise yourself with powerful techniques that will bring about changes in your experience of the world. This helps you to feel freer and much more relaxed when alone or in company. Once you see how easily you can exert some control, and make small changes to your life, you will be ready for what follows...

...what follows is an introduction to *magic*.

Confidence

"I've missed more than 9,000 shots in my career. I've lost almost 300 games. Twenty-six times, I've been trusted to take the game-winning shot and missed. I've failed over and over and over again in my life. And that is why I succeed."

Michael Jordan

Confidence is one of those things that is difficult to tie down. We all know when we see a confident person. We know, within ourselves, when we feel confident. Even if you believe you have never felt a moment's confidence in your life, then you will still know what it feels like when you have it. But confidence is not something that operates in isolation. It is connected with an absence of feelings of anxiety or stress.

But one of the odd things about confidence is that you can appear confident to others, while feeling very un-confident on the inside. I know this because there have been many times in my life when I have been filled with anxiety and fear, yet the people who interacted with me have described me as one of the most confident people they know. Remember my story about my terror at having to read to a hall filled with 600 people. I was the only one aware of my terror. All anyone else saw was confidence.

So the first thing I would like you to do is to take note of that. Frequently, how you feel is not communicated to the rest of the world. You can get away with not feeling confident and still perform well.

Knowing that gives you an edge. It means you do not have to be perfect and you can get away with it.

So, allowing that you no longer have to be perfect, it is time to have a look at how we can bring about some significant change with self hypnosis so that you can enjoy much greater feelings of confidence in your life.

To me confidence equates with a sense of inner peace. You can learn to connect with this sense of inner peacefulness in the privacy of your own space. Then you discover how to access it when you are out and about. Finally you discover how to access it when you are in situations where you wish to appear confident.

We are social animals. We need others just to survive - even if that is just to teach us survival skills. Because of this we are constantly seeking approval from others. By that I mean we are very aware of our impact on the people we come into contact with. Imagine, for a moment, you are in an unfamiliar room, alone. It may be an art gallery room, or a library. Make it real in your imagination and fill it with the objects you expect to be there. Get a *feel* for how you feel in this place - perhaps absorbed by something you see. Then imagine another person entering that room. Whether you want it to or not, your feeling state will change and you will probably be aware of this even though this is all happening in your imagination. Put twenty people in the room and notice the difference.

Become aware of this when you are out and about. Notice the emotional shifts that take place in the presence of others. Notice the difference in these shifts when the others are people you know; people you do not know; people you like; people you do not like; people you find attractive; and people you find unattractive.

There is a desire to please within us all. This is a built in survival mechanism. If our parents do not like us we will die. So we seek to please them. But when we succeed in pleasing them we feel good, and since we like feeling good, we are driven to please even more. When our parents are not pleased with us we feel bad and seek to remove the bad feeling by seeking approval. This happens when we are very young. I am not talking about the rebellious years, which are also a natural event that prepares for separation from the family unit and survival alone.

As soon as the eyes of another fall upon us we seek to be pleasing to them. You may be aware of this, you may not, but it is there. It may be hidden under layers of negative emotions like anger and frustration and fear and anxiety - but dig deep enough and you will uncover that desire to be loved.

When we lack confidence we tend to make up stories. The stories are what we imagine is going on in the minds of others. When we blush this is when we have made up a really good story about what others think of us. We do this especially when we feel as if we have made a social blunder.

When I was in my teens I used to visit the cinema on a weekly basis with a small group of friends. One evening when we were walking home after watching *A Fistful of Dollars* I made a comment about an observation of mine regarding the film. This was something I thought would impress the others with my observation skills. They all burst out laughing. It was clearly something that was old hat to them and I was the one out of the loop. I felt totally humiliated. The sting of that event remained with me for decades. It was one of the significant events of my life that encouraged me to keep quiet in the presence of others because *my opinion is of no interest to anyone.*

It is little things like this that sap our confidence and our ability to interact comfortably and confidently with others. One of the problems is that some people are much more sensitive to slights and criticisms than others. If you want to explore more of this then check out The Highly Sensitive Person by Elaine N. Aron.

It does not take many uncomfortable events to create a mind that is wary of how others perceive it.

What is most important for you to understand right now is that the past is gone. No matter what happened, it is not here now. Whatever you might imagine that people are thinking about you is most likely untrue. I know this because, in my early days of mind study, I decided that the only way I could know what people were thinking was to ask them. So I did. They were never thinking what I thought they were thinking. When I said something along the lines of "I had this crazy idea you were thinking this ... about me" they would smile as if I was crazy. The truth is that most of the time, unless you are being irritating, people are much more interested in themselves and in their own lives and problems. I am sorry to say this but you are not that important to them for them to waste their mental energy thinking about you.

So resolve now to work towards observing what *is*, and letting go of the stories you make up.

"If I say what I think, they'll probably think I am stupid" is a story you are making up. In my case that was exactly what happened. Yet, I still had a right to express my opinion and you have as much right to yours as anyone else. What you can never control is another's reaction to your words or actions. But I encourage you to share yourself with the world – how else will they ever discover how loveable you are..

"If I do this while they are watching, I'll probably mess it up, and make a fool of myself" is a story you are making up.

"I am useless at interviews. I'll never get the job" is a story you are making up.

Yet our minds are creative. If you tell yourself those kinds of stories often enough then you *will* create an appearance of being stupid. You *will* create messing things up when others are observing you. You *will* be useless at interviews.

But the worst aspect of those stories is that as you say those things to yourself you also experience pictures in your mind that go with those stories. You see yourself messing up and you feel the emotions of embarrassment and humiliation and feeling foolish. Emotions are the Power behind your mind's creative ability so the more strongly you feel those negative emotions the more likely you are to create those outcomes that you do not want.

Yes! You create the very outcomes you do not want because of your thoughts about them.

There is a difficulty though. If people frequently call you stupid, or this was the message you received as a child; or you usually mess up because you feel so nervous when people are watching you; or you never get the jobs you want because the more you want it the more nervous you are at the interview; then you expect it to happen again *because it always does*.

As soon as you look back into the past you remember those occasions where what you were expecting to happen happened. Then you say to yourself, look it always happens, why should this time be any different. Your expectation is one of failure and so you fail.

In order to increase your confidence all you have to do is to break this cycle of taking the past and projecting it into your future.

This is why it is so important for you to recognise that what is past is gone. It is gone forever.

There are two methods you can use with self hypnosis in order to bring about a change in your confidence levels.

Method 1.

Think of a time in your life when you felt confident, or when you succeeded at something. It does not matter what it was. It just needs to be something that you felt really good about. I remember when I was 12 I had a piece of writing published in the annual school magazine. That was really good. Passing my motorcycle test and then, a couple of years later, my driving test - both gave me a positive reaction out of all proportion to what I had achieved. Then I had my first photograph published in a photographic magazine, then the first one on the cover of a magazine, and then a whole article in a national magazine - these are all milestones for me that made me feel really good. I still feel good when I remember those occasions.

There will be milestones in your life, and it does not matter whether they are big or small. It does not matter whether anyone else even noticed. All that matters is that you felt good because of something you had done.

If you cannot think of anything at the moment, then just make something up. See yourself in your mind's eye achieving some longed-for dream, some life's ambition. Make it as real as you can in your mind.

If you truly believe that nothing good ever happened; if you truly believe that there was no moment when you felt good about yourself then I am afraid I still have a solution for you. What I would like you to do is to mentally relive an event that would have left you with a success had it gone your way. Mentally re-create it but change the memory so that what happened is what you would have liked to have happened. Turn it into a success fantasy about the past and connect with the good feelings. Bring this event to mind frequently and continue to replay it as it should have happened. Do this until, when you think about it, you feel good. So see yourself winning the race, giving the speech, getting the right job, or marrying the right person. It doesn't really matter, what matters is finding a way to connect with good feelings about yourself.

As you remember, or create, this event you will notice that you start to feel a little of the good feelings associated with this event. Focus on these positive feelings and allow them to intensify. Make them as strong as you can and then let them go.

That is all the preparatory work you need.

Take yourself into your trance ready to do your self hypnosis.

Recall the memory or the created event again. Feel the good feelings again. But this time intensify them as much as you possibly can. Allow those good feelings to fill the whole of your body and mind as best you can.

Then, taking those good feelings with you, allow yourself to imagine, as best you can, an event or occasion where you would like to feel more confident. See yourself moving through this event, cool, calm, responding intelligently and interacting positively with the people in your mind. If you notice the positive feelings start to dissipate, then go back to your remembered positive event, re-create the good feelings, and then come back to the place where you left off.

See the event right through to the end. Then see yourself afterwards feeling brilliant about how well you did. Perhaps you could see yourself doing something to celebrate. Then take your imagination a few days or weeks or months into the future and see the results of the positive outcome that you achieved.

Then bring yourself back gently into your normal waking world.

Do this on a daily basis. Use as many different scenarios as you can, choosing those where you would like to enjoy greater confidence. Also, once you have done this a few times, you can introduce the idea of approaching the situation while feeling a little anxious, but calming yourself and still performing well. This is essential, because it is the fear of the anxiety that is the biggest barrier to success, so if you train yourself, using your self-hypnosis, to appear confident despite a little inner discomfort - then nothing will prevent your success.

As your self hypnosis begins to impact your subconscious world what you should notice is that when you think about a situation, where in the past you lacked confidence, you will find yourself feeling less and less uneasy, until you can think about it without any discomfort. This is the point at which you need to take action and enter into the situation in reality.

The first time you 'test out' the effects of your self hypnosis, do not expect to be completely free of concerns or anxiety. Notice what you feel, remind yourself that some anxiety is to be expected but that it will remain at a level which will not interfere with your performance. The next time you repeat this activity the anxiety will be much less. This will continue until you finally feel totally comfortable in this type of situation.

It is unrealistic to expect no anticipatory anxiety or concern. But your self hypnotic training will have shown you that you can handle it and it will not interfere with your activity. That said you may have done such a good job that you are totally and completely at ease in a situation that once caused you concern.

Method 2.

This is a way to give yourself a post-hypnotic suggestion that will help you to feel comfortable in stressful situations. A post-hypnotic suggestion is an action that you program into your mind during hypnosis, but which will only activate with a specific trigger event.

Take yourself into trance.

Imagine yourself on a comfortable boat on a large lake. You have an engine, but you allow yourself to drift lazily. You settle back into soft, luxurious cushions and maybe hold a cool drink in your hand. Notice the droplets of condensation trickling down the glass. Notice the bubbles rising to the surface. Be aware of the blue sky with maybe a puff or two of white cloud. Feel the warmth of this lazy day. Maybe you could trail your hand in the water and feel its coolness. Watch birds fishing. Allow yourself to settle down and feel really comfortable while you drift and daydream in this beautiful warm, safe place. In this completely safe place you have no worries or concerns, just for now. Listen for distant sounds. Immerse yourself completely in this fantasy.

When you are as deeply relaxed as you are able to achieve. You must squeeze together the finger and thumb of one of your hands. While you do this you must say to yourself...

Whenever I do this, as long as it is safe for me to do so, I will become as deeply relaxed as I am now. Each time I do this, I will become more relaxed than the time before. Each time I do this I will feel completely relaxed and totally in control.

Repeat this two more times, relaxing your finger and thumb in between.

Now squeeze your finger and thumb together again but this time say to yourself *calm*. Draw out the word with a long *a* and say it to yourself on an out breath.

Relax and repeat this twice more.

Return to your fantasy about the boat. Trail your hand in the water once more. Notice the sky and the clouds. Feel the coolness of the glass in your hand. Be aware of your surroundings. Relax fully and allow yourself to drift and enjoy these pleasurable sensations for another five minutes.

Return to full waking awareness.

When you are out and about, initially in non-threatening situations, just squeeze together your finger and thumb and say the word *calm* to yourself. Notice how your BodyMind immediately starts to relax. Notice how deep it goes. Notice how it gets stronger on each occasion that you use it. Get a feel for how it affects you.

Then you are ready to make use of this in situation where you feel less than confident. Just squeeze finger and thumb together and say silently to yourself the word *calm*. Feel yourself relaxing and feeling more confident and in control.

This becomes more powerful each time you use it.

Do not use this when you are driving, operating machinery, or doing anything that requires your full alertness. Test it out in safe locations until you know exactly how deeply it affects you.

Affirmations

You may want to use these in addition to visualisation:

Repeat these several times while holding a mental image of the successful outcome. Always remember, if appropriate, to hear the applause or the congratulations and feel the pride that comes with your success.

I allow myself to enjoy interacting with an audience.

I allow myself to enjoy social situations.

Just the way I am is perfectly ok.

I always do the best I can do – and that is quite good enough.

I allow myself to enjoy being with others.

I allow myself to do what I want to do even though I am experiencing a little anxiety.

Self-Esteem

"Do what you do,
don't do what you don't do.
And be okay with that."

Michael Hadfield

S elf-esteem is very closely linked to confidence, and much of what I wrote in the previous chapter applies here. But I will offer a distinction that separates the two. Consider that confidence is largely about how we feel when the World is observing us. Self-esteem is largely about how we feel about ourselves. There is some overlap and one affects the other, but for now consider that confidence is pointing outward and self-esteem is pointing inward. If you see it differently, that is ok, but it is on that premise that I shall continue.

Low self-esteem is having a low opinion of oneself. But that is also projected outwards and so the World is seen as having a low opinion of oneself also. If this is how you feel about yourself, then, for a few moments at least, know that it is possible for you to change this.

You can change it because, no matter what you think, it is a state of mind rather than a state of reality.

Indicators of Low Self-Esteem

You...

- Feel inadequate.
- Believe yourself to be unlovable.
- See yourself as a failure.
- Feel unworthy of having the things you want.
- Trust the wrong people.
- Do not trust the right people.
- Have difficulty accepting compliments.

- Expect rejection.
- Always choose the wrong jobs.
- Always choose the wrong partners.
- Deny being successful even when you are.
- May engage in addictive behaviours (shopping, alcohol, food, drugs, sex).
- Overreact to innocent comments or actions.
- Have a highly developed sense of right and wrong and are overly critical of others.

That is quite a list and I could add quite a bit more, but you get the picture. If you read that list and think "but isn't everyone like that" then no, everyone is not like that. But if that is how *your* world looks then you are suffering from low self-esteem and your world will become much brighter as you take steps to improve the situation.

We all seek love. It is a natural part of being human. But imagine believing that you were unlovable, and were still driven to know that you are loved. What you might engage in is behaviour that demands constant reassurance from the source(s) of love in your life. But since you never can be reassured, you might experience anger, frustration or other negative emotions as a consequence. Life will rarely be peaceful because of this drive within to seek the necessary feedback that says you are truly lovable.

The difficulty here is that the belief is a powerful one and so any input that suggests to you that you are lovable, or adequate, or successful is immediately rejected by you – and so nothing ever changes no matter how appreciative your world is of you.

This seems to be a self-fulfilling prophecy created by past experiences. Now, while you will see me frequently drawing attention to the Truth that the past is gone and the present is what we have to deal with, I would never deny that the past has created for you a set of distorting lenses through which you view the world. You have viewed the world for so long through this distortion that it has become normal for you, and real reality would itself appear strangely distorted should you remove those lenses.

The past is a factor and needs to be honoured briefly before being dismissed.

How you see yourself, and the value you place upon yourself, is the result of your life experiences. Childhood experiences, because they take place when we are seeking to know how we can safely navigate this world, are especially powerful in this respect. Because of this, the way we are treated by our parents while growing up, is a significant factor in our self-esteem rating. Other significant adults in our young lives can also have a powerful impact on the way we see ourselves.

Parents who are overly critical, or perfectionist, can raise a child who desperately seeks to please but believes they never can. This could be a person who, as an adult, has a great deal of difficulty saying no, believes nothing they ever do is good enough, and is critical of not only small errors, but also of everything and everyone.

Parents who find it difficult to express the love that they are will probably raise children who are constantly seeking approval as adults, yet, no matter how much approval they receive, will work even harder to please.

The response to being raised by dysfunctional parents (and to some extent we were all raised by dysfunctional parents, because none of us know all the answers, and we are already thoroughly screwed up when we have our own children) can be compliance or reaction. You can give up, or you can be a super-achiever. But even if you choose the super-achiever route, whatever you achieve will never be sufficient because in the subconscious depths of your mind you are still attempting to please the unpleasable.

Know that how you feel about yourself and the effect that it has had on your life is not your fault. Nor is it your parents fault because they were doing the best they could with what they knew. Placing blame serves no purpose and only perpetuates the problem.

Knowing and acknowledging that you are not at fault frees you to make changes. Without forgiving and releasing the past it holds you where you are. Later on in the book I deal with the importance of forgiveness in much more detail.

Having dealt with the past it is time now to move forward into your better brighter future.

Repairing damaged self-esteem is not as quick or as straight forward as increasing confidence. It needs to be done in stages, and the changes will be much slower in making their presence felt.

The Art of Appreciation

Step 1

The first step is discovering appreciation.

Once each day, preferably towards the end of the day, take yourself down into your trance state. Allow your mind to recapture the events of the day. Quickly run through your day. What you are seeking are those moments when something good happened. You are looking for five of those events. When you have five of them, replay them in your mind, one at a time and feel, as best you are able, a sense of appreciation for having been given that moment to enjoy. Allow the good feeling to deepen as much as you can and then let it go and move on to the next one. Then bring yourself back to waking awareness.

You may find at first that you have difficulty with this exercise. In fact you will probably find that the lower your self-esteem the harder it is to do this. But do it anyway.

If you fail to find events that are worthy of appreciation, then use your imagination to change what actually happened to something you can appreciate. The important thing here is to connect with feelings of appreciation.

Things worthy of appreciation?

What might they look like?

I notice when a checkout operator is kind and does just a little bit more than is necessary. I notice when someone smiles at me. I notice when someone engages me in conversation. I notice a book I am enjoying. I notice good service. I notice the light shining through a leaf. I notice a road sign lovingly placed to help me to find my way. I notice the deliciousness of a cup of coffee.

Just sitting here at my desk writing this I can be appreciative of the large monitor that allows me to do several things at once. I am appreciative of the spiral bound diary that lays flat and open beside me so that I can see at a glance all of my appointments for a whole week and look forward to weekend activities that I will enjoy. I can glance at the names I have written there and spend a few moments appreciating the people I'll be spending time with. Thursday this week is looking especially good. There are pens and paper and a printer and telephones and books all of which I have chosen to surround myself with because there was something about them that I valued.

I have picked up a tin of organic baked beans in the supermarket and thought about the trees used for the label, the designers who chose the words and the shapes; the metal of the can; the drivers who brought it to the shop for me; all of the people involved in manufacturing the lorry to fetch them in; all of the manufacturing process and the people involved in picking and packing the beans and transporting them to the factory; the people who dig the ore for the tin and all of the infrastructure involved in that. But it isn't just recognising the steps in the very long and complex chain that gets a bean from a pod on a plant into a tin in my hand – it is the valuing and appreciation of all of that that is important.

Appreciation is easy. You just need to put some thought into it and you need to understand that it does not have to be big to be worthy of appreciation.

Spend a lot of time developing your skill at the Art of Appreciation. If you take nothing else from me, but do this sincerely, it will change your life.

Spend a week or two focusing on nothing more than that.

I hope you will find that after a few days your focus begins to shift towards what is going well for you. You may also find that you feel a little lighter in your mood and that your world feels a little brighter.

Step 2

The next step is to add to the above.

This time during your self hypnosis, while you are replaying your day and looking for your items of appreciation I want you to be more aware of your own participation in your day and look out for something about **you** to appreciate. Start with something small. If you made yourself breakfast, appreciate some aspect of that - or any other meal you prepared. I have just enjoyed a cup of hot chocolate carefully prepared in a way that I find especially delicious, and as I am recalling it to write about, I can feel that sense of appreciation for me in the care that I take when I make it and the savouring of the drink because it is something special I did for me. It is not something I have every day, or more than once a day, but I buy high quality organic cocoa that tastes absolutely delicious.

If you picked up a piece of rubbish from the floor, appreciate your desire to not only improve your environment but also to take action to bring that about.

If you did just a little bit more for someone else than you needed to, then appreciate your loving and caring nature as best you can. Even if it is just for a moment or two. You can go back to beating yourself up after you have done the appreciation bit.

If you smiled at anyone, appreciate your desire to brighten their day.

If you gave way to someone in traffic, appreciate your kindness.

If you opened a door, or let someone go first, appreciate your gentle nature for that moment.

Truly you can appreciate anything if you approach it from a place of lack of judgement.

Every day add one more thing to appreciate about you until you have five things about your life and five things about you to enjoy in your self hypnosis session..

Maintain this on a daily basis for two weeks.

I know this all seems very simplistic and slow, but what I am teaching you here is much more powerful than it has any right to be. It will change your life if you follow my instructions. You have been *broken* for a long time. It is unreasonable to expect to be *fixed* by reading a few chapters in a book. There has to be action to follow the reading. Without action, nothing changes. The actions I suggest are simple and possible. They ask you to do nothing you are incapable of doing. They require no co-operation from anyone else.

Step 3

The next step is to begin to honour you.

Most of the time our social training makes us behave according to someone else's rules. If the rules are the rule of law of the country you live in then it makes sense to stick to them. Here in the UK the rule is that we drive on the left hand side of the road and when everyone does that life flows smoothly. But if I were to visit the US and insist on driving the way I always have done, then I would very soon find myself, dead, injured, or in jail.

But a lot of the rules we follow exist solely in our minds and bear no relationship to the outside world. I used to have a lot of trouble driving. I would be constantly monitoring, judging, and criticising other drivers for following too closely; cutting into my safe braking space; and driving too fast in fog/snow/rain/hail/ice. Then one day I had a revelation.

My revelation was this. I was the Universe's Policeman and no one was paying me for that job.

It wasn't just rules for driving safely, I was critical of a lot more things in life. I was constantly monitoring everything and every-one for error – including myself. But my revelation helped me to realise that I had a load of rules set up in my head that no one else knew anything about. None of the people I was getting frustrated and angry with had the slightest idea that they had broken my rule because it was just my rule – in my head.

So I figured, how can anyone obey rules they know nothing about? I resigned from my job as the Universe's Policeman. I set an intention to allow everyone to do what they want – largely because they were going to do that anyway – and I would just do what I wanted to do.

I have been a lot happier since and driving is just so much less stressful.

Then there are the rules about personal behaviour that we have been programmed with: eat up, clean your plate, don't waste food, don't hurt anyone's feelings, you can't say that, that will upset someone so don't do it, don't get angry, don't cry...

Make your own list. Then tear it up and flush it down the toilet.

But we need rules to know how to operate and navigate through social situations. I mean we have all met people who have no sense of others: strangers who stand too close when they are talking to us; people who don't care what they say; loud people; people who ignore social cues, like increasing the distance between you, to end a conversation; people who you don't want to be around and avoid if you can.

You don't want to be one of those people and the fear is that you might become one if you don't have any internal rules.

My new rule is that my intention, always, is to be appropriate. Being appropriate means nothing more than taking your cues from the present rather than the past. Respond to what is happening rather than react to what happened many years ago, or what you imagine might be going on in the minds of others.

So, as always, the first step is to use your self hypnosis to rehearse and establish new patterns of behaviour that come naturally and without thought – in other words, new habits. So begin to notice those situations during your day where you feel less than adequate. These are the situations for you to use in your self hypnosis.

Take yourself into trance.

Take yourself to your favourite place and allow yourself to enjoy feelings of comfort and relaxation.

Then imagine yourself in a situation where you would like to behave differently.

Run through the situation the way you normally do and notice your comfort level with this.

Now run through the situation again the way you would like it to be.

Notice your comfort levels.

If discomfort has increased then allow the image to fade.

Go back to your favourite place and remain there until you have re-established comfort, ease, and relaxation.

Keeping hold of those feelings of comfort, relaxation and ease, run through the new situation again.

Notice feelings of discomfort.

Repeat this until you can run through the new behaviour feeling either completely at ease, or at ease enough to feel confident about doing it.

Bring yourself back to waking reality.

Repeat this until you find yourself behaving this way in normal waking consciousness.

You will probably find that one day you just behave in the new way and won't be aware that you have done this until afterwards. This is because your self hypnosis has established a new habit and as soon as something distracts you the new habit will kick in.

Test this out with small things.

If you can't waste food then leave just one pea or one chip on your plate.

If you can't say no. Then say no to something that does not matter very much to you or to the other person.

Affirmations

I allow myself to be appreciated by others.

I allow myself to accept gifts from others and I respond with nothing more than a heartfelt thank you as I recognise their appreciation of me.

I enjoy being served, or helped, by others.

I allow myself to say no whenever any request is made of me.

So now we have made some progress and enjoyed a lift in confidence and our ability to change in small ways it is time to look anxiety straight in the eye.

Anxiety, Stress, and Worry

"In any situation, the best thing you can do is the right thing; the next best thing you can do is the wrong thing; the worst thing you can do is nothing."

Theodore Roosevelt

Anxiety is the internal warning symptom that our thoughts are inconsistent with who we truly are. When we feel that we are less than the others around us, or lacking the confidence we need to succeed, then anxiety will be there establishing the truth of those erroneous thoughts.

I would like you to play with the idea that anxiety is nothing more than a burglar alarm. A burglar alarm tells us when we have an intruder and we need to take action to evict the intruder. With anxiety the unwanted intruder is a thought. When you evict that thought and replace it with a more pleasing one – the alarm turns off and peace reigns once more.

You don't leave the burglar alarm turned off in case it annoys you. Medication effectively switches the alarm off. Begin to see your anxiety as something helpful to let you know when you are off-track in your thinking. So when the alarm goes off, know it is time to take action.

But know also that you are not alone with this.

Stress is endemic in our society. In a recent interview Dr Leonard Coldwell stated that 86% of all doctor visits are stress related. He also suggested that the majority of physical illnesses have stress as their cause. This is because stress lowers immune system responses. The immune system is then unable to destroy unwelcome invaders, or malignant cell growths, that would not trouble a healthy, peaceful body. Stress is killing us. This chapter could save your life, so please take it seriously.

Anxiety, stress and worry are all very similar. As I started to write this I began to wonder what exactly the differences were. In my mind I see differences in these problems, but with my patients I

101

treat them all in a similar way because what works for one works for the others.

My thoughts are that stress is a short-term experience about something that is happening now; while anxiety and worry are physiologically the same experience as stress, but about a future event. I would further separate anxiety as worry that has deepened into something that is, or is beginning to, interfere with doing the things you want to do in life.

A quick bit of research, and by that I mean seeing what articles Google thinks are relevant to my query, found me two other experts. One of whom agreed with me and one of whom was saying the exact opposite - that stress is long-term and anxiety short-term. One of the things I remember is that my own anxiety was pretty much generalised. Some things created more intense anxiety than others, but there was always a background level of anxiety that never seemed to disappear regardless of what I was doing or thinking about doing.

What I also remember is this. My mind would play - over and over, like a broken record - the imagined terror of some event in my future. So I experienced the hell of that event for very much longer than it actually took when I finally lived through it. My thinking pattern was a huge part of the problem. But back then I used to think my thoughts were me and not something separate from me. I later discovered that they were simply other people's fears and beliefs that I had been programmed with. The door to freedom opened as soon as I realised my thoughts were not me and that I did not have to believe what they said.

At this point in my research I began to wonder what does it matter about definitions when we all have a pretty good idea what we mean when we use any of those words. So I have decided to deal with them all at once.

But, just in case you are actually wondering whether or not you have a problem that needs fixing I'll give you some symptoms.

Anxiety sypmtoms:

- Worrying and feeling tense
- Can't settle
- Easily Annoyed
- Intolerant
- Headaches
- Sweating
- Difficulty concentrating
- Frequent toilet visits
- Tiredness
- Shakiness
- Easily startled
- Problems sleeping
- Cold or sweaty hands and/or feet
- Shortness of breath
- Palpitations
- Dry mouth
- Numbness or tingling in the hands or feet
- Nausea
- Muscle tension
- Dizziness

This is not an exhaustive list. It is just to give you an idea of the ways in which anxiety can impact your life. I also need to point out that just because a symptom is on this list, it does not mean that anxiety *is* the diagnosis. Many of the problems listed here also have other causes. Your doctor is the person to see for a diagnosis. Once you have that you can choose for yourself whether or not to treat it with self hypnosis or the medication your doctor will almost certainly prescribe for you.

However, I believe that most people know whether or not they are suffering from anxiety. I spent many years in my doctor's office receiving advice and prescriptions before I realised that nothing was changing and I decided I needed to look for another way. But I always knew what the problem was. I just had no idea how to fix it. Many doctors are much more clued up these days on better ways to treat anxiety than the medication I was pre-scribed (and when the anxiety is intense, sometimes medication is needed to provide a stable psychological platform from which to seek alternatives). Nevertheless, there are still many who will hand out Valium (diazepam) and other benzodiazepines. Though I have noticed that now that the addictive nature of the benzodiazepine family of drugs is better documented, many of my patients receive prescriptions for anti-depressants instead - even though anxiety is the problem not depression. If I had to hazard a guess I'd say that the patient wanted help so the doctor prescribes something that affects brain chemistry hoping that the patient will experience some improvement in their anxiety symptoms - or maybe the drug companies, having lost out on sales of anxiolytics, are just pushing anti-depressants and claim-ing that they have an anxiety reducing side-effect.

Having filled in some background details it is now time to have a little look at what can be done about the problem.

Initially what you will need is relief from the symptoms. Relief from the symptoms gives you a little bit of freedom to think about the problems and space to take other actions that will help. Symptomatic relief is relatively easy – it is just relaxation. I write that 'just' with an awareness of how difficult that might seem right now if the anxiety is very intense, and how also it seems a little glib when your anxiety is totally screwing up your life. It took me around 20 years to find the answers I was seeking, and restore myself to a state where I could function comfortably in society once more - so if it takes you just a few months of following my instructions then be thankful that you can be free that quickly.

Relaxation alone can be achieved relatively easily by one of two methods: meditation, or self hypnosis.

To use self hypnosis purely for relaxation, you need to do a little preparation. Get yourself as comfortable as you can. If you have some music that evokes pleasant memories then play that quietly in the background or through headphones. Then allow your mind to drift back in time to any positive experiences or pleasant memories you can find. We all have these memories simply because our minds are adaptable and fun-seeking and so no matter what our life has been like there will be at least moments of pleasure somewhere in the past. Now, because of your anxiety it may be difficult to access these positive memories, so do not worry too much if nothing comes up. But if nothing comes up, do not use this knowledge to reinforce your *victim* state by thinking that nothing good ever happens to you or that you cannot even succeed at something as simple as relaxing. The memories are there, they may be hidden for now, but as you continue to seek them out, and as you continue to relax they will start to emerge from their long hibernation and you will be able to relive moments of pleasure along with all the good feelings and knowledge that you were loved. Just keep asking yourself to find good memories. They will appear. But if you cannot get hold of one right now, then make one up. The only reason you are suffering right now is because your life is not the way you want it to be. So use your wonderful imagination to dream about how you would like your life to be if everything were perfect and you were free from worry.

Having established your plan of action - the memory you want to use, or the fantasy future you want to create - take yourself into trance as I have already described. Then once you have reached your door at the bottom of the staircase, step back into the memory or the fantasy. Make it as real as you are able using all of your senses. Feel the good feelings as best you can and then, once you have connected with the good feelings allow and encourage them to deepen. Stay there for as long as you can. If you can manage 15 minutes without drifting back into worry then that would be perfect, but just 5 minutes will be beneficial.

As soon as you find yourself drifting back to your present day thoughts and concerns bring yourself back to the present.

Should you only be able to manage a minute or two in past or future, before the worries intrude, then count yourself back, open your eyes, look around for just a second or two, then close your eyes again and immediately count yourself back down, walk through the door and into the memory/fantasy again. Repeat this until you can manage five minutes of pleasure. Whatever you do, do not stop until you achieve this otherwise self hypnosis becomes another way to reinforce your idea that you are inadequate, or that nothing ever works for you.

Persistence is key.

If you can do this twice a day, then do so.

After you have been doing this daily for a week, you can move into Phase 2. Phase 2 is activating the conditioned response. When you are going about your day, at a time when there is nothing specifically anxiety-provoking. Bring back to mind the good memory you have been using in your daily self hypnosis sessions. You will notice that as you bring this image into your mind's eye that you feel your body relaxing a little. Each time you do this you will find the relaxation effect a little more powerful.

Do this until you feel confident in the power of this mental image. Now, when you enter into a slightly anxiety provoking situation (or when you find yourself worrying) again bring this image to mind and notice how your BodyMind relaxes. Notice whatever effect you experience. Each time you do this it will have a more powerful impact on your physiology (so don't do it while driving or operating machinery).

Then do this in an even more anxiety provoking situation. Work your way up until you feel confident that just bringing this image to mind will bring calmness along with it so that you can function effectively in the situation. Noticing even a small change will bring with it a new found confidence. The confidence will be because you realise at last that you are no longer powerless; you are no longer a victim of your own emotional states; no longer unable to stand up for yourself. It doesn't mean you will do these things completely free of anxiety. But once you experience a small change you will know that a big change is not far away.

And with a big change comes freedom.

Meditation

If you are still struggling with this, or you would just like to try it, then set yourself aside some time to meditate instead.

Meditation is at the same time the easiest and the most difficult thing to do.

Before I trained as a hypnotherapist I used to work in a UK National Health Service clinic helping patients who were suffering from anxiety and anxiety related problems. One of my tasks was to teach them to meditate. This allowed them to quieten their minds as a precursor to learning how to use that meditative state to access their intuition which they were then taught how to use to guide them safely through life.

No matter how simple I made my instructions, the vast majority of patients came back the following week telling me all the reasons why it was not working - but mostly how they were failing. This, despite my reinforcing the idea that it was impossible to fail at meditation because there is no goal they could fail to reach. Failure is so entrenched in the minds of anxiety sufferers that the possibility of something that was so easy that success is a given was so alien to them that they manufactured difficulties.

And all of the difficulties were because they did what they thought I wanted them to do and not what I asked them to do.

Here are the rules for a task it *is* impossible to fail at.

1. Sit comfortably with your back vertical (a straight-backed dining type chair is better for this exercise than an armchair). If you are flexible enough to sit comfortably cross-legged on the floor for 10 minutes, then you can do that, but a chair is fine. If in a chair, place both feet flat on the floor. Rest your hands, palm upwards, fingers relaxed, on your thighs. If you want to look really cool then gently touch the tip of your thumb and your index finger together so that a circle is formed. If for any reason you cannot do any of this, then just sit as comfortably as you can.

2. Repeat a word to yourself over and over again. Whenever you find that your thoughts have drifted off and you become aware that you are not repeating the word, then start repeating the word again.

3. Do this for ten minutes. You can set a timer, but you will soon discover an amazing clock inside of you that lets you know exactly, almost to the second, when the ten minutes is up.

What could be simpler?

How could anyone fail at that?

The reason most people believe they have failed is because within seconds of starting to repeat the word their busy, busy minds are filled with all of their anxious thoughts again. Despite my explanation they have decided that the task is to not have any thoughts about anything and to fill their mind with nothing but the repetitive word. Even though that is not what I asked them to do. Nor is it what I am asking you to do.

You see, not thinking is an almost impossible task. After years of mind training I can accomplish a completely quiet mind for maybe a minute on a good day. But what my mind training has achieved is the ability to quieten my mind to a much greater extent when I have something external to focus on - such as when I have a patient with me. This allows me to hear clearly my intuitive voice that guides me during these consultations.

So, because not thinking is an impossible task, I am not asking you to not think. I am asking you to fill your mind space with a word until you realise you have drifted off. You are never aware of the moment at which you drift off and back into your worry mind. Because you are never aware of this, there is absolutely nothing you can do about it. There is, however, a moment when you will realise that you are back in your worry mind. This is the only time you can return to your task of repeating your special word.

So you see, meditation is a process of engaging in a short period of focus, drifting off into your worry mind for a while, then beginning all over again. Focus... drift... focus... drift... focus... drift.

If I were to represent this as a timeline, with *f* representing *focus* and *d* representing *drifting*, it would look like:

Begin... fff...dddddddddddddd... ff... dddddddddddddddddd... f...   dddddddddddddddddddddddddddddd...   f... dddddddddddddddddddddddddddddddddd... ff... **end**.

After about a month's dedicated practise it will look like:

Begin... ffff... ddddddddddd... ff... dddddddddd... fff... ddddddddddddddd... f... dddddddddddddddddddddd... ff... dddddddddddd... f... ddddddd... fff...**end**

The drifts start to get shorter, and there are more brief periods of focus. And this is all that happens as you progress and persist. The drifts get shorter and the focus periods become more frequent and lengthen slightly.

Now I realise that I am not painting an attractive picture here. There seems to be a lot of effort for little reward. But to put things into perspective, we are talking about ten minutes once or twice a day. This is ten minutes in which you begin to discover something quite amazing about yourself - **you are not your thoughts**.

But before I get into the importance of that revelation, I need to look, in a little more detail, at this apparently simple process and why it appears so difficult.

Step 1.

If you are too comfortable there is a tendency to fall asleep, so while not actually encouraging discomfort, I encourage support for your back and a position that does not interfere with circulation. So only sit cross-legged if you can do so without any discomfort. Sit relaxed, making sure your shoulders are not hunched and that your facial muscles are all at ease. Breathe as deeply as you comfortably are able without needing to put any effort into it. The idea of all of this is so that you can focus on the task of repeating your word without any physical distraction. Though I have found that if physical distraction occurs (an itch, or an ache, for instance) the best way to deal with it is just to place all of your attention on the discomfort and make that the focus of your meditation. I find that this usually results in the irritation disappearing, but if it doesn't, it doesn't. You do not shift your attention to an irritation with the intention of making it disappear. You shift your attention there because part of your attention is there anyway. Attempting to ignore it just means you are focusing on two things rather than one because it remains as an awareness with resistance to its presence.

Step 2.

What word to repeat? In some respects it does not matter, you can choose any word. But in some respects it does. Let us for a moment choose to repeat the word chocolate over and over again. When I do that I notice that part of my attention is on sensations in my mouth, and if I kept that up for any length of time I may well find myself wanting some chocolate. So any word that has meaning for you is best to avoid.

Choose a neutral word or one that enhances the meditation experience. I sometimes use the word 'calm' or the word 'peace'. When I use these words I synchronise them so I repeat them in my mind along with my out breath and I stretch them out so they last the length of the breath.

My preference though is a word without meaning, or at least without obvious meaning - in other words a sound. My favourite is Om, a Sanskrit/Hindu word, one of whose meanings is the sound of the origin of the Universe. Some endow this sound with mystical properties. However, for most English speakers, it is just a pleasant resonant sound (pronounced like 'home' without the 'h' and with a drawn out 'm' so that it is almost a hum). But if you are alone, and repeat it out loud, you can feel it resonate within your chest. It is very centring and relaxing. It is also very like the sound from a didgeridoo.

When you realise you have drifted away from the repetition of your chosen word, then gently, and without criticism for having drifted off, return yourself to your chosen word (mantra).

There is also another traditional sound you can use. You can repeat the sound *So-hum*. Use the syllable *so* on the in-breath and *hum* on the out-breath. Using this with the breath helps you to stay focused.

Now as you develop your skill at meditation you will find that the quality of your thoughts change as you develop the ability to drop down through layers of consciousness. At first the distracting thoughts are about all the trivia and worries of the day. Then as you develop your skill in releasing them almost as soon as they appear, you will find that they begin to change in form. Perhaps they will begin by being about the meditation itself - helpful distractions; or they may start to be about really important stuff that cannot possibly wait because if you do not think about it now then you will forget. My mind has tried all sorts of tricks to get me away from my goal of repeating a word for 10 minutes.

The reason for this is that the part of you responsible for generating all of the troublesome distracting thoughts feels threatened because you are taking its power away.

No harm came to me by letting go of these deeper levels of distraction, so I can only encourage you to persist and be amused at the lengths your mind can go to in order to keep you stuck.

There is a good reason that your mind wants to keep you stuck. Stuck is safe. It might not feel like that to you, but you are the way you are because it is safer than being anyway else. That does not necessarily mean that where you are is fun or comfortable, it is just less uncomfortable than anywhere else right now. If it was not, you would be in that more comfortable place already.

Step 3.

This step hardly needs any additional explanation. Though I would like to point out that the time length is absolutely arbitrary. It could be 9 minutes, or 13.7 minutes, or 1 minute. Ten is just a nice round number that is easily measured on both analog and digital clocks by sight without giving it a great deal of thought. You can make it any number of minutes that you like. What is important are just two things. The first is that you decide on the length of the meditation before you start - and then stick to that. The second is that, in the early days, you keep your meditation periods short. If you want longer meditations when you start, it is much better to do three 10 minute sessions, rather than one 30 minute session, a day. Once you become experienced then you can increase the length of your meditations if you wish, but

I would still limit it to a maximum of 30 minutes. One, and just one, of the reasons for this is that you can be tempted to use meditation simply as an escape from an uncomfortable reality by kidding yourself you are doing something beneficial when in actual fact it is just an excuse to do nothing and avoid life. Meditation is beneficial only when it makes you more alive by bringing a greater sense of peace to your interactions with others. Avoid using it to legitimise solitariness and isolation born out of fear or social inadequacy.

Meditation, just like the self hypnosis, sets up a conditioned response. So in the same way I suggested earlier, bring to mind your mantra in a full waking state and notice the calming effect it has on mind and body. Proceed as I described earlier to make this an effective tool to combat anxiety in your everyday life.

You Are Not Your Thoughts

In my one-to-one consultations I have, on many occasions, had the idea expressed to me that

I must be bad because I think bad things.

Their reasoning being that if negative, judgemental thoughts appear then, since those thoughts are generated by them, those thoughts must be an accurate reflection of the thinker of the thoughts. I ask if they deliberately think those thoughts or if they just appear. I suggest that if the thoughts were truly a reflection of the thinker then the thinker would be untroubled by the thoughts. The very fact that you can be unhappy with the thoughts that appear in your mind means that you are not at one with those thoughts. Therefore, they cannot be you or a reflection of your true nature.

Thoughts come from beliefs. Beliefs are just programs that were installed, without our permission, when we were much younger and possessed sponge-like minds that just soaked stuff up without any discernment.

So when you are plagued by troublesome thoughts the solution is simple. You notice the thought, you acknowledge the thought, you notice the negative emotion that accompanied its arrival, and you think a new thought along the lines of *that thought is not mine, this negative emotion is telling me that this thought is not in harmony with my true nature, therefore, I can ignore it.*

In the next chapter I deal with phobias because they are a natural extension of the work with anxiety. Phobias are a demonstration of anxiety operating at an extreme. If you have no phobias then read through the chapter at least once anyway. You may gain some insights into aspects of your own behaviours. Also you may consider that the technique for curing phobias can be utilised to deal with the less intense anxiety provoking situations that you have concerns about.

Affirmations

I allow myself to do those things I want to do even though I am experiencing a little anxiety.

I allow myself not to do those things I want to do when I am experiencing considerable anxiety.

I allow myself to avoid that which I have no desire to do.

I give myself permission to say *no* when I really want to say *no*.

I give myself permission to say *yes* only when I really want to say *yes*.

I accept that even though anxiety is uncomfortable it will not kill me and I can tolerate it.

I give myself permission to let others think what they think, do what they do, and believe what they believe.

I accept that what I want is what is best for me right now.

I trust my own judgement more and more each day.

Phobia

**"If you listen to your fears, you will die never know-
ing what a great person you might have been"**
Robert H. Schuller

Phobias fascinate me. It is the way that the presence, or even the thought, of the object of the phobia can turn a normal rational human being into a quivering terrified jelly. And lest you think I am being mocking, I have suffered from a phobia or two, and cured a great many more, so I am well aware of quite how debilitating a phobia can be.

But what exactly is it that we're talking about here. How do you know you have a phobia? I mean it seems to me quite sensible to be wary of snakes. After all, a lot of them are poisonous, and even a small constrictor, if it got round your neck, could kill you with very little effort. Studies with chimpanzees show that they seem to have an inbuilt tendency to learn a fear of snakes much more readily than they learn to fear anything else. Captive bred chimps who have never been exposed to snakes have no fear of them. Captured wild chimps do.

Now, to me, there is a certain amount of evolutionary sense in being afraid of potentially lethal creatures like spiders and snakes. Though at the same time a little puzzling as to why those occasionally lethal creatures are selected rather than, to me, the very much more seriously dangerous lions, rhinos and elephants that we encountered on a daily basis back in our early evolution-ary history.

But being afraid isn't the same as experiencing a phobic reaction.

Many years ago I was visiting a place in Devon called Berry Head. This is a wonderful gorse and grass covered headland just a short walk from the very picturesque port of Brixham. Berry Head is the headland that marks the southern end of Torbay. It was May, the sky a beautiful deep blue and the whole area covered in that rich cheerful yellow of flowering gorse. The air was heady with that delicious coconut scentedness I can never get enough of when gorse is in flower. There was also a small building housing an exhibition of photographs showing the history of Berry Head. I walked in and was gently strolling round engrossed in the images and the story and some instinct caused me to look down. There, curled between my feet, was an adder. I was just ambling along, not looking where my feet were and had somehow managed to avoid stepping upon this rather torpid snake and there it was curled in the V between my feet.

Now, in the British Isles we have only three snakes - grass, smooth, and adder, and although I had never seen any of them before, my interest in wildlife ensured I knew which it was - you see the adder is Britain's only poisonous snake. Not usually lethally poisonous, but if it bit you, you would suffer. I just looked down at it fascinated and amazed that I had not accidentally stepped on it - for then I would surely have been bitten and ended my day in a hospital bed. As it was I went to find the warden, who proceeded to get a bucket and shovel and was about to chop the adder's head off with the shovel, when I stopped him. It turned out he was a little fearful of handling it and it was easier for him to kill it than to rescue it. So I took his shovel, scooped it up and released it into the undergrowth.

You will realise from this story that I am not afraid of snakes. Or maybe you think I am a little afraid of snakes since I scooped it up with a shovel. I don't think I am even a tiny bit afraid of snakes. I have since handled snakes on several occasions, but that was my first encounter with a wild snake. You will notice that I did not pick it up. However, that is just natural wariness and a knowledge of the very real danger of handling poisonous reptiles.

Someone with a phobia of snakes (ophidiophobia), in that situation, would probably have panicked and fled the building. I have seen people scream and panic at the presence of a harmless spider. Now arachnophobia (phobia of spiders) is the commonest phobia, and like snakes you can see how there is a rationality lurking at the back of it. All spiders are venomous. But with a lot of spiders, certainly almost all of those native to the British Isles, their fangs are not strong enough to pierce human skin. I have handled hundreds of native spiders, and the odd tarantula, without ever being bitten. Some spiders are able to deliver a lethal bite - Black Widow and Funnel Web being the best known - but there are also a lot of other quite innocuous looking yet quite deadly spiders out there.

Now to me it makes sense to be careful around deadly poisonous animals, and if I suddenly found a black widow crawling on my hand I would probably react before I could think. And that is the thing with deadly danger - our built-in safety and survival mechanisms tend to take care of it because thinking is usually far too slow and we would be dead by the time we decided what to do. But reacting without thinking is not being phobic.

A phobia is where the fear reaction is taken to extremes.

Going back to chimps. If young chimps never see an adult chimp reacting to the presence of a snake, then they have no fear of snakes. If they do see an adult reacting fearfully to a snake then they, in future, react the way the adult did. They have a predisposition towards that behaviour, but it still has to be learned.

Here are ten common phobias:

1. Arachnophobia: The fear of spiders.
2. Ophidiophobia: The fear of snakes.
3. Acrophobia: The fear of heights.
4. Agoraphobia: The fear of situations in which escape is difficult e.g. cinemas, supermarket queues, business meetings…
5. Cynophobia: The fear of dogs.
6. Astraphobia: The fear of thunder and lightning.
7. Trypanophobia: The fear of injections.
8. Social Phobias: The fear of social situations.
9. Pteromerhanophobia: The fear of flying.
10. Mysophobia: The fear of germs or dirt.

You'll notice that only two of them, Agoraphobia and Social Phobia, have no obvious connection with staying safe. All the rest have physical harm as a possible consequence, or in the case of trypanophobia, a definite consequence. The difference between a phobia and a rational, sensible concern is the way it affects behaviour.

Pteromerhanophobics, despite a love of foreign places and a desire for exotic holidays, will either only travel by sea and land, or medicate themselves with tranquillisers in order to reach distant lands. Others recognise that air travel, statistically, is safer than road travel and just like buses and cars crash, planes occasionally crash, but they see it as unlikely and plan for an enjoyable holiday.

Interestingly fear of flying is probably the commonest phobia that I treat because it really does get in the way of doing stuff that people want to do. But it is far from a simple phobia and it is rare that the crashing aspect is the one that is problematic. More usually it is the lack of control, a feeling of being trapped when the door closes, or a fear of panicking and being unable to escape, or hide, with all those people watching. This means that usually I am treating claustrophobia, agoraphobia, and social phobia rather than anything to do with aeroplanes.

I use fear of flying to highlight the real significance of phobias. Phobias are only a problem when they stop you doing what you want to do. Most people do not find it too difficult to avoid spiders, and most people have someone else living with them who can deal with the problem should it intrude into the home. For most people a phobia of snakes is an indulgence. Snakes are a bit sparse in the UK. In my life I have spent a lot of time in the countryside and encountered only three snakes and a handful of lizards. Snakes are easy to avoid.

Injections are generally avoidable if you are ok with never seeking medical help and never travelling anywhere you need vaccinations. Injections though, sooner, or later, will catch up with you. It is incredibly difficult to get through life without someone wanting to poke a needle into your body at some point - but you can avoid it for very long periods of time, especially if you never get pregnant.

Now if your phobia is about something like dogs or birds or thunderstorms then life gets a little more difficult.

Rather than avoidance and all the challenges that brings with it, how about dealing with the phobia?

Traditionally there were two methods for dealing with phobias. One is Systematic Desensitisation. The other is Flooding.

I will deal with flooding first because it always struck me as an especially unkind way to help someone overcome a fear. The rationale behind this is that the body cannot sustain a fear response indefinitely. So if the object of fear is never removed then eventually you will get used to it and the fear will be gone. So the way to utilise the flooding technique to remove simple phobias is to put you in a room full of spiders, snakes, puppies, birds or whatever it was that you were afraid of and you would remain in there until the fear reaction was either eliminated or significantly reduced.

But that is not really viable as a self help option so I am afraid we will have to forget about that one.

The second option, Systematic Desensitisation, is very amenable to hypnotic use.

Step 1.

Create a chart like this, write on the page, or download it from my website at:

www.self-hypnosis-mastery.com/html/self-hypnosis-download.htm

Subjective Unit of Disturbance Scale

Phobia:

100

90

80

70

60

50

40

30

20

10

0

Next to Phobia, write down the phobia you are treating.

Next to 0 write down the situation, with your phobia, (in which the phobic object must be present) where you would currently be completely ok. Spiders existing nowhere in the Universe is not acceptable. A spider sitting on the Moon is. Next to 100 write down your worst nightmare in connection with your phobia e.g. tarantula crawling up my arm, house spider crawling up my nose, body covered with spiders - you get the idea.

Then find a situation, real or imagined to fit all the other numbers, so that you have a fear scale going from 0 to 100 in increasing intensity of fear when you are in the presence of your phobic object.

Then take yourself into your trance. Spend some time creating as deep a relaxed state, in your favourite place, as you can. Then go to the first point on the scale, that is the one that evokes the least fear. Imagine that situation as best you can, make it as real as possible incorporating the smells, tastes, textures, colours, sounds & feelings into your imaginary image. If you can imagine that and remain completely relaxed then move up to the next image on the scale.

When you feel the fear reaction arising within you, just stay with it. Hold that fearful image in your mind while counting down from 10 to 1. Breathe deeply and count only on the out breath. Then let the image go. Count yourself down from 10 to 1 again. Take yourself to your favourite place until you are completely relaxed. Then return to the image that caused the fear reaction.

Repeat this process until you can imagine the situation without any fear reaction. This may take several attempts, but do not abandon it. It is hugely important that you keep relaxing and returning to the image until you can see it in your mind's eye without any adverse reaction. If you leave the process before you achieve this then you reinforce the fear and make it worse.

Do one step on the scale each day. More if you are progressing well, but there is no rush. It is far better to succeed slowly than to fail quickly.

I know that if the phobia is very severe then thinking about 100 on the scale will produce an intense fear reaction. This reaction will be so powerful that you will find it hard to believe that anything could make it ok. But that is because, at the moment, you are looking at 100 from 0 and that is a long way away. When you look at 100 from a peaceful 90, it is no further away than 10 was from 0 and no harder to achieve.

I now need to introduce to you the idea of Simple and Complex phobias.

Simple phobias are straightforward irrational fears about everyday objects. The fears that I have been using as examples: spiders, dogs, snakes, thunderstorms and so on, are simple phobias. There is one phobic object and the fear has been learned either from a frightened adult or from an unpleasant experience as a young child. The unpleasant experience is frequently forgotten, but the subconscious remembers, and warns with a fear response, every time the phobic object is encountered. It is just a buried memory saying you got hurt by this when you were two. Or your Mum is afraid of these so it probably makes good survival sense for you to be afraid too - in much the same way that young wild chimps learn their fear of snakes from other adult chimps going ape when they see a snake, but young captive chimps do not.

Complex phobias are not so straightforward. Frequently with a complex phobia the phobia itself is a fear of fear. And there is no easy escape from that one - unless you go through the exit door of the panic attack.

Agoraphobia & Social Phobia

"It's OKAY to be scared. Being scared means you're about to do something really, really brave."

Mandy Hale

There are two complex phobias that I am going to look at here: agoraphobia and social phobia. The distinction between the two is a blurred one so I am not going to make too much of the differences. I have suffered from both in my past so I know how completely isolating and terrifying they can be, and how difficult they can be to shift.

For now, just know that they can be completely cured, but remember what I said about the SUDS scale. When you are at 0, 100 seems impossible. When you are 90, 100 is just another small step like the previous 9 you have successfully taken as you climbed up the scale.

Agoraphobia: fear of the market place.

…not, as many people imagine, a fear of open spaces.

There are no phobias that are fun to have, but agoraphobia is one of the worst, simply because it is almost impossible to avoid the object of fear on a day to day basis. This is because the object of fear is Life itself. Fear of Life manifested as a fear of social encounters; a fear of being trapped; a fear of feeling foolish; a fear of looking foolish; fear of humiliation…

Another deadly aspect of agoraphobia is the speed with which it develops to a point where the sufferer is afraid to leave the house alone. Often its onset is started by a panic attack – in itself frightening enough, without this possible consequence. The closing in of a personal world within a matter of weeks is a terrifying experience, and one that friends and relatives find almost impossible to understand and to cope with.

I have observed eleven factors that are frequently present with agoraphobia:

1. Low self-esteem
2. Lack of interest in job
3. Lack of a creative outlet
4. Insecurity
5. Lack of individuation
6. Insecurity in Relationship
7. Strong dependence
8. Fear of the cure
9. Nothing to live for
10. Lack of play/fun
11. Lack of regular exercise

You will notice that they also resonate with social phobia. You will also notice that I have not mentioned going out, or super-market queues, or cinemas, or meetings… and that is because they are just symptoms and you do not cure anything by treating symptoms. When you deal with causes then you produce cures. I am not suggesting that this list, long as it is, is exhaustive. I present it simply so you can see which items resonate with you so that you can begin to take action. If you make a shift, even a small shift, on half of the items in this list, then your life will be noticeably easier and you will experience much more enjoyment from it.

You can use self hypnosis to help you to bring about a shift in all of these areas.

Low Self-Esteem

I hope that you have already read the earlier chapter on self-esteem. Unfortunately self-esteem has become a bit of a buzzword. However, from an agoraphobic's perspective it is something that needs to be explored and for the purposes of this discussion it is going to mean: how important you think you are in relation to others.

Now, if you think you are about as important as a worm, then you are not going to want to mix with anyone else, because they will be able to see how unimportant you are. If you can see it, then it has to be clear to everyone else. This alone is a good reason to avoid others. But I would like to point out that just because *you* can see it does not mean that everyone else can. You can see your dreams - but no one else can!

Everyone wants to feel important. From a Mum getting a spontaneous hug from her child, or a thank you for a well-cooked meal, to a degree ceremony with a huge audience – we all like to have at least someone recognise and honour our worth. Consequently we will avoid circumstances that make us feel unimportant. If we feel less important than everyone, then we will avoid everyone. If we need an excuse then our wonderful, self-protective subconscious mind will come up with a solution – it might even create a socially acceptable (i.e. medically identifiable) health problem.

Lack of Job Interest.

In my experience most people do not *enjoy* their livelihoods. For the majority, what they do is ok, but not what they would do if they had a free choice. And at the lower wage end of the employment world, work is seen largely as drudgery – something necessary in order to pay the bills and just survive until it is time to draw a pittance of a pension, or until life is over.

Work is often a trap. An individual somehow ends up doing what they do without knowing quite how it happened. It pays well. They used to like it. Now they do not like it. Unfortunately, as the salary increased the lifestyle improved with it. Then as salary increased, expenditure increased also until we finally arrive at a point where life is lived in a certain amount of luxury. There is probably also pressure from a spouse and children who would not be pleased were you to substantially reduce their affluent life-style.

So the job is tolerated.

How can you give all of this up and do something fun for a lower salary?

Once more you are trapped trying to survive.

Lack of Creative Outlet

This I have identified as a key element in psychological problems. Changing just this one aspect of life brings about profound changes in all the other aspects without doing anything else. We are, each of us wonderful creative beings. Each one of us has a mind that is beautifully and wonderfully imaginative. But what happens is that we are frequently taught that our creations are not good enough. I see this reflected in the eyes of so many who come to see me for help. Let me give you an example from my own childhood - Art. My drawing skills are still around the level of a five year old, they never developed beyond that. I remember many hours, right up until age 15, in art classes. But I was rubbish.

I have identified two problems. They were a lack of encouragement and a lack of teaching. I never once in all those years of art classes saw a teacher demonstrate a technique, show anyone how they could improve their work, or give a word of praise to anyone whose work was not already high quality. All art teachers did was to state what was to be drawn/painted, and then select the most *life-like* to go on the wall.

This lack of encouragement for demonstrating our unique view of the world; the lack of praise for an effort that is the very best we could produce given our personal skills abilities, and eyesight; the lack of being lovingly shown, without criticism for what we've already achieved, a better way to achieve what WE want to achieve; is the source of much pain and failure in later life.

I have since discovered that with the right teacher anyone who wants to enough can be an artist at an acceptable level. And the right teacher is one who demolishes the barriers to the success that we carry within. The right teacher is one who knows that we can do what we want to do, but we are afraid to do it. The right teacher allows, praises, and encourages pure expression of self.

Creativity is not just about art. Art is just an example. Cooking a meal with love and arranging it beautifully on the plate is a work of creativity. Planning or planting a garden or a window box is a creative act. Walking down the road and daydreaming is a creative act. Starting a business is a creative act. Putting together a jigsaw puzzle, or solving a crossword puzzle are creative acts. Writing an article, or designing a web page, are creative activities. Creativity is putting you out into the world and changing that world, making that world different, either in your dreams or for real. Your creativity does not have to be better than anyone else's. It just needs to express YOU.

If you do nothing else after reading this, add a few moments of creativity to your world every day.

Insecurity

This shows up as a lack of feeling safe in your world. It can manifest as an unhealthy obedience to, and fear of, authority figures – like parents, teachers, employers, and supervisors. It can show itself as an inability to say 'no' when you really want to say 'no' but feel guilty about letting someone down. Maybe you think that because someone asks, you have to say 'yes', otherwise they will think badly of you or stop liking you. In truth if you start to say 'no' when you want to, you will find that people like you more because they value your honesty, and they know that when you say yes you really mean it and are a genuinely willing participant.

Lack of Individuation.

This is a nice way of saying you never really grew up. But telling someone they have not grown up can be perceived as an insult. What this means is that you may well have had over-protective parents who were fearful for your safety, and in your best interests they prevented you from taking those risks – like getting lost, falling out of a tree, exploring a graveyard at night, staying out a little later than was safe – that children actually need to take. These risks are necessary in order to discover that although their world can be a frightening place at times, it is possible for them to experience those fears AND discover that they can survive them and be whole and alive and ok. You even need to fail publicly as a child and feel embarrassed, but be reassured by your parents and learn that this too is a survivable event. This is what I mean by *growing up*. I have to admit that falling out of a tree, as an adult, is a lot more physically risky than doing it as a child. And if you have already arrived at severe agoraphobia then the graveyard at night time is probably a no-no. So go back to creativity and just imagine yourself doing those things that were forbidden as too risky, even though all your friends were doing them and you just ended up feeling isolated and alone. Imagine how your world might be different now, if you had done those things then.

Insecurity In Relationships.

You know you are with the wrong partner, you know the relationship you are in is not working, yet you are terrified of being alone. You are not loveable, so you had better put up with what you get, because if you give this up, there will not be anyone else and you will spend the rest of your life alone and die all alone. But quite often with agoraphobia, the agoraphobic partner is totally dependent on the other. Although they will not venture outside alone, they will quite often go to places with their trusted companion who knows about their difficulty. So doing something about an unhealthy relationship means having no one to support you and help you to maintain your problem. Yes, that's right, your trusted partner is actually helping you to cultivate and sustain your agoraphobia.

This is what the fear says. And while you believe what it says it is perfectly true for you. You will be alone if you give up what you have. Not because you are not loveable, but because you believe it. Beliefs are not truths. But if you believe you are not loveable that is what the world will see, someone who does not love themselves. And if you cannot love yourself then no one else will.

But you might be seen as vulnerable and consequently find yourself being used when you thought you were being loved.

Seems a bit harsh that, but agoraphobia is what you do to yourself when your world becomes so intolerable that you will go insane if you do not find a way to escape from it. And that is exactly what your subconscious mind does, without your permission; it creates a way for you to escape. What it creates is not pleasant, but it means you do not have to face anyone who might see the truth of you – that you are not loveable, or clever, or artistic, or have any value whatsoever.

Dependence.

In a loving relationship with a caring partner, there is often an unhealthy dependence. This is frequently because of the partner's need to be needed. This is the most difficult aspect I face treating this problem, because the partner's need to be needed resists, and occasionally even sabotages, the changes that I am working to bring about.

This problem is again born from your childhood if you were raised with:

- Parents who, because of their own beliefs about what was in your best interests, failed to ensure that you experienced the world in safe ways – on your own.

- An early life that did not provide you with challenges to overcome.

- Parents, teachers, significant adults who found it difficult to watch you fail (and learn) and gave constant correction or took over when a task was not being completed fast enough or accurately enough.

- Adults who were over-critical, creating this feeling of inadequacy that leaves you with a sense of 'I can't do it on my own' I need you there 'just in case…'

Fear of the Cure.

At the end of the day, if you want to be free of this problem, you know that you will be able to go out whenever and wherever you want. You will have to go out alone. You will have to go shopping in supermarkets, go to theatres, travel in trains and planes. You will have to make decisions and choices for yourself. You will have to do things that others may look at and judge unfavourably.

Right now, in the safety of the fear, all of those things seem horrific and just thinking about them will produce an intense anxiety reaction simply because you cannot see how you can get from where you are to where you want to be without lots of pain. So it is probably safer to stay where you are.

Nothing to Live For.

If there is no interest in life, no fascination for the world, or an aspect of it, no joy, or pleasure; if every morning when you wake, your waking thought is 'Oh no! How will I get through today.'

if every moment of that day is longing for nighttime and the oblivion of sleep; then you will experience no *drive* to be well. If you want to change, if you want to be free of this incapacitating fear that is destroying your life, then you have to want freedom. You have to want it more than you want to stay in bed. You have to want it more than you want to sleep.

Lack of Play/Fun

What do young children do more than anything else? They play. They turn everything into a game as long as they are contented. What do adults not do much of? Play. You need to play. You need to be playful in your approach to life. Life can be serious all on its own. It does not need your help. You can have fun and it will not mind. When was the last time you had a good laugh? When was the last time you knocked a ball around without trying to win or beat anyone? When was the last time you flew a kite without needing to have a bigger/better/faster/more colourful kite than everyone else? When was the last time you made a mud pie? When was the last time you wore a funny hat?

Lack of Regular Exercise

Lack of regular exercise – for obvious reasons is also a factor of significance. Exercise releases endorphins, which raise your mood state. It lets your body know you care about it and a sense of routine is always important to the healing of any psychological illness.

Healing with Hypnosis

Hypnosis is wonderful because it can make the healing process easier. It can make the healing process easier without losing sight of the fact that at the end of the day you are going to be doing what terrifies you right now. With hypnosis it is all in the mind. Your fear is all in your mind. Your fear arises out of your thoughts and your thoughts arise from your beliefs and ideas about you and your world. Your fear comes from your deep subconscious mind and this is the area that hypnosis can impact. You are still going to have to walk out of the door on your own one day, and you may still feel a little anxious, but you will do it and feel good about having succeeded and each success will build on the next and the next until you look back on this period of your life as an interesting excursion into the Shadow energies within your mind.

Self hypnosis is not a magic wand that will make everything go away in a flash. But it is a magic wand that makes the process of healing gentle and caring and never takes away your sense of achievement at having accomplished the shift from hiding away at home to being free and comfortable and confident out in the world.

So how can you use self hypnosis to free yourself from this particular prison?

First of all have a look at the eleven points that I have outlined and get a piece of paper and copy them down or download them. Next read through the list, dwell on each one and notice your emotional reaction. Some will resonate more strongly than others. After feeling your way through the list give each one a score from 0 - 5 depending on how strongly it resonates with you. Then cross out any that scored zero. The one's that are left are the ones you need to work on. Start with the lowest score. If you have more than one with the same score, either pick one, toss a coin, or roll a dice to choose which one to work on.

For example, say you selected Lack of Interest in your Job. What you need to do is to take yourself into your trance and gently daydream about what would need to change in your job to make it more interesting for you. Bear in mind you are only looking for tiny improvements here - just small shifts to make the intolerable a little more tolerable. If having your desk in a different position might do it for you then imagine all the ways that might come about and play through each scenario in your mind.

If having a colleague treat you with a little more respect would do it then imagine that happening, and if you wish, imagine how that might happen.

Need more appreciation? Again see it happening in your mind.

Then look at all the separate aspects of your job and find just one small thing that you like. Maybe you work flexible hours, maybe there is a creative aspect to your work, maybe you really like how organized and tidy your desk is. Maybe you are especially helpful with customers; maybe you enjoy lunchtime when you can get away on your own. Whatever you find, spend a few moments appreciating that aspect of what you do and see yourself doing it while connecting with a sense of appreciation for you and know deep down inside that there is some small part of your work that you enjoy and whenever you feel overwhelmed bring this memory back and reconnect with as much of the good feeling as you are able.

On your next session you can repeat this and focus on this one aspect until you feel a small shift in your real world experience, or you can move on to the next item. I would stick with items with the same score until you feel a shift, even a small one, before moving on to those items that scored higher.

For the other items the procedure is just the same.

Take yourself into trance.

Imagine yourself in a situation that relates to your difficulty.

Either

Make small changes in your imagination that cause you to feel a little lighter about the situation.

Or

Go into the past and make the changes to the event that you believe caused you to be the way you are. Make peace with it. Then go into the future and imagine how it is now different.

Bring yourself back to waking reality.

The key to this is to see the situations through your own eyes. Ensure that you experience positive emotions. If the positive emotions are absent then make small changes until you feel a positive shift in your emotional state.

So in your self hypnosis sessions look for small things that are ok and magnify them. Imagine things just how you would like them to be. Look for small things to appreciate about things just the way they are.

Trapped

If life is so closed down that going out of the front door on your own is a real problem, then here is something you might want to try.

Stand behind the door with eyes open and take yourself into trance. In other words, do whatever you do when you are going into self hypnosis, but retain enough muscle tension to remain standing. When you feel relaxed just open the door. Notice the level of fear response that brings, then stop and repeat the going into trance process. When you feel relaxed again take a step forward. Then repeat the process and keep up with this repetition until you step onto a public thoroughfare. Repeat the process. It is most important that when you reach the place of maximum fear intensity that you take the time to relax before you return. Then return one step at a time, relaxing between each step until you can close the door. Then turn around and do it all again. Then do it all again. Then do it all again. Keep doing it, not until the fear overwhelms you (because it will not) but until you are truly fed up with the whole process and could not care less which side of the door you are on.

Then give yourself a treat because you have just made a tremendous achievement.

Repeat this process again and again (at least once a day) until you can walk into the public space without doing the self hypnosis.

Then you do the same thing with your next landmark -maybe the end of the street, maybe the post box, maybe the bus stop, maybe the shop.

Now you have some successes under your belt it is time for pen and paper again. Make a list of all your target locations - the places you want to be able to be okay visiting. Might be things like, hairdressers, newsagent, supermarket, cinema, bus, train, flying, walk in the park, day out in the country or at the coast... It really does not matter, but make it a list of things you cannot do at the moment but that you want to do. Those things that the lack of is ruining your quality of life.

Again score each of them from 0 to 5 in order of difficulty. Select the lowest score and write down the individual steps you need to take to achieve it. A trip-to-supermarket list might look like this:

- Go out of front door.
- Unlock car door
- Get in car
- Start engine
- Drive to end of road
- (whatever your route entails)
- Park in supermarket car park
- Get out of car
- Lock car
- Walk to entrance
- Select trolley/basket
- Enter supermarket
- Select item
- Select next item (and so on)
- Join checkout queue
- Unload shopping/Pack shopping/Pay for goods
- Take shopping back to car
- Return home

Your list may be longer or shorter.

I have been in a place in my mind where a supermarket trip was my worst nightmare - especially the queuing and paying part. I cured myself and have cured other agoraphobics for whom the same was true.

Now, with the supermarket trip broken down, what that list represents is just a series of discrete and separate steps. Each step can and will be taken without needing to proceed all the way to the end of the list.

You have already sorted go out of the front door so you move to unlocking the car door. Proceed with this in exactly the same way as you went out into the public space. One step at a time until reach the car, unlock it, relax, re-lock it, and return to the house. Then repeat this until it bores you all in one session. You have to reach boredom in one session if that is at all feasible.

When you get to the end of the road, you find a place to safely turn around and come home. If you are feeling anxious, park safely, and take yourself to your favourite place and relax before returning home. If you are using public transport, go one stop and return home, then go two stops...

Never, ever start to return in a state of fear.

If you do this you will undo all of the benefits you have worked so hard to achieve. Always work until you can reduce the fear reaction before returning.

When you get to the supermarket car park you relax and immediately return home. Then you go back and do it again... and again...

When you eventually select your trolley (or basket) you go through the supermarket entrance and IMMEDIATELY turn around and leave.

Because the next step is the most difficult there are two things I need you to do. I want you to visit several times and not buy anything. Just walk around looking at stuff. Then when that is ok I want you to put one or two or three items in your trolley or basket and then walk out of the shop leaving the trolley or basket somewhere with the shopping still in it. DO NOT put the shopping back on the shelves.

It is really important that you learn to feel comfortable doing this. It is perfectly ok. Someone will put the stuff back. I have worked in a shop, people leave shopping all the time, It is no big deal putting someone's shopping back on the shelves. I leave my shopping even now when the queues are too big and I am not prepared to wait. The reason you must do this is because, in my experience the area of maximum difficulty is the queue. That is where the trapped feelings come on most strongly. But the trapped feeling is just because of the programming that says 'I have got shopping, I can't just walk away and leave it. What will people think?' Well you *can* just walk away and leave it because you have already demonstrated that you can not only do that but also that you can go back to the same shop and do it again. And what people will actually think is 'great that is one person less in front of me in the queue'.

So remember - one step at a time. Stick to that step until it bores you. And if you possibly can, reach boredom in one session.

As soon as you realise this works you will feel so much power returning to you that you will know that you can do anything you want to.

Affirmations

> **I allow myself to be just as scared as I am.**

> **I allow myself to enjoy different experiences from others even though we are all in the same place.**

> **I allow myself to experience fear symptoms without giving them any power over me.**

> **I can always become just a little bit more relaxed than I am.**

> **I allow myself to leave at any time my fear begins to over-whelm me regardless of where I am, who I am with, and who is watching.**

> **I allow myself to feel safe.**

> **I allow myself to feel unsafe.**

> **I recognise that what I interpret as fear is just a set of symptoms. Symptoms are just physical sensations. Physical sensations do not make my decisions for me.**

Relationships

"You need to associate with people that inspire you, people that challenge you to rise higher, people that make you better. Don't waste your time with people who are not adding to your growth. Your destiny is too important."

Joel Osteen

Whenever people seek out help or advice to change their lives, three areas come up time and time again: money, health, & relationships. In this book I look at each of those subjects and offer you some guidance as to how you can use self hypnosis to bring about change in these areas of your life. Relationships I will discuss now and return to later in the book. Health is covered in the following Body Section while money, oddly enough, makes its appearance in the Spirit Section.

There are five common problems in relationships: poor communication; not feeling loved; not being in a relationship when you want to be in one; not being in the relationship you want to be in, and abuse.

I am not saying these are the only relationship problems, and if there is another problem you want help with then go to this book's web page and post a comment at the bottom. But for now, these are the ones that I am going to show you how you can use your mind to bring about change.

Abuse

Let's look at the last one first - abuse. If you are in an abusive relationship then get out of it NOW. Self hypnosis is not your priority here. If you try to use self hypnosis to change your partner's behaviour, all you are doing is making excuses for not leaving. If you have nowhere to go, ask friends, get on the internet, there are places that will help you, but get out.

Of course, physical abuse is easy to identify. If someone hits, or physically hurts you for any reason, that is unacceptable. It is simple.

Psychological, or emotional, abuse is not so easy. But that is partly because the abuse wears you down until you believe that this behaviour is normal and you deserve it.

It isn't, and you don't.

But just to help you out here, here are some of the signs that will let you know for sure that you need to get out if your partner...

• Uses money to control you
• Is verbally abusive
• Puts you down in front of others
• Causes you to feel afraid
• Expects you to be a servant
• Experiences jealousy
• Doesn't want **you** to talk about your problems to anyone else
• Doesn't trust you
• Checks up on you
• Makes light of the abuse and is not taking your concerns about it seriously
• Frequently criticizes you
• Isolates you from family and friends
• Is upset or angry with you several times a week
• Avoids conversation about your problems
• Engages in secretive behaviour
• Always disagrees

...and how that makes you feel is...

• Lack of enthusiasm for anything

- Uncertain about how others see you
- Feeling that you are faulty in some way
- Lack of confidence
- No longer able to believe in yourself
- Always finding fault with what you do (before anyone else does)
- Feeling lost and isolated
- Wanting to be different in order to please your partner
- Never sure about your own decisions and ideas
- Fantasising about when it is all going to get better
- Wanting to escape or run away

If this is you, get help and get out. You deserve better than this.

So now that we've had a look at the worst case scenario, just consider that any other situation can be improved. But don't think, because what you have just read makes your problems seem trivial, that maybe you should just put up with it. If you aren't happy in your relationship then you owe it to yourself to do everything within your power to fix it. And I need to remind you that your Power is far more powerful than you think.

Down to business.

In the paragraph above I mentioned being happy. Now I have some bad news for you.

No one can make you happy.

That is right, I know you don't believe me, but I am afraid it is true. No one can make you happy. Happiness comes from within you. I have been happy in miserable circumstances and miserable in fantastic circumstances. Happiness comes from within you. It is different from pleasure. Pleasure is what we feel when people do nice things for us. Pleasure is what we feel when things seem to be working out. The trouble with pleasure, and there's nothing wrong with pleasure, is that it is transient. It is totally dependent on external circumstances. It is totally dependent on the World behaving in ways that we like. The minute the World stops complying with our set of 'rules' about how things should be, then the pleasure is gone.

People mistake pleasure for happiness.

Happiness comes from within. It is something that is there when we believe in ourselves. It is there when we feel confident in our ability to overcome challenges. It is there, whenever we choose to allow it to be there. Worries and concerns cover it up and make it difficult to access, but it hasn't gone, you just covered it up because you believe that to be happy in difficult circumstances is just, well... wrong.

I am not suggesting for a minute that you *should* be happy in difficult circumstances. I certainly feel I have every right to feel miserable when circumstances are difficult, but I also know that I have every right to feel any way I want to under any conditions. Sometimes I can manage happiness when other people would be unhappy, and sometimes I can't. What I don't do is blame externals for how I feel.

So consider this, as a thought experiment for a moment or two...

How you feel is a choice that you can make moment by moment.

It is hugely important that you **get** this, because if you don't, you will be attempting to solve the wrong problem with your self hypnosis. Consequently you *will* fail.

Accept, just for now, that happiness is a choice that you can make or not make. Accept, just for now, that happiness is always present within you. Accept, just for now, that you don't know how to tap into that happy feeling when you want to.

Make Me Happy

A serious problem in many relationships is that one partner expects the other partner to 'make me happy'. When the other partner fails (which is what has to happen because they have no control over another's internal emotional state), they think that there is a problem with the relationship. They are right, the problem is *their* unreasonable expectations.

I made a distinction between pleasure and happiness earlier. I am not saying that your partner should never please you, or do those little things that bring a smile to your face and a warm glow to your heart. Those things are an essential to any successful relationship. But, in my experience, they happen spontaneously when happiness is present in the heart first.

When you work with self hypnosis it is really important that you understand that all you can change is you. If you attempt to use self hypnosis to control another you will fail. If you use it to become more peaceful and loving yourself, the other will change without you having to control or orchestrate that change. The really odd thing is that when you seek to control another's behaviour, you fail, when you change your own behaviour, their behaviour changes just the way you wanted it to. So you change others by working on yourself. This is because your world is a reflection of your inner state - they cannot resist changing along with you. Either that or they find life so uncomfortable that they withdraw from your world. Either way, you get what you want.

You see, the world, and that includes your relationships, reflects back to you what is inside of you. So when you are happy, good things tend to increase in your vicinity. Now that may mean that your current relationship ends, quite naturally, because you need to be with someone else in order to have the relationship of your dreams, or it may mean that your relationship moves rapidly in the direction of perfection. But all you are doing is to use these techniques to change your mind and your attitude.

That is enough theory. Time now to do some work.

Think about how you would like your communication with your partner to be different. Make some notes about this. When you see things written down it activates other areas of your mind and so ideas flow more freely than when you try to hold them all in memory. Be sure not to attach blame to yourself or your partner for the state of things as they are now. Focus totally on how you want things to be in the future.

So now you have some ideas about how you would like things to be different. While you have the pen handy also think about the rest of your interactions with everyone else you know and don't know. Make notes of those people who communicate with you the way you would like your partner to. Think about those interactions and get in touch with the good feelings you have when you are communicating in that way.

Take yourself into your relaxed trance state.

Then, in your imagination, recreate one of those good inter-actions and feel the good feelings as fully as you possibly can. Enjoy the moment and the conversation. Notice how you stand or sit; notice whether your body feels relaxed and open; notice the angle of your head when you are speaking and when you are listening; notice whether you are actively listening or just search-ing within your own mind distracted and looking for the next thing to say. Notice every nuance of posture and emotional state.

Now while hanging on to the good feelings and the memories of posture, position, and comfort, imagine a conversation with your partner. Play it through, but make sure you reproduce how your body was, your state of comfort, and what you were thinking about. See how that feels. If there was any discomfort at any point, or difficulty in maintaining the same stance then just go back to the good conversation, feel everything fully again and then come back and repeat it with your partner in your imagination.

Repeat this until there is no difference in your levels of comfort.

Allow all of these images and thoughts to drift away and take yourself to a comfortable place of relaxation and peace before gently bringing yourself back to waking reality.

Repeat this daily until you are aware that a shift has taken place in your waking reality.

Now, when you engage in 'real-life' interactions with your partner be mindful of what is different from the way you were in your successful (imaginary) communication. Your self hypnosis will make it much easier to be aware of where the differences are. Notice the differences and seek to bring them into alignment with those you know are normal with effective and clear communication.

Love is like happiness. It is inside you and your job is to let it out. When you let the love out, it comes back to you. When you believe you don't have love in your life, then rather than attract it - you push it away. The only problem is that when you believe no one loves you, or when you believe that the person you need to love you doesn't, it is because the love inside of you is being blocked. You can imagine it like a wonderful, beautiful, golden light at the very centre of your being, or if you prefer a warm golden candle flame.

Now imagine that you suddenly found yourself arriving, as a baby, with your bright light of love, amongst a group of cave-dwellers. People who had been in the dark for a long time and were used to feeling their way around - even though their eyes were fully functional.

Now I have been in the dark a few times in my life and when someone turns on a bright light it physically hurts. So you'll understand when people react negatively to your brightness. In order not to be rejected (because at this time you are unaware that there is a world of light & beauty just outside the cave) you cover up your light. And because it is covered up, you forget it is there most of the time, but on those occasions when you do remember, you remember the pain it caused others and the pain their rejection of your light caused you. In order to be accepted you made a choice not to be who you are. Then you chose to forget to remember who you are because whenever you did, it brought along with it the memory of the pain of rejection.

But the light is still there.

All you have to do is remove the cover.

But like the others, if you remove the cover completely the light will hurt your eyes too because they have become adjusted to the dark. So remove the cover a little bit at a time. Exposing yourself to a dim light, then a little brighter light and so on, will allow you to acclimatize without discomfort.

The problem never lies with anyone else.

When you make the changes within yourself the world has no choice but to rearrange itself around the new you.

What you do now depends on how much light you have covered up. If all of your light is hidden you might be having a tough time with the idea of loving yourself. You might even believe yourself to be unlovable. If that is the case with you then pretend, just for now, that it is not only possible, but also perfectly ok, for you to learn to love yourself. Then pretend that you are going to discover how, but it is going to take a while so there's no immediate threat of finding out that you are actually ok after all. Therefore, you can breathe a sigh of relief. Then what you are going to do is to start to learn how to like yourself. When you have done that you can move on to loving yourself.

Whether your first step is loving yourself a little bit more or just liking yourself a little bit more, the process is the same. After all, all you are doing is exposing a little bit more of however much light is already showing. If none is showing then you are going to make a crack in the cover and let a little out.

When I think about how to love myself I tend to think in terms of treating me with respect; being encouraging and enthusiastic about those things that interest me; being supportive when I am finding things a little difficult; and encouraging me to follow my heart and my intuition, even when 'common sense' would suggest otherwise.

In my own journey from not really liking myself very much, to recognising what a great guy I am, I found that learning three new skills were key to success. Those skills were appreciation, respect, and how to say no. Those are the skills that we're going to explore using self-hypnosis.

Almost as soon as you start to practice these skills you will notice that life is getting better and better for you. I've touched on all of these already in other chapters but they are so important to your sense of well-being that I make no apologies for reinforcing these ideas.

Appreciation

In the chapter on Self-Esteem I introduced you to the idea of the Art of Appreciation. There I suggested that at the end of each day you use your self-hypnosis session to connect with a sense of appreciation and realize that some good things happened to you during the day that might otherwise go unnoticed. In relationships that appreciation needs to be a real-time, present moment thing. Not something you do hours after the event. Here are ways you can improve your sense of appreciation for your partner by noticing the good in others at the time they are being kind to you.

So, when a waitress brings you a cup of coffee, you can ignore her as if she's part of the furniture, you can say thank you from your head, or you can make eye-contact and say thank you from your heart. A thank you from the heart is appreciation. A thank you from the heart recognises that she needs to be pleasant even though her heart is breaking, even though she had a row with her boyfriend last night, even though she's been working eight hours with just a half hour break and is dead on her feet... A thank you from the heart recognises that even though she is serving you at this moment, she is your equal. A thank you from the heart has the same meaning as Namaste - the Light in me acknowledges that same Light in you. We are one.

When I reach the checkout in a supermarket I think about what it might be like to sit in one spot all day (unlike writing, where I get to go to the toilet without having to ask permission), picking stuff up, scanning it, and putting it down and doing that a gazillion times every day; having to fake smile at customers and thank them for waiting and getting paid peanuts for providing this service.

When I am driving I think about the people who designed the road signs and chose a font that was clear and easy to read from a distance; and the people who erected them so that my journeys would be a little easier 'cos I don't have a satnav.

When I buy stuff I think about the amazing chain from the raw materials grown or dug out of the earth to the designers and manufactures and growers and transporters and packagers and all the amazing connections like the people who built the lorries and the roads and the aircraft and the huge interconnected web that links us all together from consumers to producers.

When the sun shines I can be transfixed by something as simple as the way the light shines through a leaf, or backlights a flower. I look out at the natural world in awe at the small and the big.

All of this is appreciation. And it is dead easy to do. I hope you have been doing this in your evening self-hypnosis sessions, but now I want you to move that moment of appreciation to the item of the actual event. In other words, it is time to get out of your head and start to notice what is going on around you. You live in an amazing world, filled with amazingly kind and thoughtful people. It is time you started to notice them and acknowledge them and all the other wonders that surround you whether they be natural or someone's amazing ideas turned into physical reality. Remember everything that is man-made was an idea in someone's mind before it ever existed.

Now you have shifted your awareness towards real-time appreciation, I still need you to acknowledge these things in your self hypnosis sessions. That way you get twice as much benefit from them. Now I have given you some clues as to the type of thing you can use...

Take yourself into your trance and allow your mind to drift towards something in your day (if this is morning then think about the previous day) that you can appreciate and value. When I first started using this exercise I would appreciate things like the taste of a cup of coffee, the smile I received at the checkout, the weather, a flower I noticed, the fact that a shop had what I wanted, a good book... there is always something you can find. Then enjoy it again in your mind and feel the appreciation and the connections. Then find four more things and repeat this with each of them.

Do this daily.

After you have been doing this for a week or two you need to introduce a variation. You need to introduce something about yourself that you appreciated that day. It doesn't matter what it is - big or small, but find something you did, something you thought, even something you didn't do, to appreciate and value. There are no excuses here. You have to come up with one thing. It doesn't matter if you didn't do it very well, or you could have done it better, or that other people are so much more deserving of appreciation than you - find something about you to value - just a little, just for the duration of the exercise.

Then, in a similar way to the way we worked with your Self-Esteem, after your five appreciations, include one about your partner. Then each day add one more appreciation about your partner until there are five about your day and five about your partner.

Then when you have reached five things, I want you to imagine that, at the time they happened, you expressed your genuine appreciation for whatever it was and that your partner received it graciously. Don't worry about whether or not it is in or out of character. This is your imagination. Make it the way you want it to be. We can deal with reality later.

Come back to your waking reality.

Take this exercise seriously, no matter how bad your relationship is. If you need to, be prepared to work hard to find even small things about your partner that you like and appreciate.

Respect

No relationship is worth having if there is no respect between the partners. But, unfortunately you cannot make your partner respect you. However, I would suggest that you entertain the idea that, if you feel your partner fails to respect you then somewhere within you is a lack of respect for your partner. Yours may not be as *big* but it will be there. Before you do this work you must have made some significant progress with both the Confidence and Self Esteem exercises. Without the awareness that those exercises raise you will not succeed with this.

Take yourself into trance

Go to your favourite place.

Run through your day and initially notice any occasions where your partner, in your eyes, failed to respect you.

For each instant:

Replay the incident but this time see your partner behaving in a more reasonable, but still realistic way.

Replay the incident with your partner behaving in the most amazing way that you can imagine.

Replay the incident with your partner behaving in a more reasonable, acceptable, but believable way. This will be a way that is better than the first but not as good as the second.

Imagine yourself doing something nice for your partner as a gesture of appreciation for their consideration for you.

If any negative feelings come up then return to your favourite place and return to a state of calmness and peace before repeating. Do this until you can run through the events peacefully.

When you have finished return to your favourite place and relax for a few moments before bringing yourself back to full waking awareness.

Remember relationships are about companionship, support, encouragement, intimacy, often parenting, and most of all friendship.

Relationships are not about selling yourself into slavery, or giving up on your dreams, hopes and desires.

Relationships are not about being at someone's beck and call, nor about losing yourself and becoming the role of mum, dad, husband, or wife.

I have finished with relationships for now, but I will return to them again in the Spirit section of this book where I will teach you one or two more tricks about how to have what you want.

Body

Pharmaceutical companies are not interested in creating cures.
What they do is to create customers.

A recent study revealed that drug companies spent
nearly $84 million on marketing pharmaceuticals in the
District of Columbia during 2011. Almost $19 million
of this amount was for "gifts" to hospitals, physicians and
health care providers. Researchers at George Washington
University School of Public Health and Health Services
report that 12 physicians in the area received lavish gifts
that totaled more than $100,000 each in one year.

thealternativedaily.com

Body

"The cells in your body react to everything that your mind says. Negativity brings down your immune system."

Loretta Lanphier

While it is quite acceptable to believe that a body's weight can be changed simply by making choices, and that hypnosis is a well-known treatment to effectively stop a body's *addiction* to nicotine dead in its tracks; using hypnosis to impact disease processes is much less well known, even less frequently used, and frowned upon by the medical profession more often than not – despite most of the early success being accomplished by highly qualified medical doctors.

This section is an introduction to the real power that lies within your mind.

The Healing Room is key to this process and so I spend some time describing this and how you can make use of it. I refer to it in most of the treatments from this point onward. Part of the reason for that is that the more frequently you visit a place in your mind, the easier it is to imagine it and the more real it becomes to you. Also there is an element of ritual involved here. Once you have succeeded with some small changes, there will be a subconscious expectation of success, and change, whenever you bring this room into your thought-space. This is the power of ritual. Please do not ignore it.

There is a lot of visualisation from this point onward in this book. Remember visualisation is just imagination or fantasy. There is nothing difficult here and, as with everything else in this book, the more you do it the easier it gets.

By the time you have read The Healing Room and Health you will be in a position to use your new-found knowledge to impact anything going on in your body. I do not, in these pages, look at specific disease processes but I have provided enough information for you to create the imagery you need to deal with your physical problems.

I have specifically not mentioned cancer here. The main reason for this is that I recently discovered that in the UK it is a criminal offence to suggest any treatment for cancer that does not require medical intervention. The *Cancer Act 1939* gives the medical establishment a monopoly on cancer treatment and the promotion of cancer treatment. This law, though very out-dated, was recently used by a member of the medical profession to **prevent** the Totnes Cancer Healthcare Conference from taking place because the conference was focused on effective alternatives to chemotherapy, radiation, and surgery.

If the use of natural processes to heal cancer is of specific interest to you then I highly recommend that you read:

The Journey: Brandon Bays

The Healing Journey: O Carl Simonton MD

You will find that Dr Simonton's techniques can be incorporated easily into your self hypnosis sessions.

Chronic pain is something that so many people suffer from. I have provided some solutions here. They have all worked with many individuals. They have all failed to work with other individuals. However, these techniques have succeeded many more times than they have failed. But I need to be straight with you, since I have no desire to mislead you or create false hope. If chronic pain is your problem then give these techniques your very best shot. Please do not give up because the pain isn't all gone in a couple of days. It may be gone rapidly, but it may take a while, so give it at least a month of daily practice before moving on to something else. If you *get* that pain is something your mind creates to let you know there is a problem, then you will almost certainly manage to reduce it.

Weight loss and smoking I include in this section largely because they are the treatments that hypnosis is best known for. Blood pressure reduction is a great one to experience the power of mind over body largely because there is an excellent chance that your blood pressure is higher than it should be and, unless it is dangerously high, you will have the breathing space to spend time working on lowering it before resorting to medication. Finally I explore sleep. Insomnia affects many, many people and again I offer some simple solutions that should increase quality and quantity of sleep without the need to resort to unsafe medication.

By the end of this section you will be feeling as if your world is coming back under your control. With this new found confidence you will be ready for the next leap forward – creating the reality that you want rather than the reality that you have.

The Healing Room

"The quieter you become, the more you can hear"

Ram Dass

I highly encourage you to create a healing room. I don't mean a real one. I mean an imaginary one. When you do this you will find that you have an amazing resource that will assist you when your physical body experiences the occasional malfunction.

Before I continue with this I need to reiterate that if you have any physical problem that concerns you, then at least get it checked out by a medical professional. All that I offer within these pages is support and assistance. I am making no claims that these techniques will give you the ability to heal or cure any physical affliction.

That said my words will reflect a belief that these things are possible – simply because I have experienced the power of a mind utilising self hypnosis to change physical outcomes. I cannot and do not, however, make any claims that this will be true for you. I simply offer techniques that I know have been effective with others. But, I encourage you to use these techniques with the support of your physician.

So from this point on consider that nothing I say is true and that I am simply guiding you through the techniques of a thought experiment for you to play with.

The Healing Room must be considered a sacred space. As with all sacred spaces there is a modicum of ritual associated with it. Please do not ignore the ritual, it is just as important as the healing work that you do.

The Healing Room is simply a space in your mind. In other words, a fantasy creation of your own imagination. But it is a special place. It can be as elaborate or as simple as you wish. But what I suggest is that you follow my guidelines and only when they no longer serve you and you have a strong inspiration as to what you need instead, *then* create your own variations.

You will enter your healing room from a light filled hallway.

Your hallway may be the entrance to a building. Your mental approach should see you walking towards the building, aware of the beautiful gardens that surround it. If you prefer to remain indoors then create this hallway at the bottom of a grand staircase. Start your approach at the top of the staircase and count yourself down 20 steps from 20 to 1.

Once in the hallway approach the door to the Healing Room.

The door can be any kind of door you wish, but it must be lockable. This keeps you secure when you are making use of its facilities and ensures that no else can enter.

When you enter your Healing Room you will be aware that it is actually several rooms. But first of all design your main work space. Create a comfortable chair or lounger. A desk, only if you wish. Plants definitely. Include a large picture window looking out over a view that pleases you. I would suggest that this vista be one of nature. Water is associated with healing so a view of the sea, a lake, river or waterfall would be good. Surround it with an appropriate landscape. Make it bright warm and appealing. If you like you can have a door that leads you out into this space, but that is not necessary.

This room can be decorated any way you desire as long as it creates a sense of peace, tranquillity and the possibility of healing in your mind. If you like candles, incense and mandalas on the wall then include those. If you prefer a more clinical space then create that for yourself. But if you just want something simple, warm and comfortable then it is yours for the imagining and a big fireplace with a warm welcoming log fire burning in the grate may be appropriate.

The more time you spend creating this perfect space, picturing it in your mind before you use it, the more powerful will be the effect it has. Attend to the details. If you are artistic, draw it so it is even clearer in your mind. If you are not artistic then find images and either print them or cut them out and stick them on a page so you have a clearer idea of whatever your room contains.

Now the rooms that lead off from this one.

The most important is the control room. This will contain either a desk and chair, with computer monitors, or will be a room filled with switches and dials – depending upon your preference. This is the room where you can control bodily functions. You will find here controls for things like blood pressure, pain sensitivity, blood flow - anything in fact that you wish to exert some control over. Your imagination is the only limit to what can be influenced. When you have a problem with some aspect of your body you simply imagine the appropriate control and alter it. For blood pressure, say, you can imagine lowering the two settings for systolic and diastolic to 120 and 80. For pain you can imagine a sensitivity control that you can lower a little bit at a time. When you make small changes you can be encouraged to continue as you notice the immediate changes in your body's responses.

You don't have to imagine all of the controls now. Just get a sense of the type of layout and know that whenever you need a specific control that it will be there waiting for you to adjust it.

Submarine Room

The second room is the Submarine room.

Just for fun, and to create the mood, you may want to include a large marine aquarium here along one wall. Fill it with anemones and brightly coloured, inquisitive fish. The most important piece of equipment in here though is a very comfy lounger.

You may have seen the film Fantastic Voyage, based on a story written by Isaac Asimov, where a submarine, along with its crew is miniaturised and then injected into a patient where it sails the arterial seas until it gets to the problem and the crew then perform micro-surgery or something.

Well this room is where you do that.

But not exactly like that.

You imagine yourself, and any expert you wish to take with you, getting into a submarine and shrinking. Then you find yourself transported to the area of the body where there is a problem. But this is where it gets a little weirder than the purely biological take of Fantastic Voyage. You don a protective suit and step out into the space where there is a problem and look around. But you don't need to know what your anatomical insides look like. You allow your subconscious mind to present you with a symbolic image of the problem. Then you set about restoring it to normality.

Here are some examples:

Inflammation may be represented by a bright red balloon. Your task would be to change the colour of the balloon and deflate it.

An arthritic joint might be imagined as a rusty set of gears and pulleys. Your job would be to clean them up with a wire brush (yes power tools are allowed), make them all shiny, and oil or grease them so they rotate smoothly. Or simply remove the old rusty cogs and replace them with new ones. Make the new ones out of stainless steel, or gold, or platinum.

High blood pressure may appear as a dam about to burst and all you need to do is open the sluices to release the excess pressure before repairing any damage to the structure of the dam.

The trick is to allow your subconscious to present you with an image, and then you need to work with that image. You will know if you are working with the right image because you will be able to feel things happening as you *play* with the images.

So the procedure is:

Take yourself into trance.

Deepen the trance with a count down (See Appendix 1).

Approach your healing room – either by finding yourself in the gardens or at the top of another staircase.

Take a moment or two to relax and enjoy the view from the Healing Room window.

Engage fully with this.

Express your willingness to be free of whatever ails you.

Spend a few minutes imagining yourself in your own future free of this problem.

See this through your own eyes.

Feel the difference in your body as best you can.

Imagine yourself experiencing those pleasures that are unavailable to you now because of this problem.

Experience it through all of your senses.

Allow the good feelings to expand.

Now go through into the Submarine Room.

Continue as described earlier.

Return to your comfy chair in the Healing Room.

Give thanks and express appreciation for the healing as if it had already happened.

Enjoy the view a little more.

Bring yourself back to full waking awareness.

Always approach using any aspect of the Healing Room in this way, but feel free to substitute other rooms or procedures.

Most of the healing work you do will take place in either the Control Room or the Submarine Room. From here we move into more esoteric territory. I add these more for completeness and for those of my readers who prefer to seek out more spiritual solutions.

Portal Room

The third room is the portal room.

This room is filled with soft white light. Once inside this room you will have no awareness of walls or the door. But the light is brighter in one area and this is the portal to another dimension (remember you are just making this up so enjoy it). When you call, your Healing Guide will appear. This Guide may appear in any form: spirit, human, or animal. You can ask your Guide questions about your health problems and listen for the answers. You may receive the answer there and then, or it may arise within you at some time in the near future. Do not consider this exercise a failure just because your Guide chooses not to speak at the moment of you asking the questions.

If you are unsure what kind of questions would be useful, here are the ones I use with my patients when I do this exercise with them.

- What does this illness want from me?
- Why does it want that?
- Does it have some need that I am not giving it?
- Why is that part of my body unhappy?

- Does it believe that it is helping me in some way?
- What do I need to do to get better?
- Are there any medicines, herbs, vitamins etc., which I should take?
- Are there any treatments that would be beneficial to me right now?
- How long will it take for my body to heal?
- Am I doing anything that is preventing healing?
- What benefits am I receiving from having this illness/disease?
- Is this illness/disease representing some suppressed emotion?
- If this illness disappears, what will I have to face that the illness helps me to avoid?
- Will anyone suffer if I am healed?
- What else can you tell me?

This usually brings up a whole host of information that may well cause you to realise that there is a very good reason why you are suffering right now. It also frequently shows you some steps you can take that will allow the illness to disappear quite rapidly and naturally.

Once you have finished your conversation always remember to thank your Guide – even if it appears they were silent. Look around and you will find that the door has re-appeared and you can leave.

The Garden Room.

When you walk through the door to the Garden Room, you find yourself in a beautiful garden, filled with brightly coloured flowers, shrubs, trees, fountains, waterfalls and ponds. If you wish you can even add some beautiful butterflies and the buzz of bees busily collecting nectar to make a delicious healing honey. The garden has a winding path that leads eventually to an open space. Here the ground rises and on the top of the rise sits your Healing

Temple. The Healing Temple is surrounded by a stone wall with an arched gateway, but the gateway is blocked by a golden mesh. You need to walk through this mesh and your body seems to dissolve as you pass through it, returning to normal on the other side. But, trapped in the mesh, is that which you least need.

Continue on up the path and enter the temple. You are greeted by Light Beings (or Angels if you prefer) and taken through into what appears to be the spiritual version of an operating theatre. You are asked to lie on a table where, surrounded by Light Beings, you drift off. The light beings work on your light body, healing your aura and opening your chakras. This will then result in a rapid healing of the body.

When you awaken you find yourself back in your Healing Room.

This healing space gives you the freedom to explore and create, adding rooms that satisfy your own specific needs.

Have fun with this. Visit daily. Try out all of the rooms. In fact you will probably find that the room that appeals to you least will be the one that brings you the most benefit. Then, once you find out what works, keep on using it until the problem is gone.

There are also two doors leading to the Room of Rest and the Room of Inspiration. I shall introduce you to the workings of these particular rooms later on in the chapter on wealth.

Health

"If we are creating ourselves all the time, then it is never too late to begin creating the bodies we want instead of the ones we mistakenly assume we are stuck with."

Deepak Chopra

I am writing here about your physical health rather than your mental health. You can consider that this whole book is about your mental health, but if you have physical problems then, depending upon their severity, they will take some or most of your mental energy – at which point dealing with physical problems actually improves mental health.

Now, before we start work on using the *magic* of self hypnosis to bring about physical change, I need to insert an additional disclaimer –for my sake as well as for yours.

I am a hypnotherapist with over 15 years of experience helping people to solve their mental and physical challenges. I have experienced success in both of those areas. However, I need to emphasise that I am a hypnotherapist, I have no medical qualifications, and therefore, I am not allowed to advise you regarding your medical condition. If you have a medical problem I have to encourage you to see your physician and to follow their advice.

Everything else you read here reflects my opinion and experience – nothing more. If you choose to use self hypnosis to help yourself with a physical or mental problem do so with the support and knowledge of your medical practitioner.

Unfortunately we are not encouraged any more to be responsible for ourselves and our own well-being. That is not in the best interests of the medics, health insurance companies, or the pharmaceutical giants that live well from our consumption of what they want to market as the latest Superdrug. In fact Dr. L. Coldwell has such a low opinion of these pharmaceutical giants and their greed that he states "They murder our loved ones for money".

Strong words but they are born from the frustration of the power of these organisations to block low-cost solutions. Those of you who use health food supplements and vitamins and prefer to use natural medications will be familiar with the recent legislation that threatens the supply of vitamin, mineral and plant-based supplements.

We are not considered wise enough to know what is best for our physical bodies, nor are we considered fit to refuse pre-scribed medication even though there is a wealth of professional research available suggesting such medication is potentially seri-ously damaging to our health. But that is just my opinion and I am certainly not suggesting that you will find cures for any life-threatening or other illnesses within these pages.

Ok so disclaimer in place, I will continue.

Let me tell you a story. This is a true story and there were half a dozen witnesses to this. But I need to set the scene a little first.

So first let me tell you something about me. I was raised as a Roman Catholic and the stories about Jesus that fascinated me most were the stories about miraculous healings. As an adult I always wanted to be able to heal in that same miraculous way.

The trouble was, without any experience, how did I achieve this. I mean from the point of view of trying it out without appearing to be totally crazy. I mean you can hardly walk up to someone who is perhaps talking about a health problem and say "Hey! I'd love to work a miracle. Would you be my Guinea Pig?" At least I couldn't do that. My concern would be failure and embarrass-ment as well as the fear of disappointing someone – and that is if they would take me seriously enough to let me have a go.

Then there is the problem of how to do it. I have seen healers holding their hands over people, so I could do that but where and when and how would I know when I'd finished? These were all questions and fears that stopped me from even making the attempt.

Then my teenage daughter was house-sitting for her Mum. Her Mum had a pet rabbit and my daughter had the job of looking after it. But there was problem. The rabbit had been diagnosed with a bone disease that was causing disintegration of its skeleton. The rabbit had only been given a few weeks to live. I knew nothing of this when I popped round to check that my daughter was ok. But the rabbit was in the house, listless and totally lacking any energy or enthusiasm for life. My daughter, I could see, was really worried the rabbit was going to die while she was looking after it. I thought – what the heck – and held my hands over the rabbit and thought healing thoughts.

When I'd finished there was no change in the rabbit's condition. It was just as listless. So I thought well that was an interesting experiment I will not be trying that again.

I saw my daughter again about a week later and since she hadn't mentioned that the rabbit had died I asked her how it was. She said that the next morning it was full of energy hopping around, interested, and eating again. A few months later she gave me an update. The vet now referred to this rabbit as the Miracle Rabbit. It should not be alive and well but it was.

Some time after that I was in a pub with some friends and one of them was complaining that she had a really painful finger. It doesn't sound much but apparently it was causing a lot of discomfort and she asked me to heal it. I hadn't ever mentioned my interest in healing to her. But, put on the spot – I did. The pain left and normal movement returned. No wait this time – it was instant.

That was just a little background, now to the story I promised earlier.

I spent six months of my life reading tarot cards in pubs with several other psychics and mediums. As we were setting up one evening, one of the bar staff came over and asked if there was a healer among us. I decided to keep quiet. Several fingers pointed right at me. (I had done some healing for a couple of the other readers.)

The landlady came over. Two years earlier she had fallen down the steep cellar steps. She had been in constant pain ever since. Not only that but she had limited spinal movement and could bend forwards only very slightly. As you can imagine life was very difficult for her. The doctors had done what they could and there was nothing left.

I spent ten minutes working with her. At the end of that time she bent over and touched her toes for the first time in two years. The pain had also gone. The entire bar staff were amazed.

Now, I am not sharing this with you to build myself up, or to suggest that I have amazing abilities. Because I don't, and I don't have amazing success every time I try. But the reason I could do this amazing stuff is because I had a very strong desire to do it. Anyone, I believe, with an equally strong desire can achieve similar results.

No, the reason I share this with you is so that you can begin to consider that miracles are quite normal. Just entertain that possibility for a moment. Entertain the idea that illness is malleable and changeable and is no more real or permanent than an idea. Now this is no easy task. The more serious the illness, the stronger the pain, the more difficult it is to entertain the idea that it might be possible to let go of this if only you knew how. I mean when the pain fills your mind, or the cancerous bulge is eating away at your body, no one in their right mind would suggest that you could, in the blink of an eye, just disappear it all.

Even if that was possible it would trivialise your suffering. Make it pointless. Even make you angry that it wasn't fixed immediately.

If you can just shift a little way in your mind to believe that it is possible to impact your illness using nothing more than your thoughts, then you make change easier to achieve. It doesn't even have to be much of shift. If you could drop the pain from a 7 to a 6 on a 0-10 pain scale then that would demonstrate, quite clearly, to you not only that change is possible but also that if you can make a small change you can make a big change.

I have already mentioned that while I was training to become a hypnotherapist, my tutor encouraged me to attend a Masterclass she was holding about a subject called PsychoNeuroImmunology or PNI. This was a journey into the history of using the mind to bring about physical healing and to then use those techniques within a hypnotic trance to enhance the power of the mind to control the body. Check out The Cousins Centre for Psychoneuroimmunology for more information on this fascinating subject. Norman Cousins was a man who cured himself of *ankylosing spondylitis* with vitamin C and laughter. You might consider the laughter the *mind medicine* that activated his body's healing response.

This subject fascinated me. The part that particularly fascinated me was the idea that mental images can be used to change what the body is experiencing. I used mental images of healing light when I was working with those people that I healed. Remember, I mentioned the patient with the headache, another with arthritis, and another with fibromyalgia and how PNI techniques removed their pain quickly and effortlessly.

Well these experiences fueled my interest in the whole subject of MindBody medicine and I have done a lot of research, and gained a huge amount of experience in the 11 years that have passed since then.

Now you may be thinking, that was just a headache (actually it was just a headache but on a scale of 0-10 where 10 is about the worst pain you can imagine, this was scoring around 6) and headaches come and go, and the painful knee well that was just coincidence, but I have got arthritis - rheumatism- chronic fatigue syndrome – real fibromyalgia - IBS - toothache - low back pain - upper back pain - slipped disc - hernia... and these are real physical problems caused by physical deterioration of my body and no amount of words are going to fix that...

...well...

If, deep down, you weren't hoping that I would have a solution to your problem I doubt very much that you'd still be reading this...

so forget all about what the physical world doctors say, just for a while (bearing in mind of course that they make a living out of your illness). Then come with me into a fantasy world where, occasionally, amazing things happen.

But before I do that I want to tell you a cautionary tale about one of my failures. This tale is to introduce you to the idea of something we call Secondary Gains.

You might consider that a Secondary Gain is a benefit created by the illness. If there is a Secondary Gain involved there will be no healing until and unless some other way to obtain the Secondary Gain is found.

Just because the illness brings with it a benefit does not mean that the illness itself is pleasant, imagined or in any way tolerable. It is just more tolerable than the world would be without the illness.

I received a phone call from the husband of a potential patient who was pretty much housebound and suffering chronic pain. I'll call them Jane and John to make the storytelling easier. The pain was so bad sometimes that it was impossible for Jane to get out of bed. Walking was difficult. Housework was difficult. Sitting down and lying down were difficult. John explained to me, over the phone, that I might have appointments cancelled at short notice because sometimes Jane just couldn't get up. John, very thoughtfully, wanted to make sure I was ok with that before I committed to taking on Jane as a patient. I would also have to visit Jane rather than have her come to see me.

I turned up at the arranged time. Had a long chat with them both and then set about doing the hypnotic treatment while John went out to pick up the kids from school. Luckily Jane was used to meditation so inducing trance was much easier than I anticipated. Unfortunately pain can get in the way of trance work, but all of the pain reduction techniques I use are also effective in a fully waking state – it's just a little easier in trance.

I worked my magic and the pain dropped from a 6 to a 5 on a 10-point scale.

This was not as much as I normally manage but it was movement. It just meant the removal of the pain would take a little longer.

Jane was very pleased and felt wonderfully rested after the session and we made another appointment for the following week.

The morning of the next appointment John phoned, very apologetic and cancelled. We made another appointment for the following week.

The morning of that appointment John phoned, embarrassingly apologetic and cancelled. We made another appointment.

On the morning of that appointment Jane phoned and cancelled. We made another appointment.

If this had been anyone else I would not have continued to make appointments, but I had met and spent a considerable amount of time with these two lovely people and met their children and I knew how badly they needed my help so I was a lot more tolerant than I would have been otherwise.

On the morning of the next appointment no early phone call. But John did call around lunchtime to check if I was coming.

To an outsider it might seem puzzling. After all Jane and her whole family were suffering. After years of ineffective medical treatment I had, in around 30 minutes brought about a significant reduction in the intensity of the pain. You would think, that anyone suffering would want as much of that as they could get just as soon as possible.

But the truth is that I had demonstrated quite clearly that I was a threat.

When I arrived for my second visit I explained to Jane exactly why I was a threat. John's financial income resulted solely from his being a carer for Jane. Jane's financial income depended on her being ill. If I were to *cure* Jane they would immediately be in serious financial trouble and might even lose their home. Their whole way of life, and the freedom from having to please an employer, was dependent on Jane remaining ill. I spent an hour explaining about Secondary Gains and how they can create and maintain quite serious physical ailments. There is no suggestion here that Jane was making anything up. Her illness was quite serious and she had been poked, prodded, and tested by various medics for several years. Yet she totally accepted and understood when I explained just how her BodyMind had created something very real to free her from the pain of the consequences of childhood experiences. Jane's self-esteem and confidence were zero. Because of this, functioning in a social world was almost impossible and incredibly emotionally painful. I believe Jane's mind simply transformed this emotional pain into a physical pain.

Jane agreed with my assessment. We did a hypnosis session from which Jane returned feeling much better.

For homework I handed Jane the documents in Appendix 2 and Appendix 3. I include them here so that you may take advantage of them if you think that they may help you to get clearer about your problems.

As I was leaving Jane said that John would call me to make the next appointment because it would depend on his calendar.

I never heard from either of them again.

If you have no way to resolve Secondary Gains you may have to accept your illness as the price you pay.

My own nervous breakdowns, and eventually agoraphobia, that I mentioned in earlier chapters gave me the Secondary Gain of not having to interact with anyone because that interaction was difficult for me. My mind gave me an escape (without my permission, I might add) from the intolerable by creating something that a doctor could diagnose as a reason to stay at home.

The problem itself was dreadful but slightly better than having to face the world and allow the world to see the state I was in. If I could have accepted that and just stayed inside, never interacting with anyone else, it would have been a workable solution. But I wanted to be free. Without that drive for freedom – the illness will win.

Pain

"When we are willing to accept our experience, just as it is, a strange thing happens: it changes into something else. When we avoid pain, struggle not to feel it, pain turns into suffering."

Brenda Shoshanna

In the US more than half of the population lives with chronic or recurrent pain. Their most common sources of persistent pain are head, back and neck. 40% of sufferers claim, quite reasonably, that pain interferes with sleep, mood, leisure and work activity, as well as the enjoyment of life. In a two-week period 13% of the workforce experienced a loss of productive time because of pain. The cost of this is $61 billion – though three-quarters of this is because of reduced performance rather than absence.

My earlier comments may have left you with the idea that I believe that pain is trivial and simple to remove. That is not the case. There is nothing trivial about pain and I don't always find it easy to remove. Sometimes pain removal is a long and slow process. This is because everyone is different and so if chronic pain is your problem then you may need to spend some time using each of these techniques until you find the one that works for you.

The reason I mention my success stories are so that you can know what is possible. These are not stories about people who thought they were suffering severe pain. The pain was real. Doctors had been consulted and diagnoses given. These are stories where Western Medicine failed and the Mind succeeded.

I'm going to introduce you to three different techniques for pain removal. In my experience each of these methods produces results. But that does not mean they all work with everyone.

So now I'll teach you the three methods of pain removal: Fluffy Bunny, Quantum Healing, and Focused Attention. For each of these techniques - take yourself into self hypnosis and make yourself as comfortable as you can in your Healing Room. Do the work I describe in your comfy chair, then, if you wish, you can visit the Control Room, the Portal Room, or the Garden Room to reinforce the work you have done.

Fluffy Bunny

I have called it this for two reasons, the first is that I hope it made you smile; the second is because it was once a fluffy bunny.

I was attending a meeting with my Paranormal Investigation Group (Eximius) at our local pub and one of our members had been suffering from severe lower back pain. It had been checked by a doctor and, as usual, was still hurting. I asked if I could try some healing. So I waved my hands around for a bit with absolutely no change to the pain. That was disappointing (I did say it doesn't always work) so I shifted to the next technique in my armoury. Bear in mind we were sitting in a pub with lots of other people around so it wasn't really the place to induce hypnosis. But I'd done this before in a full waking consciousness state so I started to ask about the pain. These are also the questions you need to ask yourself.

Stage 1:

How big does it feel?

Think in terms of width, breadth and height. It is a good idea to close your eyes and measure with your hands. Avoid trying to constrain the size and shape to the physical size and shape of the part of the body that is painful. The idea of this is to get a sense of how big it *feels.*

What colour is it?

Just allow your subconscious mind to give you a colour. If it doesn't then just pretend you know what the colour is, or just guess.

What texture does it have?

Check if it is smooth, rough, hard, soft, warm, cold, anything that would be communicated through your sense of touch.

How heavy is it?

Just get a sense of its weight and density.

Anything else about it that you are aware of?

Just take a moment to explore it fully and see if anything else about it comes to your mind or catches your attention. Pay attention especially if it reminds you of anything from your past.

Stage 2:

Now, and this is the key to changing the physical sensations associated with this problem, you are going to make some changes.

With your answers to the questions you have created a mental image of your problem or pain. This is how your subconscious mind represents the problem. So now we are going to use the subconscious mind to solve the problem by dealing with the problem in the language of the subconscious.

You see the mind has two major modes of functionality – logic and creativity. Logic is the analytical mind. This is the list maker. This is the part of you that sees cause before effect. This is the part of you that needs to know the hows and the whys and the wherefores. Creativity has a simpler approach and it works with images and feelings.

Take each of the aspects of your image in turn and change it somehow. Make it larger or smaller, lighter or heavier, smoother or rougher, warmer or colder. Play with it. Make it twice as big, four times, 8 times as big. But with each change you make check in on the discomfort level and measure it on your 0 to 10 scale. Notice if any change makes it better or worse. Either is good.

What you are looking for here is the connection to the discomfort. Once you have identified it – and you identify by noticing which change to the image causes a corresponding change in the pain.

If making it smaller reduces the pain, then make it smaller and smaller – but do it in little steps and watch the pain shrink with the image. If making it smoother reduces the pain then get your electric sander out and make it really smooth and finish it off with a coat of varnish.

Use your imagination to change these aspects in any way that makes a difference. If one change doesn't work try another. Keep changing the colour until you get a response then make that new colour more intense and vivid or paler and more pastel. Be creative.

When I was working with my friend in the pub the image was a hard shiny ball. We covered it in fur and it turned into a fluffy bunny – hence the name of this technique. The moment it became a fluffy bunny the pain reduced from a 6 to a 2.

It may be that as you begin to describe the attributes of your discomfort in Stage 1 you become aware of an image that seems to represent the discomfort. If that happens then work with that image. With my patient with the headache we turned it into a rugby ball. Stabbing it several times to let the air out and then thoroughly flattening it was what relieved the pain totally.

The key to success with the Fluffy Bunny Technique is to work with whatever pops into your mind. Then be creative in your approach to changing it.

Quantum Healing

I know this is the title of my favourite Deepak Chopra book, but it is also my name for this technique. There is no connection between the two – though I highly recommend having a read of the book.

This is the sciency bit.

When I was at school I was taught that everything was made up of atoms and that atoms were like tiny solar systems with a nucleus (Sun) surrounded by orbiting electrons (planets). What I wasn't taught, and only my own curiosity led me to this discovery, is that there are 92 naturally occurring different sorts of atoms. These are the elements – things like hydrogen, gold, silver, carbon and all the other stuff that our planet is made of.

Then it got even more interesting. The nucleus was made of two things protons and neutrons and, depending on the particular element, there were different combinations of these. The electrons, unlike planets, could have more than one in an orbit – but there seemed to be rules. Two electrons in the lowest orbit, 8 in the next one, and I don't remember learning any more than that.

Then it got even more interesting. Electrons didn't spend all of their time in our Universe. Sometimes they were here and sometimes they weren't. Sometimes they behaved as if they were waves (like light) and sometimes they acted is if they were solid. And the protons and neutrons were made of all sorts of tiny little sub-atomic particles. And they keep finding more.

Then it got even more interesting. It seemed that the more they tried to pin down these little beasts the more difficult it became until finally it was realised that nothing solid actually existed. All of these things were just energy.

It is just that when there were a lot of them the energy was so dense it seemed solid and real. That is not even taking into account the fact that each individual atom is almost completely empty space because the protons, neutrons and electrons are very like the solar system because that too is almost totally empty space.

Ok! So in a book about self hypnosis I have just given you a very quick lesson in quantum physics which would probably horrify any quantum physicist. But the point I want to get across is that you don't exist and your discomfort is just an illusion.

Yes I know you bought the book and if you didn't exist you couldn't have done that. But I am only really talking about the physical universe here, not about your mind or your conscious awareness. I also want to get your attention and stretch your thinking a little because it will help to release you from your pain.

That you are reading this is a reasonable assumption. So as you look out of your eyes you see the words and the words communicate ideas which may or may not form images in your mind's eye along with understanding in your consciousness.

But where do you see the words?

I make no apologies for repeating myself. Understanding this is key to healing.

There is no tv screen in your head. No projector projecting an image onto the back of your skull. What happens is that photons of light (energy) hit cells at the back of your eyeball. An energy transformation takes place and bio-electrical signals move along the optic nerve. Note that the image does not move along the nerve, just the bio electrical signal – an energy pulse. There are about 120 million rods (light sensitivity) and 6 or 7 million cones (colour sensitivity) in the human retina. So there are lots of these messages moving information as you follow these words with your eyes. But at no time is the image that is projected onto your retina by your eye lens transmitted as a complete image.

Your brain then decodes all of these messages at the other end of the optic nerve and the Optical Cortex somehow sorts it all out and fools you into thinking that you can see an image – an image that exists nowhere except upside down on your retina. You do not see what's on your retina. You see with your brain. Your brain makes it all up. Seeing is an illusion.

Every other sense works exactly the same way.

Your external reality is an illusion and that includes any pain or discomfort you are experiencing.

Now you don't have to believe any of this. But play with these ideas. Think about perception and just exactly how you know that your reality is the way it is because the truth is that you could be dreaming the whole thing. That doesn't make it less real and it doesn't make pain any less painful – but if you can accept that reality is not quite what you thought it was then you can change it.

I experience a dream with a theme from time to time. The theme is that my car vanishes from outside my house and then re-appears some time later. I always think about calling the police to report the theft, but never do. The reason I never do is because I know that the car always returns, undamaged as though it had never moved. How do I know my car always returns? I know that because in my dream I remember the other dreams and all the other cars this has happened to. In my dream I remember those past events as if they were real. My dream world has memories just like my real world and in my dream world they are just as valid. Yet I am making it all up. But in that dream state it is as real as my computer screen is in front of me right now.

You may have heard about lucid dreaming. Lucid dreaming is when the dreamer is not only aware that they are dreaming but they are also able to manipulate and control events from within the dream.

The reason I have explored these ideas in this book is that I want to help you to loosen your grip on reality, because your tight grip on reality is one possibility for the source of your pain. If you loosen your grip, you may experience a lessening of your pain.

Just because your pain is an illusion doesn't mean it is painless.

Just because you create your own reality doesn't mean that you have everything you want.

But the minute you are willing to accept that reality may not be quite as real as you used to think it was, that is the minute you take your power back.

To summarise:

- Physical matter is actually just energy
- Your brain makes stuff up based on what its senses are telling it
- You imagine your reality into existence
- Pain is part of the illusion you have somehow created

So the challenge now is to somehow use this knowledge to create a different experience of reality – and experience it free from the pain.

Here's how:

Take yourself into trance.

A:

Notice your discomfort.

Notice the space it takes up in your body.

Notice its boundaries.

Focus on it.

Feel it fully.

Allow yourself to recognise that this is just energy in motion.

Allow yourself to understand that this is just the motion of molecules and atoms.

As best you can feel it fully as energy.

Focus on this for a few moments then,

184

Switch to...

B:

Feel all of the space outside of the pain boundary.

Notice that what surrounds the pain goes on forever.

Allow yourself to ponder on the infinity of the Universe

Allow yourself to remain aware of the space outside of the pain boundary

Notice all of its limits

Notice the boundaries as a 3-dimensional object.

Become aware that the space that surrounds the pain is made of energy in motion.

Allow yourself to understand that this is just the motion of molecules and atoms.

As best you can feel it fully as energy.

Stay with this for a few moments then,

Switch back to the pain and repeat from A:

Spend a little time inside the boundary and then a little time outside the boundary. Continue to switch between the two. Noticing each time how it is the same energy inside and outside. Noticing also how the boundary shifts and the pain penetrates the space and the space penetrates the pain.

Keep doing this until you feel some shift in the sensation of discomfort. It may take some time the first time you do it, but even if nothing happens the first time keep coming back to this. It is a valuable and effective technique for healing.

What you may find each time you switch is that it becomes more and more difficult to define, or feel, the boundary. That is fine and indicates change taking place.

Focused Attention

Focused Attention is probably the easiest of the three techniques, so if the other two seem like too much effort then try this one first, but be aware that the effort it takes to learn and use Fluffy Bunny and Quantum Healing will be well rewarded.

Take yourself into trance.

Allow your awareness to settle fully in the most painful, or uncomfortable, part of your body. Fully focus all of your attention in that spot and keep it there. Just keep your attention in the centre of the discomfort, and feel the discomfort as fully as you can. Let the pain intensify or reduce as you maintain your attention and focus on that spot.

That is it.

What you may discover is that the centre of discomfort is a little elusive. If, once you have found it, it shifts away from you, then you know you have it on the run. That shifting is an indication of the technique working. Just follow it wherever it goes, never letting it out of your attention until the pain disappears. Resistance is futile. It will go if you hang in long enough and follow it. Only allow yourself to stop once the pain has reduced in intensity – even if it is only by a small amount. Next time you will move it a little more until you feel in control of your life again.

So there you have three useful techniques for the removal of pain or discomfort, but I urge you to use this only after getting yourself checked out by your physician. For each of them make yourself comfortable, take yourself into self hypnosis and then apply whichever technique you feel most drawn to. If it doesn't work the first time then don't abandon it. Try each technique several times. This might be especially necessary if you have a strong belief in the power of the pain, or its cause, over you.

I know it is difficult to persevere when something seems not to be working, but in this instance it could well benefit you. Re-read the chapter each time so that your grip on what you believe to be your reality becomes a little looser.

Also remember that sometimes it is just a case of developing your skill at using a new technique. Just ten minutes of doing this each day will eventually lead to mastery and success.

If the pain is so intense that you find it difficult to focus on remembering the steps in these techniques, there is a Pain Relief Hypnosis recording available to download from my website. It incorporates some of the material above along with an induction designed to work with pain.

Weight

"My idea of healthy eating is blowing the sugar off my donut"
Homer Simpson

I will only explore weight loss briefly here from the point of view of simple techniques you can use with self hypnosis to assist you in breaking your addiction to fattening foods. I have written much elsewhere on this subject and if you want a fuller exploration then check out my book **How to Lose Weight Easily**

For the majority of individuals who are overweight losing weight is something of a challenge. The problem is that although the desire to be slimmer is strong, the emotions that surround food are so much stronger. This means that weight loss entails a lot more than cutting down a few calories each day – weight loss is a battle against being deprived of what you deserve and makes you feel good.

The emotional connections with food are strong and generally derive from childhood experiences where sweet treats were frequently used as rewards and so sweet, fatty foods become an indication that we are loved. As adults, when our mood is low and we crave those protective loving arms around us once more, we seek out sweet, or fatty 'treats' because deep within our subconscious we feel good and deserving once more, at least while we feast.

Once the feast is consumed, we are consumed by guilt for having given in and failed in our diet. Frequently what follows this is a binge because we've failed in our calorie restriction for today so I might as well forget the diet and start again tomorrow.

All of this comes about because of a lack of understanding of how your mind operates and rationalises.

So remember whenever you are losing weight. Every time you are tempted to eat more than you need ask the food, as you hold it in your hand, "Are you Love?" and wait a moment. Then either eat or don't eat. Just get used to asking that question of every mouthful that you don't need.

Also you have to decide upon your priorities.

Which of these is more important to you?

Being slimmer and buying the clothes you like rather than the clothes that fit.

or

Eating more than you need.

If you would rather eat, then forget about taking any steps to lose weight. In fact just skip the rest of this chapter. Recognise that you have made that decision and you are going to stop beating yourself up about your weight and appearance. Accept that as you get older you may well experience health problems that slimmer people don't suffer from. Accept it as a consequence of your decision. Make up your mind now, that in 20 years time, you will not complain about having to take heart medication, or be concerned about the difficulty you have in getting around. Know that whatever happens – you chose it and will happily accept your shortened life, and will not be concerned about time not spent watching your grandchildren grow up.

These are some of the possible consequences of being overweight, but you really have to see that you have a choice. You can be slimmer or not. If eating a little less and exercising a little more is just too much trouble and you would much rather enjoy a cream cake and three spoons of sugar in your coffee and not torture yourself with thoughts about missing those 'treats' then be happy with who you are at the weight you are and forget about what society thinks is best for you. Yes, there are negative consequences, but if you want to take the easy way out, that is your choice and no one has the right to tell you that you are wrong for choosing that.

If you are still here (and not forging ahead with the next chapter) then I guess you are serious about losing weight. So what I am going to do is teach you how to use self hypnosis to make that process a little easier.

But first you need to know the rules.

The rules are that there are just two rules and two guidelines.

Rule Number 1:

Stop eating either when you are full, or when the pleasure is gone – whichever comes first.

Rule Number 2:

Eat when you are hungry and not otherwise.

Guideline 1:

Eat a little less.

Guideline 2:

Exercise a little more.

Got that?

Simple isn't it.

I am not suggesting, or encouraging you to diet. My reasons for this you will find explored fully in **How to Lose Weight Easily**. I realise you may not have read that, but I don't want to go over ground that I have already covered thoroughly. **How to Lose Weight Easily,** by the way, is not a book about using hypnosis to lose weight. It is a book that shows you the ten simple steps you need to take to lose weight easily and explains the background about why those steps will work and why dieting leads to eventual weight gain.

Here I will show you how you can enhance the message in that book by using the power of self-hypnosis to assist you.

At this point you must have an idea of what your weight loss goal is.

Take yourself into trance.

Take yourself into your Healing Room and then go into the Portal Room.

As you stand before the Portal the light seems to solidify, and as you watch the Portal itself becomes mirror-like.

Stand in front of the mirror.

The reflection that looks back at you is not the present you, it is the you that you wish to be. Slimmer, attractive, dressed in clothes that show off your figure and allow you to look really good.

Allow the reflection to turn around so you get a really good look at what you are about to become.

Imagine yourself stepping into the mirror, a little like Alice Through the Looking Glass, and step into the Portal and into your reflection.

You become that reflection.

You become the slimmer more attractive you.

You find yourself in another space and time that is your future. Bend, twirl, dance... do whatever you need to do to allow yourself to feel the sheer pleasure of being in a lighter, fitter, healthier body.

Now take yourself, and your new body, off to explore somewhere you would love to be. Sunbathing, a tropical paradise, walking in nature, anything at all that you would love to do. In this magical space you have only to imagine it and you are there. Imagine yourself doing it and engage fully with this vision of your future. Enjoy doing things that your excess weight prevented you from doing.

Have fun.

Spend as much time here as you wish.

When you feel it is time to leave, transport yourself back and step out of the Portal.

Now imagine a beam of light coming into the top of your head and travelling down through your body. Imagine, with every breath you take, that light is spreading out and filling every cell in your body. As the light fills your body, feel yourself getting lighter and lighter.

Return to your Healing Room.

Bring yourself back into full waking awareness.

Do this exercise on a daily basis until you reach your desired weight.

Now whenever you have thoughts of food, or experience a desire to eat when you are not hungry, bring to mind that image of the slimmer you and hold it in your mind.

Look at the food you desire and ask yourself "is this what I really want, or would I rather be slimmer?" Answer the question honestly and do whatever you want to do. Eat if you still want to. Don't if you have changed your mind.

If you choose to eat it is most important that you do not consider this a failure – because it isn't. It was just a choice to eat something you didn't need. No big deal. Later on today, or maybe tomorrow, you can make a different choice.

Eating when you don't feel hungry is just a choice that doesn't help you get to where you want to be. It does not mean you are bad, useless, a failure or whatever negative term you **used** to apply to yourself.

I know I said there were two rules and this means you broke one of them – but so what. You have to get that you are in charge. You make the decisions about you. And you accept the consequences. Losing weight means eating less. There's no way round that.

But eating less is never a problem. Eating less is just a choice.

Whatever you do is ok – even if it is sabotaging what you want.

And if it is sabotaging what you want then recognise that you will not get what you want if you keep doing it. And if you intend to keep doing it you may as well stop kidding yourself that you want to be slim because your actions suggest the exact opposite. So own up. Say "actually I want to be fat".

Now, if you would like to try something a little simpler.

Take yourself into trance

Repeat the following mantra until you have had enough.

I have **no desire** to eat sweet, sugary, fattening foods.

Once the habit is broken switch to:

I enjoy eating my healthy nutritious meals.

Smoking

"Many of life's failures are experienced by people who did not realize how close they were to success when they gave up."

Thomas Edison

To begin I would like you to entertain the possibility that the only difficulty with giving up smoking are the beliefs you have about the difficulty of giving up cigarettes.

Smoking: the Myth of Addiction

The Myth of Addiction is the reason many smokers don't attempt to give up, or give up giving up at the first twinge of a thought about smoking. The most popular aspect of this Myth is that nicotine is more addictive than heroine. Smokers love this one. It gives them permission to just carry on killing themselves.

What we are talking about here is a physiological addiction - a need by the body itself. When a heroine addict's body needs a fix, it needs a fix. It doesn't matter whether the body is asleep or awake, and the need, the physical suffering, gets worse the longer the body has to wait. It doesn't matter that it is inconvenient right now, as long as the drug is withheld, the suffering intensifies.

I live in the UK and a great many of my patients holiday in US and Caribbean resorts - this entails 10 or 12-hour transatlantic non-smoking flights. I have never once had anyone who couldn't manage that flight without a cigarette, or who chooses holiday destinations based on flight length. Oh! Yes as soon as they get into a space where they're allowed to smoke they light up, but it isn't a problem during the flight because they've told their body it just isn't allowed so forget it. And their body forgets it for the duration of the flight.

I have treated smokers who smoke 40 a day. Not one of them is woken from their 8 hour sleep by a body craving for nicotine.

Yes they light up almost as soon as they get out of bed, but they weren't woken up by a need.

There is another aspect of clinical addiction that is conveniently ignored by those with a vested interested in smoking i.e. tobacco companies, and drug companies peddling drug-based solutions that require you to continue to purchase their products. This aspect is habituation. When you introduce a drug into a body and continue to put that drug into a body the body habituates. That is the body gets used to the drug and so the effect of the drug lessens. This causes a physiological need for an increase in dose in order to maintain the effects of the drug. This is why addictive substances are addictive because you need more and more.

Cigarette smokers tend to smoke the same number of cigarettes per day for decades!!!! And the number of cigarettes a typical smoker smokes in a day has more to do with the number of cigarettes in a packet than it has with any physical craving. I always ask my patients how many cigarettes a day they smoke, so I have a lot of data on the things that smokers do. Smokers tend to smoke 20, 30, or 40 a day, with an occasional 10 or 15. No one ever smokes 27 cigarettes a day, or 32, or 41.

What cigarette smoking is is a habit.

That is all, just a habit.

That doesn't mean it is easy to break. Nail biters know this only too well. But it does mean that the problem is only a problem of the mind, not a problem of the body. If a smoker can tell his or her body not to have any need for a cigarette while they sit in a plane for half a day, why can't they give their body that same message about sitting at home, or driving or having a meal or socialising?

This is because a habit has a trigger. The trigger is usually environmental. Picking up the phone, getting in the car, finishing a meal, getting up, having tea or coffee, sitting in the pub, commercial breaks during tv programs, boredom, being with other smokers - these are all environmental triggers.

If you're a driver you have probably experienced the effect of these environmental habit triggers. A driver who is a front seat passenger will often discover their foot pressing the brake when someone cuts in front of the car they are not driving. Or if you are driving a car where the controls are reversed you might have found yourself turning on headlights instead of wipers. Non-drivers don't need to feel left out, just think about those times you were watching action films, fast cars, fight sequences and so on and realising that you were tensing muscles as if you were part of the action.

Breaking the habit is easy with hypnosis.

A meta-analysis of 600 studies of around 72,000 smokers who used different methods to quit found that hypnotherapy is consistently the most successful way to become a non-smoker.

(New Scientist, 1992)

Hypnotherapy is the most effective means by which people quit the smoking habit.

(Iowa University study)

Be convinced that your cigarette smoking is just a habit before continuing with this process. While you believe you have an addiction you will not succeed. Habits are broken by becoming conscious of them rather than allowing them to act out automatically.

The world is full of ex-smokers. They are the ones who frequently start smoking again. Become a non-smoker instead. Focus all of your work in self hypnosis on reprogramming your subconscious into accepting that you are a non-smoker. Non-smokers do not think about cigarettes. Non-smokers do not long for cigarettes. Non-smokers do not miss cigarettes.

Now you are ready to investigate your smoking habit more closely.

Get your pencil and paper out and, in your mind, go through your smoking day.

Make a list of all the times of the day that you light up a cigarette.

A typical smoker may smoke:

- immediately on rising
- after showering
- while waiting for the kettle to boil
- before, during or after the first cup of tea/coffee of the day
- before, during or after breakfast
- in the car on the way to work
- smoking breaks or tea breaks in work
- before, during, after lunch
- driving home
- before, during, after evening meal
- commercial breaks on tv
- during phone conversations
- just before bedtime
- while out walking
- while socializing with other smokers

If you live where smoking in public places is allowed:

- When you visit a pub/club/bar
- Restaurants
- Theatres, cinemas…
- While out shopping

Make a note of all your 'smoking points' during the day and if you work, note how your smoking pattern differs on your days off or weekends? Just to make it a little easier you can download a template, from this book's website, to fill out if you wish.

When you have completed this exercise have a look at the patterns. How many times have you written 'because I craved one'? You will notice that all or most of your cigarettes are smoked because of what the clock says or what the activity says. In other words your cigarette smoking is nothing but a Pavlovian Conditioned Reflex – a response to an external stimulus. Conditioned reflexes, as Pavlov discovered, die out when they are not continually reinforced.

Your list of smoking circumstances will be used in your self hypnosis, so make sure you are fully conversant with it because you will be referring to it from memory.

Take yourself into trance.

Go to your Healing Room.

Allow your mind to drift back to that very first cigarette you smoked. Remember the unpleasant taste. Bring to mind all of the things you didn't like about that experience. Think about why you smoked the next one. Was it because you wanted to fit in, to feel grown up?

Remind yourself that you are grown up and you don't need to pretend any more. Remind yourself of all the people who are your friends and acquaintances and ask yourself do you really need to smoke in order to keep them in your life? Or are you pushing everyone away now because smoking is no longer acceptable in our society.

Now bring to mind your list of cigarette smoking times and places.

For each item on the list say, quite firmly, to yourself: I have no desire to smoke when…

Fill in the details from the first item on the list.

Then: I have no desire to smoke when…

And complete the sentence with the next item on the list.

If you fancy a little variety you can ring the changes a little with

When I… (list item), I have no desire to smoke.

And continue until you have covered all the items on your list.

So it might be like this

I have no desire to smoke when I wake up in the morning. I have no desire to smoke while I am enjoying my cup of coffee after my breakfast. When I get into the car to drive to work, I have no desire to smoke.

…and so on.

From time to time add in something along the lines of…

And when I am watching my favourite tv shows in the evening I become so engrossed in what's going on that I *forget about smoking.*

When you have completed all the items on your list finish off with something along these lines. The actual words aren't important so you don't have to memorise this.

I am now a non-smoker. I feel pleased that smoking is now a thing of the past. In fact smoking is now so far in the past that I forget about smoking. I forget all about smoking. When I come back to waking awareness it will seem as though I have never smoked. I am a non-smoker.

Then bring yourself back to full waking awareness.

This may only need to be done once, or you may need to reinforce it. You may find that certain cigarettes just drop out of awareness, but others still hang around. If this is the case, then repeat the session just focusing on those stubborn occasions when you still feel the need to smoke.

Afterwards, in the unlikely event that you experience any *craving* – remember that this is *not* an incurable addiction. It *is* the natural discomfort experienced during any healing process. When you break an arm, or cut yourself – you don't expect to heal free of pain or other discomfort. But as the healing progresses the discomfort eases, and as each day goes by you know that your body is becoming healthier and healthier.

However, there are one or two things you can do to ease any immediate discomfort – just as you might take a painkiller for the pain of a broken bone.

Suck an ice cube, or rinse your mouth out with iced water. This will remove any discomfort.

Should you find yourself thinking about cigarettes, or other tobacco products, then just find something to do that occupies your mind more fully – like a crossword or other puzzle, do some creative writing, painting or craft work…

Remember any mild discomfort is only short-term, but you can make it seem bigger than it is by focusing on it. So distract yourself and it will remain small and insignificant.

Good luck – because we all enjoy some of that, and have a wonderful and healthy life.

And if you are truly committed to becoming a non-smoker then there are some additional things you can do that will ensure your success.

Throw away all of your smoking paraphernalia like ashtrays and lighters. Nothing shouts commitment to your subconscious like throwing away any remaining cigarettes. If you keep a few - just in case – then you are planning to fail and so you will. If you feel any discomfort, go for a walk, or if you are fit and otherwise healthy engage in some vigorous exercise.

Increase intake of fluids, just not coffee, alcohol, or soft drinks (sugar & caffeine). More fluids help to wash the nicotine from your system. As the nicotine leaves you will feel better. It takes about four days.

If you need something in your mouth then chew something that isn't full of sugar. Carrots, celery, or nuts, perhaps. Eat three or four oranges a day for those first few days, and if you can't manage that take a high dose Vitamin C tablet and some B Vitamins to ease any stress you may temporarily experience.

Continue this regime for ten days.

Then congratulate yourself for doing easily what so many people have found to be difficult.

Blood Pressure

"If a drug company finds out that celery juice lowers
blood pressure, and if they tell it to people, they
can't sell their drugs. They get three bucks for a pill.
Why should they tell you to use celery juice?"

Jacque Fresco

Manipulating your blood pressure is a great way to demonstrate the impact that your mind can have on your body. It is also a great way to show you how your self hypnosis is much more powerful than you may imagine. With even a little success here you will develop a belief that will allow you to tackle more serious health issues with confidence in your ability to relieve your own suffering.

So why blood pressure?

Well, there is a good chance that your blood pressure is high enough to negatively impact your health. I can say that with certainty because 1 in every 3 people has blood pressure that is too high. So if you think of two people who are close to you – then one of you probably has high blood pressure.

Now, the trouble is that blood pressure gets too high without letting you know. Most people only discover they have high blood pressure during a routine visit to their doctor for something else entirely. Then that discovery usually results in even more unnecessary medication. Blood pressure, however, is something that you can, in most cases, do something about yourself. Even without the use of self-hypnosis, blood pressure can be lowered with some small lifestyle changes. But I want you to lower it purely with the use of self hypnosis. After you have made even a small change, you can make the lifestyle changes to bring it down even more – but first you need to find out how easy it is to keep track of your own blood pressure so that you never get that unpleasant surprise when you visit your doctor.

Now you may think that your doctor's surgery is the best place to have your blood pressure measured, but it isn't. The best way is to do it yourself. You see, anxiety is one of the things that pushes blood pressure up and a lot of people suffer from what is known as White Coat Hypertension. This is high blood pressure caused by being in a medical environment. White coat hypertension can easily push your blood pressure up from a normal 120 to a hypertensive 150.

Also blood pressure (Bp) varies, quite naturally, throughout the day. Your blood pressure is lower when resting and relaxed than it is when you are active. When you measure it yourself you can, if you wish, measure it several times a day, or just once a day when you are relaxed. When you do this regularly and keep a record this gives your doctor a much more accurate picture and helps them to help you with much more relevant treatment, because many of the pharmaceutical treatments for hypertension are quite harmful in other ways.

In the days when blood pressure was measured with a column of mercury and a stethoscope you had little choice but to get it measured by your doctor. Nowadays there is a huge range of accurate, electronic Bp monitors that are so simple and easy to use that anyone can take accurate Bp readings.

So in order to see the effects of your self hypnosis you will need to obtain one of these blood pressure measuring devices. The correct term for one of these is a sphygmomanometer (sphyg for short) but Bp monitor is a little easier on the tongue so I'll stick to that. I encourage you to get hold of one. They are handy to have and are an easy way for you to keep an eye on your own cardio-vascular health. I bought one around 12 years ago and it still works fine so it is a good investment and they are considerably less expensive nowadays.

One suggestion though. Avoid the wrist cuff monitors. Rather than using a cuff that you have to undo sleeves and slide up your arm, these just wrap around your wrist. It makes sense and is much easier to use – but the wrist is not a good place to measure Bp. The position of your wrist is much more variable, in relation to your heart, and this effects the Bp readings. Readings taken with an arm cuff fastened above the elbow are much more reliable and consistent.

Before we get on to the practical work; I have not written this chapter because Blood Pressure is simply an easy way to demonstrate the power of self hypnosis. As I mentioned earlier 1 in 3 people suffer from high blood pressure. But moderate hypertension, like smoking, produces no noticeable symptoms. However, just like smoking, after a few years of ignoring it, you start to suffer serious health problems. The worst of these, heart attacks and strokes, can be lethal or severely disabling.

High blood pressure causes:

- Artery damage and narrowing
- Aneurism
- Coronary artery disease
- Enlarged heart
- Heart failure
- Transient ischaemic attack
- Stroke
- Dementia
- Mild cognitive impairment
- Severe kidney damage and failure
- Eye and sight damage
- Erectile dysfunction
- Loss of sexual desire, lack of arousal and orgasm (women)
- Osteoporosis
- Sleep problems

So you can see that by working with your blood pressure, you can save yourself, and your loved ones, a great deal of heartache in the future by taking action now.

The first step is to order your Bp monitor. If you want some help with this go to the book's website and click *Mentioned in the Book* on the right hand side.

Then take a few readings over several days to establish your average Bp.

The monitor will give you three numbers, systolic pressure, diastolic pressure, and pulse rate. Systolic is the higher of the two numbers. If your blood pressure is in the healthy range then systolic is 120 or below, and diastolic is 80 or below (120/80). Now it is actually unlikely that your blood pressure will be in that range because most adults have blood pressure above that but below 140 over 90 (140/90). This is what is now known as pre-hypertension. If you are in this range then you need to be taking steps to reduce your blood pressure anyway. Above 140/90 and you definitely need to have a word with your physician. Though by all means suggest that he gives you a couple of weeks to work on it by yourself before resorting to medication. Then you can go back and he'll think his original measurement was a mistake when he sees how much your blood pressure has dropped.

So there are two things to do.

The first thing is the self hypnosis. The second is all the other stuff. Now although this is a book about self hypnosis and I want you to use that first, I will let you know about the other things you can do to reduce your blood pressure because it is so important for your general health and well being to keep your blood pressure within the normal range.

If heart health is a particular concern for you then I would strongly encourage you to read The Wellness Book and The Harvard Medical School Guide to Lowering Your Blood Pressure, both by cardiologist Herbert Benson.

Ok so how do you use your mind to lower your blood pressure.

Well first of all there is some bad news.

Unfortunately, Bp does not respond well to direct suggestion so going into trance and simply affirming a mantra such as "my blood pressure is now 120 over 80" is going to do you no good at all. By the way, direct suggestion is not the same as the Healing Room visualisation I touched on earlier.

The good news is that what Bp responds extremely well to is simple hypnotic relaxation. So just going into trance, making yourself comfortable in your Healing Room, and remaining there for around 20 to 30 minutes twice a day will be powerfully beneficial.

So, all you have to do is to get nice and comfortable, count your-self down, go to your Healing Room, and then let yourself drift away on an imaginary journey to your favourite place of relax-ation where you can lie on a beach, wander through the country-side, or stroll through a beautiful garden filled with flowers and fountains, pools and paths, or whatever is your heart's delight. Deep relaxation alone can bring about up to a 20% drop in Bp. That is from 200 down to 160. When you do this regularly twice each day this becomes a permanent state of affairs.

Now if you want to do something more and include a little bit of visualisation that relates to the problem then by all means do so, but your self hypnosis work is primarily deep relaxation. If you wish, you could also visit your Control Room before returning to full waking awareness. In your Control Room notice where your blood pressure controls are set and reduce them a little. As you do so feel yourself relaxing even more and feel the tension releasing itself from deep within your blood vessels.

Another image you can use is that of a pressure cooker with the safety valve released and steam rushing out. As you imagine this, again feel the relaxation deepening within you as you sink deeper and deeper.

Another variation you can use, after you have settled comfortably in your Healing Room, is to create an image of an old fashioned Bp monitor with a column of mercury. See the column of mercury at your current blood pressure and count down 160, 159, 158… or whatever is appropriate for you and see the column of mercury slowly dropping as you do this. Count from where your blood pressure is, to where you want it to be. As you count down feel yourself sinking a little deeper into relaxation with each number that you count. When you reach your target number (probably 120) then allow yourself to enjoy your relaxing visualisation. When you bring yourself back to normal waking awareness, allow yourself to slowly become fully aware and alert while maintaining a state of relaxation.

It is a good idea to measure your Bp before and after your hypnosis sessions so that you can see the effect. But don't forget to keep a record so you can see the overall trend also.

Another powerful way to use self hypnosis to reduce your blood pressure is slow breathing while in trance. Use a relaxation technique to induce trance, count down from 10 to 1 and then, aware of your state of relaxation, allow your breathing to become easier and easier, slower and slower.

The average respiration rate is about 12 breaths per minute. You need to reduce this to 6 or lower. I can do 4 breaths a minute quite comfortably, and with a little practise I can breathe at a rate of two breaths per minute. If you feel any discomfort, or breathlessness, just relax all of the muscles around your chest, breathe normally for a breath or two and then resume slow breathing. All of your focus, while remaining deeply relaxed, is on slowing down your breath. This needs to be done for 30 minutes twice a day and it is an incredibly powerful way to reduce blood pressure. You may need to do this with your eyes open at first so that you can watch the second hand of a clock and count your breaths per minute. As soon as you get a feel for the correct slow rate of breathing then you can revert to eyes closed, but allow your mind to remain focused on your breath. If you imagine that each breath is the first slow breath that you are taking then you will be unaware of the passage of time.

Most people breathe very shallowly and much more rapidly than necessary. The trick is to gently pull air into the lower part of your lungs by pushing out your abdomen. Once this area is full then allow air into the area of your ribs and finally into the very top of your lungs where you may feel a lift in the area of your collar bones. Breathing into this area may invoke feelings of tightness and breathlessness, but as always, if you notice any discomfort, relax, take a few normal breaths and then resume deeper slower breathing. Deep breathing is easy and effortless when you are very relaxed, but it does require concentration because it is not usual.

So that is how hypnosis can help you with this problem, and if your blood pressure is only slightly elevated this may be sufficient. However if your blood pressure is very out of control then there is much more that you can do to reduce it naturally.

The things you can do fall into three areas. If you make small changes in all of these areas you will find it much easier to incorporate them into your life as permanent changes. Small steps are easier to develop into new habits than bigger steps.

The three areas of change are Activity, Diet, & Supplements.

Activity:

This one is simple. Just exercise more. If you walk just one mile a day, an activity that will take just 15 or 20 minutes, this is enough to make a difference. However it needs to be aerobic activity so get yourself a Heart Rate Monitor to ensure that your exercise is sufficiently vigorous to push you into the aerobic zone – moderately fast walking will do this – and then get into the habit of doing it every day.

Lack of fitness is a major factor in cardio-vascular disease and you only need regular moderate exercise to change this and lengthen your life.

If you smoke then stop. Nicotine is a vaso-constrictor that causes narrowing and hardening of arteries. The body, however, is capable of repairing some of the damage so the sooner you stop the sooner your blood pressure will drop. If you need help with this then check out the earlier chapter on stopping smoking.

Stress is a major cause of hypertension. Following my self hypnosis prescription above will go some way to alleviating this, but you really need to look at how you are dealing with life's problems and seek alternatives. Doing the work in the early chapters on confidence and self-esteem will reduce stress in your life.

Diet:

I don't mean go on a diet, I mean change what you eat. If you are overweight then you need to read my book **How to Lose Weight Easily and Free Yourself from Diets Forever** in order to discover how to modify your eating in a way that helps you to lose weight without having to endure the deprivation that diets create. Losing weight causes a drop in blood pressure. It's not a big drop, but it helps.

Reduce **sodium** intake. For most people this means add much less salt to food. Manufactured foods are loaded with sodium because manufacturing processes destroy flavour, so if you are going to eat it, then cook it yourself from fresh ingredients.

Alcohol in small amounts can drop Bp by 2 points, but in larger quantities will push it up by considerably more.

Caffeine affects blood pressure so cut out or cut down coffee and caffeinated soft drinks.

Eat a handful of **raisins** three times a day. Recent research showed that raisins reduced systolic Bp by up to a value of 10 and diastolic up to 5.

Dark chocolate caused a 2 point drop in Bp in research conducted by Dr Karin Reid in Melbourne, Australia.

Supplements:

Vitamin C lowers blood pressure so take a 500mg supplement twice a day.

If your diet has insufficient **magnesium**, which helps with the flexibility of artery walls, then take a magnesium supplement.

Just before we move on to the next topic I want to share with you that I have personal experience of all of this, and the reason I am confident in these techniques is that on 24th February, 2010, I measured my Bp and found it to be 204/92. After a period of panic I did some research and established a plan of action. Just one week later, on 3rd March, 2010, my blood pressure measured 136/80 and all I did was the things I have described to you above. Deep relaxation with slow breathing; CoQ10, & magnesium supplements; a small daily quantity of alcohol (2oz wine); a couple of squares of dark chocolate, some raisins, and I reduced my intake of manufactured foods and cooked more of my own meals from fresh ingredients. I also made sure I walked around 2-3 miles each day for at least 5 days of the week.

Reducing blood pressure does mean you have to do stuff, it's not difficult stuff, but it does need commitment and record keeping. Without the constant feedback of lowering Bp values when you measure them, or the reassurance of healthy values, you will slip back into old habits so, once you have restored your blood pressure to good health, set a time once a week to check it and make sure you keep a note of it.

Sleep

> "But [Pooh] couldn't sleep. The more he tried to sleep the more he couldn't. He tried counting Sheep, which is sometimes a good way of getting to sleep, and, as that was no good, he tried counting Heffalumps. And that was worse. Because every Heffalump that he counted was making straight for a pot of Pooh's honey, and eating it all. For some minutes he lay there miserably, but when the five hundred and eighty-seventh Heffalump was licking its jaws, and saying to itself, "Very good honey this, I don't know when I've tasted better," Pooh could bear it no longer."
>
> A.A. Milne, Winnie-the-Pooh

Sleep is probably the only thing we do each day that really matters. So we need to do it well. The majority of adults need between 7 and 9 hours of sleep each night. If you don't get enough sleep, or you have poor quality sleep then you fall into *sleep debt*. Sleep Debt increases for each night you fail to restore your sleep credit.

Now that might seem a strange thing to say because, on the face of it, sleep appears to be a quite natural process that we have no control over – largely because we are *unconscious* when we do it. But, we can actually do quite a lot to improve the quality and quantity of our sleep without having to resort to medication to help us.

A survey by the National Sleep Foundation showed that 35% of the people surveyed had sleep problems (I told you sleep was important, it's *so* important it has a *Foundation*).

The problems fell into four categories:

1. Difficulty falling asleep
2. Frequent waking during the night.
3. Waking up too early and staying awake.
4. Waking without feeling any sense of refreshment.

I think all of those things happen to all of us at some time, but there comes a point when they are happening frequently, or worse still, nightly, and that is when you have a problem. The problem is twofold. First of all you no longer look forward to bedtime because you know what's going to happen. Secondly you are not energized by your night's rest and so fatigue sets in early along with problems concentrating and staying focused. Enthusiasm is difficult to find, temper gets short, energy goes, and relationships suffer. Lack of sleep can even be painful, with headaches a frequent consequence. Insufficient sleep is dangerous and needs to be taken seriously. Over 100,000 road accidents a year are attributed to driving while drowsy.

The interesting thing is that poor sleeping patterns can usually be fixed quite easily and without resorting to medication.

Anxiety

Anxiety is one of the major causes of sleep disruption and that is quite understandable if it is just an occasional disturbance. But when the anxiety is a background state that is always present then it is time to take action.

Anxiety falls into two main categories:

1. Anxiety about things you have no control over.
2. Anxiety over things you have control over.

If you can do something then take action. If you can't do anything then recognise that you are powerless, it is in the lap of the Gods, and make peace with it.

I realise that simplifies things a little, so here is another angle.

Anxiety is all about thoughts that wander through your mind. The thoughts will be thoughts that cause your emotional energy to drop into the territories of anger, fear, or grief. Anxiety is either a fantasy about what might happen, or a regret about what has happened. Neither of those is going on in the present.

The problem is rarely what has happened, or might happen, it is your thoughts about that. The thoughts are the problem. It is the thoughts that disturb your sleep, prevent you from dropping off, and wake you early.

So attend to the thoughts.

Now you may think that you are powerless to impact your thoughts. After all you only know about them once they appear and once they appear it is a little late to do anything about them.

At least that is what your thoughts would have you believe.

Worrying is a choice and an addiction.

You can control it, but not directly. You have to sort of sneak up on it through the back door.

Here are three simple things you can do to begin to take back control of your mind.

They are designed to facilitate a quieting of the mind, but they require something from you.

They require that you do them rather than think about doing them - that sounds like a good idea but I cannot be bothered right now. They also require that you trust that your world will not come crashing down around your ears if you relinquish thinking about your problems for a little while.

Bathe

Just before bedtime, run yourself a nice warm bath. If you like bubbles and candles and soft music, do that too. Get in, then just lie there soaking in the warmth and allow your mind to drift to somewhere pleasant. Plan a dream holiday to a place you'd love to visit; fantasise about a new *toy* you'd like to possess; start to write your novel in your mind by developing the story line and characters; let your mind run free to explore anything at all that you find fascinating. If at any time you realise you are back on your favourite worry subject, then just let that go and return to your imaginary world. After about half an hour of this, get out and *go straight to bed*.

Turn off TV

About an hour before bedtime turn off the TV. Instead listen to some relaxing music, something drifting and dreamy if you have it, definitely not something that makes you want to get up and dance. Read a really good book that takes you away and engrosses you, or read something really boring.

Exercise

Fit some vigorous physical activity into your evening routine. One of the primary reasons for poor sleep quality is that, in these days of sedentary occupations, our bodies just don't get physically tired. Physical tiredness is an aid to deep and restful sleep.

So join a gym, go for a fast walk, or buy yourself a rowing machine. It doesn't really matter what the exercise is or where you do it but get physical. The exercise generates endorphins which make you feel good. When you feel good it is much harder to get hold of negative thoughts.

There are also some don'ts.

Cut down on caffeine and other stimulants. Caffeine isn't just found in coffee, it comes in tea and some soft drinks have oodles of the stuff hidden inside. It is pointless complaining about being unable to sleep while maintaining a life-style and diet that stimulates your physiology.

Don't expect to get a good night's sleep if you nap during the day. Falling asleep while watching TV is something you need to particularly avoid. If TV is so boring get up and do something more interesting instead. Find something to stimulate your interest until around an hour before bedtime and then start to wind down – but still avoid napping in the armchair.

Go to bed to go to sleep. So don't read in bed. Don't watch TV in bed. Don't listen to the radio, or anything else, in bed. And most important of all, don't nap during the day or evening.

If anxiety is disturbing your sleep then doing these simple things will improve your sleep quality, and quantity. Elsewhere in these pages you will find more details on how to reduce anxiety, so make sure you study that section of the book and take action.

Reading about how to solve your problems does not solve them.

Acting on the information will.

If you feel that you are not sleeping at all at night time, then it may be that your sleep rhythm has been completely disrupted. A good way to restore normal sleep patterns is to force yourself to stay awake for two full days and the night in between. The following night, when you go to bed at your normal bedtime, you will almost certainly sleep.

OK, I have given you some real world solutions that you can try, it is time now to look at how you can support improved sleep patterns with self-hypnosis.

Turn your bedroom into a Sleeping Space. Make sure you can keep it dark, quiet and pleasant. This might be a room where you need to consider the principles of Feng Shui as an aid to removing clutter and ensuring the *energy* of your room is conducive to restful sleep.

Before you retire for the night, get a pen and a pad and write down your important tasks for the next day. Those things it is essential that you accomplish. Put it somewhere safe.

Ensure your room is warm enough. If this is not possible then ensure your bed is warm enough. I use additional quilts in the winter so even though the room becomes quite cool overnight, I stay nice and warm.

Make yourself comfortable and arrange your pillows so that your neck is supported.

Now begin the process of self hypnosis.

Initially count yourself down from 10 to 1. Counting each number on each out breath. As you breathe out imagine that you are relaxing a little bit more.

When you reach number 1 then move into the Appreciation Process.

Here I want you to drift lazily through your day becoming aware of those moments you appreciated. I covered how to do this more fully in the Self-Esteem chapter. The idea is to pick just five occasions in your day that you would like to express appreciation for. Bring the moment fully back into your mind and relive it but this time with a sense of full appreciation for the blessing you received with this gift.

Once you have processed the five moments give yourself a moment or two to bask in the glow of your appreciation.

Now we begin a progressive relaxation. This is based around a Silva-Method process that I especially enjoy.

First of all bring into your imagination a big chest with a pad-lock. I like a pirate-type treasure chest, but you can use whatever appeals to you.

Into this chest place carefully all of the thoughts, worries, and concerns that are wandering through your mind, all of the things you need to deal with tomorrow and the day after, all of the things you need to forget, all of your regrets about the day, all of your guilt or any other negative emotion you are experiencing. They can go in as anything you like, words, thoughts, objects, energy... you can even put into it any individuals who are caus-ing you problems.

When you have emptied out, then shut the lid and close the pad-lock with a big key that you put somewhere safe. I like to bury the chest on a desert island (like the pirates did with treasure) but you can bury it in your garden, put it in your loft, or create a special imaginary place for its safe-keeping until the morning. You see, in the morning, if you wish, you can open it up and take out all the stuff and put it back in your head. But you don't have to do that, for you will find, if you just forget about it, that when you come to repeat this exercise the following bedtime, that your chest has magically emptied itself and all of the previous day's problems have completely disappeared.

Now take yourself deeper into trance by once more counting down from 10 to 1.

Go to your healing room and...

...then allow yourself to become aware of any muscle tension in your scalp area. Release and relax any tension in the muscles of your scalp – as best you can. Once you have done this allow yourself to become aware of a subtle tingling sensation within this area of your body. It is a little like a gentle pins and needles without any discomfort. You may find it difficult to sense at first but be assured it becomes much easier with practice. You may consider this tingling sensation to be your life force, or the energy that you are.

Allow yourself to become aware of any muscle tension in the area of your forehead. Release and relax any tension in the area of your forehead – as best you can. Once you have done this allow yourself to become aware of a subtle tingling sensation within this area of your body.

Allow yourself to become aware of any muscle tension around your eyes and eyelids. Release and relax any tension in the area of your eyes and eyelids. There are several tiny muscles in this area and they hold a lot of tension so spend a little time ensuring they are fully relaxed. Once you have done this allow yourself to become aware of the subtle tingling sensation within this area of your body.

Allow yourself to become aware of any muscle tension in the area of your face; this is primarily your cheeks. Release and relax any tension in the area of your face – as best you can. Once you have done this allow yourself to become aware of a subtle tingling sensation within this area of your body.

Allow yourself to become aware of any muscle tension in the area of your mouth. Release and relax any tension in the area of your mouth. Just like your eyes, your mouth has a lot of tiny muscles that hold tension so spend a few moments focusing on this area and releasing all of the tension. Once you have done this allow yourself to become aware of a subtle tingling sensation in this area of your body.

Now allow yourself to become aware of any muscle tension in the area of the skin of your neck. Release and relax any tension in the area of the skin of your neck. Once you have done this allow yourself to become aware of a subtle tingling sensation in this area of your body.

Now we need to begin to work a little deeper so allow yourself to become aware of any tension within the neck area. Release and relax any tension within the neck area. Once you have done this allow yourself to become aware of a subtle tingling sensation in this area of your body.

Now allow yourself to become aware of any muscle tension in your arms and hands. Release and relax any tension in your arms and hands. Once you have done this allow yourself to become aware of a subtle tingling sensation in this area of your body.

Now move to the chest area and allow yourself to become aware of any muscle tension. Release and relax any tension in this area of your body. Once you have done this allow yourself to become aware of a subtle tingling sensation in your chest area.

Now we go a little deeper again, so imagine you can feel your way into the organs of your chest and allow them to relax. Feel your heart beating regularly and know that it will continue to do so as you rest and sleep the night away. So release and relax any tension within the chest area. Then once more, allow yourself to become aware of the subtle tingling sensation in this area of your body.

Moving now to the abdomen and you allow yourself to become aware of any muscle tension. This is an area of the body that holds a lot of tension – this is why we have gut feelings. So spend whatever time you need to release and relax any tension in this area of your body as best you can. Once you have done this allow yourself to become aware of a subtle tingling sensation in your abdominal area.

Now we go a little deeper again, so imagine you can feel your way into the organs of your abdomen and allow them to relax. Know that they will continue to do their work as you rest and sleep the night away, but that their work will help you to awaken refreshed and revitalised. So release and relax any tension within the abdominal area. Then once more, allow yourself to become aware of that subtle tingling sensation in this area of your body.

Moving down now to the muscles of the thighs, allow yourself to become aware of any tension here. Then just release and relax that tension in your thighs. Once you have done this allow yourself to become aware of the subtle tingling sensation in your thighs.

Finally, moving down now to the muscles of the lower legs and feet. Allow yourself to become aware of any tension here. Then just release and relax that tension in your calf muscles and feet. Once you have done this allow yourself to become aware of the subtle tingling sensation in this area of your body.

Now we reverse the direction, but change the process. This is purely an exercise in imagination.

Focus on your feet and allow yourself to imagine that your feet are no longer a part of your body. This is a bit like forgetting your feet exist by allowing yourself to pretend that you have no input from your feet.

I know this sounds a bit mad when you are just reading about it, but believe me, it works when you have arrived at this point in the process after following the earlier relaxation.

Then allow yourself to feel as if your lower legs are no longer a part of your body.

Move up to your thighs and allow yourself to forget about your thighs.

Then do the same with your arms and hands. Allow yourself to behave as if your arms are no longer a part of you.

Then do this again with your abdomen and chest.

Now count down from 5 to 1, with the usual rules for counting on an out-breath and imagining that you are relaxing even deeper with each breath that you breathe out. (Not that there's a lot of you left to relax at this point.)

When you reach number 1 then move yourself in your mind to a place of relaxation. This can be anywhere you like. My favourite is relaxing on a hammock slung between two palm trees on a tropical beach, but it doesn't really matter where you go as long as it is a place of peace and relaxation for you. Enjoy it fully by allowing all of your senses to have input into your imagination. I enjoy the sounds of seabirds, waves gently washing up the beach, blue sky, fluffy clouds and golden sands, the feel of sand between my toes, or the warm water washing across my feet, maybe the weight of my body pressing against the colourful material of the hammock and the gentle swaying of the hammock that lulls me into a deep and restful sleep. Taste and scent are perhaps more difficult to include, but I like the scent of coconut, so a drink of coconut milk served in a coconut shell does the trick for me.

If after you spend ten minutes or so exploring this fantasy you are still wide awake, then you go back to the beginning and start all over again.

Continue to do this all night if necessary. At least this way you are enjoying a restful and rejuvenative lack of sleep, because the deep relaxation this process will create is of great benefit to your body.

What you will find though, as you do this self hypnosis as part of your going to sleep routine every night, is that each night you will manage less and less of this procedure before you find yourself in a deep relaxing sleep. If you awaken early then simply start the process again.

That is all there is to it. But don't rush this process. Take your time – after all you were going to be awake anyway, so there's no rush. You don't have anything else to do. Relax, take your time to explore the feelings and sensations fully, and take it seriously. It works if you follow my instructions. If you skip bits, or do your own variation, then you probably have issues about sleep that you need to explore.

Spirit

"I have looked in the mirror every morning and asked myself: 'If today were the last day of my life, would I want to do what I am about to do today?' And whenever the answer has been 'No' for too many days in a row, I know I need to change something."

Steve Jobs

Spirit

The Body heals with play, the Mind heals with laughter, and the Spirit heals with joy.

Proverb

From this point on I want you to consider that you have done all of the hard work and now it is time for some well-deserved fun. Treat this section with a sense of playfulness. If you take it too seriously then it will slow you down.

I begin by giving you a feel for how you manage to create your own reality even if you say, as I did on many occasions, "if I actually created my own reality, don't you think I'd have created a better one than this?"

You don't actually need to believe this in order to benefit from the techniques in this section. I offer some real world, as well as magical world, reasoning for why it will be effective.

Without the experience of a deep sense of happiness life is a bit of a struggle so I start this section by showing you how you can begin to experience more of this in your life. A lack of money is also problematic in enjoying life so that comes under scrutiny too. There is a look also at a different level of relationship harmony, a last minute chapter on the essential nature of forgiveness and we end with capturing that sense of freedom of spirit that allows us all to live the life we want rather than the life we have.

I sincerely hope that you reach the end of this section feeling at least a little uplifted and ready for some new adventures.

Create Your Own Reality

"Thought creates your world and then says, 'I didn't do it.'"
David Bohm, Quantum Physicist (1917-1992)

From this point on in this book I want you to have some fun. I have introduced you to some new ideas about the mind-body connection and shown you how you can utilise that knowledge to your advantage in a way that helps you to bring about physical, as well as mental, shifts that allow you to have much more control over your life.

However, everything that you have read up to this point has been designed to bring you from a place where life has been difficult for you, to a place where you are at or very close to what most people call *normal*. By that I mean you are learning to function again and do some of the things you enjoy, and that other people enjoy, regardless of your history.

I do not want to leave you there.

I want you to move beyond this point and see that life has so much more to offer you. I want you to move beyond this point and start to live your life just as fully as you wish. Now, one of the problems with wishes, when you suffer from low self-esteem, or severe anxiety, is that they tend to be limited. So if you worry a lot about things going wrong, you may not be that keen on planning a trip round the world. But when you are free of that concern, travel may suddenly become something that you love to do.

So allow your wishes to change as you grow and heal.

In this chapter I want to introduce you to the idea that you create your own reality. If you have not read The Secret, or any of Esther & Jerry Hicks' books then I encourage you to do so. They go into this subject in much more detail than I am able to cover in a book on self hypnosis.

But it is essential that you understand these ideas because you can then utilise your self hypnosis to its maximum benefit for you.

First there is a problem that we need to get out of the way. It is a problem that frequently prevents people from moving forward with this and using it to their advantage. The problem is that you are reading this book because you have had some problems negotiating life. You have not found it as easy as most other people seem to. So if you accept that you create your own reality then you have to accept that you created all of the pain in your life. Then when you discover that you can create pleasure instead, you will almost certainly have a tough time reconciling the fact that if only you had discovered this knowledge earlier on, then you could have avoided an awful lot of pain and you could have lived a wonderful life.

This surely is a recipe for grief and regret?

If it didn't have to be the way it was then my life has been wasted is an idea that not many can live with. This creates resistance to change and prevents you from further exploration of these ideas.

The past is just a memory.

It might be a painful memory, but it is just a memory.

The past does not exist now.

One of the things that I love about the magical way things work is that it is full of contradictions. One of the contradictions is this: you create your own reality, but you can only do what you do.

I used to be very rigid in my thinking (some of my friends think I still am – but I love them anyway), and hypocrisy was something I loved to judge in others. Until I found myself holding two opposing points of view, both valid, simultaneously. This is the nature of your spiritual journey. It brings you into conflict with everything that is in the way of your living a peaceful, joyful life.

Consider the past. You always did your best. The decisions and choices you made were always the best you could make - given what you knew at the time; given the life experiences you had had at that time; and given your level of anxiety at the time. With hindsight, or knowledge of the future, we can all make better choices. But we don't have that, so the way forward is to acknowledge that you always did your best – even when it didn't work out.

The past isn't where you are. Where you are is the present. The present is your moment of power. It is only in the *right now* that you can ever do anything. In the *right now* you can create your reality.

Create your reality?

What exactly does that mean?

What it means is:

- Being responsible for your actions.
- Deciding what you want.
- Taking appropriate mental actions to bring about what you want.
- Taking appropriate physical actions to bring about what you want.
- Never giving up on your dream unless you decide you no longer desire it.

What doesn't it mean?

- Never having a problem to deal with.
- Never having people disagree with you.
- Never experiencing any anxiety.
- You can control the weather (though I have made it rain on three occasions).

Consider that creating your own reality has two aspects. It has a real, physical world aspect to it. It has a mental, magical, mystical world aspect to it. For a long time I made the mistake of thinking there was just the mental aspect and suffered years of the frustration of things not working for me despite doing everything *right*. The truth is I wasn't doing everything right, I was missing out an important part. But you need both the mental and the physical to bring about results.

This is a subject that has held a fascination for me for almost 20 years now. It started when I began to study the workings of my own mind in order to find a way out of the hell I'd been in for so long. So I began to notice odd coincidences. I'd think of something – just a fleeting thought of something that I felt would be nice – and then it would happen within a day or two, or occasionally within hours. I've already touched on this subject in the chapter on Visualisation.

I discovered two things about the effectiveness of the power of thought.

Brief fleeting 'that would be nice' sort of thoughts frequently manifested. Thoughts that had a lot of intense emotion surrounding them also manifested.

The stuff in the middle rarely seemed to have any impact.

Ok, so how do you make use of this?

What I am going to do, in the next few chapters is look at the four things that most people desire and show you how to use your new found self hypnosis skills to enhance the power of your thoughts and bring about an increase in your Happiness, greater Freedom, more Wealth and better Relationships.

Happiness

"Keep away from people who try to belittle your ambitions. Small people always do that, but the really great make you feel that you, too, can become great."

Mark Twain

The trouble with common words is that we all think we know what they mean, yet they don't always mean the same thing to different people.

Here are some of the things my dictionary associates with Happiness: fortunate, content, well-being, pleasure, carefree, confident.

There is false happiness, and there is contentment.

False happiness is the idea that things will make you happy. The idea that the next iPhone, latest tablet, new car, new puppy... will change your life in a positive way forever. The buzz is down to anticipatory excitement and soon palls once the new 'toy' is acquired.

You see this in young children when they want a pet. What they really want is a live teddy bear that is cute and cuddly. What they don't want is something that poos on their bed and needs cleaning up and exercising and the novelty soon wears thin.

Just think back in your life to all of those things, those material objects, or people, that you wanted in your life because they would make you happy. Then remember how long the buzz lasted before you wanted something else. If you happened to marry the object of your desire then it probably wasn't so easy and you maybe learned to take the good with the bad.

Let me suggest to you that the happiness that you really seek is something that is within you.

The happiness you seek is an attitude of mind, rather than a possession.

Does that mean that in order to be happy you shouldn't want things?

Of course not! I like new toys just like everyone else. I just enjoy them fully while I have them and while they are novel. I don't give them magical powers to change my life and I don't immediately start looking for the next new thing to fill the happiness gap.

Because of this I find that I enjoy my 'toys' for much longer than I ever did when I believed that happiness could be delivered by the postman.

I remember when the iPad came out a few years back and I was playing with one in an Apple store. I thought it was brilliant. I realised it was just a giant iPhone (without the phone), but I really, really wanted one.

Much to my surprise I received one for my next birthday, and it is one of the loveliest gifts that I have ever received. Not so much for what it was, more for the love and care that went into its selection for me and the kindness and generosity of my daughters for thinking of it. I am not an easy person to buy gifts for but this one blew me away.

Less than a year later it was superseded, and is now very out of date and will no longer accept updated operating systems because Apple don't seem to care about customers who don't buy every new thing they want to sell.

I still love it and use it daily. And every time I use it I am amazed at the technology that went into it and I still find it quite magical that I have a powerful computer that I can carry under my arm and use almost anywhere. I used to be a computer programmer working with mainframe computers that needed a huge air conditioned room to work safely. The first one I worked with had just 138K RAM and was the size of two big wardrobes. The disk drives were each about the size of filing cabinets. But now I have in my hand something with a screen about the size of an

A5 sheet of paper that connects me with the world, lets me play games, send letters, and all sorts of fun stuff.

But I know people who, as soon as iPad 2 came out had to have it because as soon as something new arrived on the scene, it destroyed their pleasure with what they had and left them with an ache to acquire the latest offering.

And the reason I am telling you this story is to introduce you to the first step in the acquiring of happiness. This is a step that is totally under your control and completely independent of any desires. It is also the keystone of my recommended treatment to improving your Self Esteem so you will be quite familiar with this...

Appreciation

The first step is that of appreciation.

Appreciation of what you already have is probably the most important skill to learn in the search for happiness. But before you switch off, that doesn't mean you can't want new stuff. Nor does it mean you cannot have new stuff. It just means that new stuff and happiness are no longer intimately entwined.

When we spend our lives looking over the hill for the next adventure we reach a point where we no longer exist in the present. We cease to be at peace because our thoughts are always in the future. Acquiring the Art of Appreciation is the way to bring peace and happiness into the present moment and I make no apologies for revisiting it here. Appreciation is the key to happiness.

What I would like you to do is to take the exercise I gave you in the self esteem chapter and enhance it.

Take yourself into trance, you could use your healing room or a favourite place as your starting location and then relive those moments of appreciation as fully as you can. Remember all the details, the nuances, and the good feeling. Then, connecting with that good feeling, encourage the good feeling to grow and fill your whole body. Once you have achieved this all-over glow then allow yourself to relive that moment of appreciation once more.

As I mentioned earlier these appreciation moments do not have to be huge events. You do not have to be a lottery jackpot winner to express appreciation. But what you will discover, and this is where the pieces of the jigsaw start to come together, is that the more fully you express appreciation for the small things in your day, the more you will attract bigger things to appreciate and enjoy. This is the how you start to create your reality – a reality filled with what you want, rather than what you do not want.

So see just how much appreciation you can enjoy over the smile of a stranger; a particularly flavoursome, hot cup of coffee; a delicious donut; or a scintillating sunbeam illuminating autumn gold on your woodland walk.

There is an old saying: *want what you have.* There is much wisdom in this. It is not so much a call to stop accumulating, it is much more a call to look around you and enjoy what is present with you right now.

As you learn to do this more and more, what you will find is that your world slows down and becomes more leisurely and enjoyable. Because you take in more. You take time with people. You begin to actually listen to what people are saying and instead of looking for a way in – a way to replay some of your own experiences – you will make a profound connection with the people you meet, and they will wonder what exactly happened. The reason for their wonder is that they will have been heard, possibly for the first time in their lives.

Acceptance

Do you love yourself?

If you don't, do you like you?

One of the questions I ask in my initial interview with a new patient is this:

If you could completely change your personality, what is the one quality that you have that you would keep?

I asked this of a young lady yesterday and she almost started squirming in her chair. Her body language changed completely and instead of looking at me (which she had been doing up until that moment) she was looking anywhere but towards me.

Some people don't like themselves. Some people have such a bad impression of themselves that to be asked to find something about them that they like is, for them, torture. However, I persisted and eventually we discovered that she was compassionate. So here is your next exercise.

Get out pen and paper and write down 10 qualities that you have that you like. 10 good things about you. It doesn't matter whether they are big things or small things as long as they are positive qualities

You cannot be happy unless you are okay with who you are. If you are not ok with who you are then happiness will elude you until you find a way to become ok with who you are.

The reason most people have a problem with who they are, is because of things they carry with them from the past. Regrets about what they did or didn't do. Guilt about what they did or didn't do. *Shoulds & Shouldn'ts* they carry around in their heads and constantly ignore. Well, they ignore them until after the fact at which point they start to beat themselves up about the particular *should* or *shouldn't* they failed to comply with.

We need to bust through this if happiness is to be achieved.

Remember a little earlier I suggested that **you do what you do**. Look into your past *now* and see if there was ever a time when you **did not** do what you **did**. Keep searching in your memory until you are totally satisfied that:

You do what you do, and you don't do what you don't do.

So what is there to feel guilty about if you can only have done what you did?

To look at this another way – you can only choose what you choose. In any given moment we have a memory of our life experiences; we have our fears and concerns; we have no absolute knowledge of the future; and we have our current mental ability to figure things out.

In other words everything that makes you who you are exists as a summation of your past and your personality. Given a choice to make we use our mind to assess the situation given what we already know and given our mental state, and we make a choice based on what already exists. That choice can be the only one we choose because we base it on what already exists.

What we choose, therefore, is the only thing we can choose – *in that moment*.

In another moment with fresh information, new experiences, and a different mood state we might make a completely different choice. But that also would be the only choice we could choose *then*.

So, since you cannot change the past and since your guilt and regret is about past choices that you wish were different, you can gently move to a state of recognition that having happiness by changing the past is never going to happen, so you can either give up on wanting happiness or let go of wanting to change the past.

This is acceptance.

How it is right now is just how it is right now.

That does not mean it is to be like that for all time. Just for right now. Once you accept that you can change it.

What you resist persists.

Acceptance releases resistance and allows for change.

Release the past to allow in a new future. When you hold on to the past you continue to re-create it in your future.

Time for another pen and paper exercise.

Write down your story.

Don't skip this one, it is really important. It doesn't have to be long. It can be as brief or as detailed as you like, but I don't really want you to write a book – just a paragraph or two, a page at most. Include the best bits and the worst bits.

Then read it.

Cry or laugh.

Now write down the story of the rest of your life *just as you expect it to be* based on what you have just written about your past. Read that. If that is what you want then stop at this point. If that is not what you want for you, then write down the story of the rest of your life *just as you would like it to be*. This can be total fantasy if you wish. Make it as good as you possibly can.

Now, in your mind, move forward to the last day of your life on this earth. Look back at the time between that day and now sitting here reading these words. But look back as if the first story of that time was true. Then look back as if the fantasy story was true.

Then ask yourself the questions:

Which of these would I most like to have memories of?

Which of these do I deserve?

Acceptance is the state of recognising that how it is is how it is *right now*. It is not a state of resignation. Acceptance is the place from which great change takes place.

Your acceptance self hypnosis exercise:

Take yourself into trance either in your healing room or favourite place.

Imagine yourself standing on a stage. The audience is everyone who has had either a positive or a negative influence upon your life. Connecting each one of them to you is a golden chord. It connects the heart area of their body to the heart area of your body.

Imagine yourself reaching down and disconnecting one of the chords and handing it to the person it is connected to. Thank them for being in your life. Thank them for the lessons they have taught you and then move on to the next chord.

Do this until you are free. You may want to add in a healing of the area of skin where the chord was attached to you.

Come back to full waking awareness.

You will notice that I have asked you to include positive as well as negative influencers of your life. It is important for you to release judgement, as well as you are able, in this exercise. I would also like you to notice that this is not a technique to remove people from your life. Your loved ones will be there too, and you will disconnect from them also.

This exercise has one purpose and one purpose only – it frees you from the constraints of your past. It allows you to be spontaneous. It allows you to make choices based on what's going on right now, not based on something that happened 30 years ago. It also allows you to realise that the people in your life are just passengers you met on a journey. Some were fun, some less so. You don't live your life based around the thoughts and ideas of the people who were on the bus or the train yesterday.

Please also release the connections from loved ones during this exercise. It doesn't mean that you will love them less, or be loved less by them. What it does do is free you to love them more. Quite often in loving relationships there is fear of displeasing the other, or fear of losing the other. This fear constrains behaviour and prevents us from being ourselves. When you release the connection you will find that you are more able to be fully present with those who are important to you. Without the fear – happiness will be present with you. Consequently your relationships will deepen and grow richer.

As you release the final connection notice how much freer and lighter you feel. Notice that you are free now to move in any direction you wish. There are no constraints.

There is only one reason not to accept yourself. That reason is that you believe thoughts and ideas that others have put into your mind. No child comes into this world in a state of non-acceptance of self. Non-acceptance is something that is learned. It is learned from others who do not accept themselves either.

We discover very early on that we can do things that cause physical or emotional pain. We discover that we are not liked when we pour sticky stuff all over the carpet – even though we have so much pleasure doing it. We discover that painting on stuff called paper makes our parents smile and praise us – but painting on stuff called walls – causes our parents to shout and smack us. This is even though walls are obviously bigger and better. Eating pleases them – whether or not we are hungry. Not eating displeases them – whether or not we are hungry.

There is a huge list of things from your life that seemed like fun, or good ideas, to you but that displeased other people in your life. So we quickly learn to feel guilty about what we do and guilty about somehow hurting others. We very quickly grow a policeman in our head. This policeman turns into law everything that has displeased another in our young life. We have a controlling voice in our head that is constantly on guard reminding us when we are treading dangerous ground and forever denying us our freedom and the right to be ourselves.

We can never accept ourselves for who we are while this voice has control of our actions. We can never make truly inspired, or even spontaneous choices, while everything needs to be referred to this echo from the past that needs to make sure no one will be upset by our actions.

There is a much easier way. Just ask yourself what is appropriate right now. Not what was appropriate 20 years ago.

The world is full of critics.

But that is the way we are trained. Now the internet, with sites that invite customer reviews, gives every critic a voice – even when that voice has no qualifications to offer criticism.

Take this book for instance. There will be those who love it; those who like it; and those who dislike it. I hope you love it. Some will like that I have deviated considerably from (yet another) standard text on self hypnosis and included some of my own personal story. Some will find that that personal touch helps them connect more fully with the information. Some will dislike that I have not just written a script for every situation. Some will love that there is a process – each step of which brings them closer to mastery of their own mind. Some will dislike the Spirit section feeling it offers them nothing practical, yet others will see it as the most important and illuminating part of the book.

But all it means is that those who don't like it picked up a book that wasn't meant for them. Criticism says much more about the critic than the object of criticism. So when you feel in the mood to criticise, recognise that all you are doing is revealing the inner workings of your own mind and your own likes and dislikes about yourself. The world reflects itself back to you. When you see something out there that you dislike, there is some of that in you.

Here's a new way to be.

Allow everyone you encounter to be themselves freely. Allow the judge within you to fall silent and discover that the world does not collapse around you. As best you can, see that everyone is doing their best, given their knowledge and life experiences – just as you are. Look for the love within. Look for the desire to share and help. Everyone has kindness within them. Only those who have been given reason to be afraid of life have difficulty expressing it.

So be aware that this book has one purpose and one purpose only. That is to serve you by helping you to change your mindscape so that the world reflects back to you a more pleasant experience. It can only do that if you follow my guidance. Just reading the words will not change very much at all. You need to do the exercises regularly in order to experience the change that will occur.

That gives me a bit of a conflict though. You see I have been devouring self help books for a couple of decades now, and I enjoy reading them. The ones where I have to stop and pick up pen and paper and do exercises are the ones I hate. It is not always convenient to do the exercise, yet it is difficult to continue in the flow of reading without doing the exercise. Those are the books I frequently fail to finish reading. So why am I writing a book that falls into the category of what I like least?

I will tell you.

I am writing a book that falls into that particular category because the books that are easy and enjoyable to read never changed my life. They just kept me afloat when I thought I was drowning. The ones that made me stop and think and ponder and write things down, or take out half an hour to do a visualisation or meditation exercise are the ones that changed my life and actually pulled me out of the water and onto dry land.

So start to notice your judgements, reflect upon them, and look within yourself for whatever it is you are judging in another. It will be there in you – maybe much reduced in intensity – but it will be there.

As you disconnect from the past and begin to release judgement of others so you will move into a state of greater and greater acceptance of yourself.

Appreciate what you have, accept you for being the wonderful person you are and you will find that happiness begins to appear more and more in your life. You will become more spontaneous, feel more inspired, and become more loving not only to those you care about, but also to the strangers you meet.

Happiness is who you are. You do not need to seek it. Just be yourself and it will emerge.

Wealth

"The real opportunity for success lies within the person and not in the job."

Zig Ziglar

Think for a moment. What exactly does *wealth* mean to you? Is it money? Is it property or goods? Is it the cash in your pocket or the amount that arrives in your bank account each month? Is it what you have to spend or how much you have saved?

How much do you need? Is there a figure, a monthly income, an annual salary, that, if you had it, would mean you are wealthy? Where is the line between poverty and wealth for you?

What are you prepared to do to get what you want? Are you prepared to think about it? Are you willing to take some small action? Would you spend 12 hours a day in order to have it?

So before we continue think for a few moments about exactly what it is that you want and exactly what you are willing to do in order to have it.

You probably want more than you have. Most people do. I certainly do. But in order to use the power of your mind to assist you in manifesting the **more** – you need to understand the power of *wanting* to keep what you want out of your reach.

Did you follow that?

Wanting stops you from getting what you want.

Let me give you an example:

I want a new camera (I always want a new camera by the way, it is a permanent state of affairs with me, I just love cameras). That wanting is experienced a little like lust, a powerful desire, but the desire is born from not having and the feeling of *wanting* reinforces the not having and keeps it in place.

Hale Dwoskin, teacher of the Sedona Method (which I highly recommend) puts it like this: Would you rather want it, or would you rather have it?

There should be no problem with that. I am guessing you went for the have it. Wanting is a constant reminder of not having and since we are in the process of learning to use the power of our mind we need to understand the attractive power of strong emotions. When we really want something what we are intensely aware of is its absence. So our wanting is really a concentrating on the fact that we do not have it. Our mind, aware that we are spending a lot of time thinking about what we would like, is aware of the accompanying emotional undercurrents that are focused on the lack of what we want and the longing for it. This creates a negative undercurrent that accompanies each want.

The process of manifestation is one of sending out an intention wave, like a light wave or a sound wave, which the Universe matches in frequency, reinforces and returns to us. We send out a little wave and the Universe sends back a matching bigger wave that has enough energy to become a physical manifestation. But when we send out an intention wave and simultaneously send out a resistance wave, then the two waves effectively cancel each other out and the result is no change in circumstances because what we are sending is nothing.

So it seems as though the problem is how to want something without wanting it, and in a way it is exactly that and I will show you how to do just that with a mind trick. After all this is a book about how to use the power of your mind in order to improve your circumstances.

What we cannot do is lie to ourselves or pretend that something is true that we know is not true. This is the big problem with affirmations. Affirmations are lies that you tell to yourself again and again in the hope that eventually you will believe them. If you ever do eventually believe the lie then at that moment your affirmation will bear fruit.

But there is a much easier way that does not require you to fool yourself that anything is true that clearly is not true.

For me, when I was a young child, I always knew, when I went to bed on Christmas Eve, that the following morning there would be a stocking filled with goodies at the end of my bed and some brightly wrapped presents waiting for me under the tree in the living room. I never knew what I was getting but I knew I would like it and have a wonderful day with a very special dinner and lots of chocolates. I did not have to affirm anything, I just knew it would happen. It was a magical night followed by a magical day. I did not understand the mechanism, or the work that my parents put in to make it so special for myself and my sister. I did not worry about where the money would come from.

I just expected it. There was no wanting. Just enjoyment. The wanting came when I was much older and developed interests that allowed me to request particular gifts.

So think back to a time when you expected something to happen. Expectation is an inner knowing that something will manifest. What you need to do is to shift your wanting to an expectation. The expectation reinforces the desire and creates a more powerful signal that the Universe has no choice but to fulfil for you.

Christmas was easy. I'd be really happy with a new locomotive for my trainset. Life is much more complicated now. But one of the things that is really needed, before doing any hypnotic work on manifesting greater wealth, is clarity. You need to know what it is you expect.

It is pencil and paper time again.

Take your sheet of paper. Make three columns. Head them Health, Wealth, Happiness. Then under each heading write down whatever it is that you would like to attract into your life.

Make sure you get at least ten entries in each column. I have provided a template sheet for you to download from the book's website. I am going to work with the Wealth column, but you can repeat the process later with the other two.

Look down the column and allow yourself to become aware of whether or not the entry is a need, an ambition, or just something you would like. Make a note next to each entry to indicate which it is.

You do not have to use my definitions but I would class a *need* as something like a utility bill that requires payment; a job or other source of income; a roof over your head and clothes on your back; or enough food of sufficient quality to keep you fit and healthy. *Ambitions* are things like running a multi-million dollar corporation; getting a promotion; starting your own business; or completing a marathon. *Likes* are things like the latest smartphone; a new car; a holiday; or even a lottery win.

The definitions are a bit blurry, so do not be too concerned about which category things go in. For instance, some people might consider a loving intimate relationship a *need*, others might consider it a *like*, while there may be one or two who regard it as an *ambition*. The importance of this exercise is for you to think more deeply about the desires you find within you and to realise that there are differences between them.

Needs need your immediate attention, so attend to them. They will be at the back of your mind in your worry corner anyway, so you may as well focus your attention on them. That way, you will feel much more in control of your life and your destiny.

The question then is, how can you use self hypnosis to pay a utility bill or satisfy any other immediate and pressing need? Well I am afraid you cannot. But what you can do is to use self hypnosis to release any worries or concerns you have about the payment, and then, in that freer mental space you can explore solutions to the problem – immediate solutions and long-term solutions.

Needs

I will take you through this as two separate exercises, but there is no reason you should not combine them if you prefer.

Make yourself comfy in your self hypnosis chair. Count yourself down into trance and step into your Healing Room. Stand in front of the door to the Room of Rest. Beside the door is a chest with a key. Open the chest and place into it the specific worry that is causing you concern right now. If you want to use my utility bill example, then imagine placing the utility bill into the chest and locking it with the key. Now, allow your mind to drift and wander and decide where in the world you would be most at peace right now. This is your doorway to anywhere at all, so allow your imagination free rein – skiing, sunbathing, exploring jungle trails, watching wild animals on safari, relaxing on a luxury cruise liner. As soon as you step through this door you find yourself wherever you have decided to be. You can be alone, or with others; you can be on holiday, or enjoying an adventure; you can go anywhere you desire. When you open the door to the Room of Rest, you notice a curtain of light. As you step through the doorway, and through the light, you feel the light penetrating every single cell of your body and sweeping out of your body all of the molecules of concern and worry. As you step through the light curtain, and find yourself standing in your destination, you feel freer, lighter and easier than you have in a long, long time. Spend some time in this place and return whenever you wish.

When you step back through the doorway you will retain all that you have gained and when you open the chest to retrieve your bill, notice that the bill has been transformed into a pile of cash. Retrieve the cash and see yourself paying the bill, while giving thanks and feeling appreciation for whatever the money is paying for – maybe keeping you warm, maybe watching TV, maybe heating your food, maybe supplying water to your taps, maybe firing up your computer and facilitating your enjoyment of the internet... If your worry is something else then find a way to transform it from a problem to a solution and see the solution having replaced it when you open the chest.

Always be thankful and appreciative.

Bring yourself back to full waking awareness.

Now for solutions.

Take yourself into trance once more and into your Healing Room. This time you are going into your Room of Inspiration. Decorate this room anyway you wish, but I would strongly encourage you to line the walls with inspiring images. Perhaps a short quotation that reminds you of who you really are and what you are capable of. Have some portraits on the walls of figures from history who are famous for problem solving. If you like science you might want Einstein, Newton or Edison. If you favour art, da Vinci might be more suitable. If you see life as a battle then include some great campaigners – Wellington, Nelson (I am British), Alexander the Great, George Washington – whoever it is that, in your eyes, was able to overcome insurmountable odds and provide solutions. Maybe also include some of your favourite entrepreneurs – Richard Branson immediately springs to mind, but you probably know of others.

If you don't know many people who fall into the category of being successful, then get hold of some biographies of entrepreneurs, or other genuinely successful celebrities who have overcome challenges and found success doing what they want to do. Make this an on-going work so that, over time, your Room of Inspiration becomes filled with images and objects that immediately put you into the frame of mind that solutions exist for the challenges you face. You may not know what they are yet, but you know they exist.

If you wish, this room can hold a desk, filing cabinets, a computer, but the most important object in here is the Solution Chair. This is just a really comfy swivel chair. It can rock as well if you like that. Think about small objects, or models, you can decorate this place with. These will be, or represent, solutions to problems. Things like an aeroplane (overcoming gravity), a telephone (speaking with someone so far away they can't hear even if you shout), a book (how to let lots of people own and read the same story at the same time), a public library (how to let lots of people access tons of knowledge without them needing to be able to purchase the books), a train (how to move lots of people around a country quickly and easily), a car (freedom).

It doesn't matter what you choose, I have just made a few suggestions to get you started. But choose things that are meaningful either to you or in your life. Choose things that you use daily – like a car, or public transport – that provide you with a magical solution that is much more convenient than a horse for getting to work.

Spend a lot of time furnishing and decorating this imaginary place. You will probably need to do some research in order to do a thorough job, so see it as an ongoing exercise rather than something you have to complete in one go.

For the first time you use it, have just one portrait, and one model of a solution.

So sit in your Solution Chair and focus on the face in the portrait. Think about this person. Imagine, you can somehow connect with them telepathically. If they are dead, then imagine your thoughts are travelling back in time to when they were at their most brilliant, or imagine your thoughts are connecting with their spirit. Do whichever feels most comfortable to you. Reflect on their achievements. Reflect on how they found a solution for what many considered impossible. Tell them about your current challenge. Then allow your mind to quieten and listen for a response. A response may come in the form of a thought, an image, a sound, a feeling... it may not be in the form you feel it should be, but do not sit in judgement. Judgement blocks the flow. Allow to appear whatever appears, and if nothing appears to appear then allow that to be okay too. You may need to visit this place several times before the thoughts and images begin to flow more freely. You may also find that challenges that you have a high emotional investment in finding a solution to are also more resistant to providing solutions.

Now, move on to whatever model you have chosen and reflect upon all the problems that it provided a solution to and how it changed the world. Think of all who have benefitted from its invention and how lives have been changed. Allow your mind to reflect deeply on all aspects of this.

Let me give you an example that I have already touched on in my Art of Appreciation class.

A tin of baked beans.

Baked beans are one of the few tinned products I buy, but for me it solves a problem. If I make some toast, beans on top gives me a delicious simple lunch that I really enjoy. When I want a quick meal, or am just not in the mood for preparing the fresh vegetables I normally eat, baked beans are the perfect solution. They work with mash, chips, salad, fish, meat...

They are a handy size, easy to carry, not too heavy, easy to open and pour.

But someone needed to have already invented the tin to make it work. Someone had to work out a sauce and spice recipe to make them taste just as good as they do. There were probably months of trials and taste tests, and many failures before the product was fit for sale. Then I might reflect on how it got to the supermarket shelf. Who put it there? How my purchase helps to keep them employed. Who put the tin in the cardboard box and loaded it onto the lorry? Who drove the lorry? Who built the lorry? Who mined the steel and the tin used in the manufacture of the can for the beans? Who designed the label? You can go all the way back to the haricot bean farmers and the fertiliser manufactures. You can take it anywhere you like following the multitude of individual threads that are all pulled together in a tin of baked beans, but all the while look for the innovation and the solutions to problems. The latest of which is that ring pull thingy that means you no longer have to struggle with a tin opener and risk slicing your hand open with those lethally sharp edges any more.

Then reflect upon your problem as if it were a tin of baked beans. Look for solutions, follow threads in just the same way. Imagine you have a team of whatever experts you need and ask them to provide you with solutions. Then quieten your mind and allow any thoughts, ideas, images, sounds and feelings to emerge. Know also that if solutions do not emerge now, then they may well pop into your mind later when you are focused on something else.

This exercise is designed to move you from a state of disempowerment to one of solution seeker. Just this shift in your thinking will make you feel better and when you feel better your natural inspiration is much more likely to come up with ideas.

When you are finished leave the room and bring yourself back up into normal waking awareness.

Each time you visit, add another portrait and model, or object, until you have sufficient to work with. Then each time you visit you can choose who you want to work with on that occasion.

When you are fully back then take a pencil and paper and write down any thoughts or ideas that came to you. It is most important that you do not edit or judge these in any way. Just record them. Quite often you need to open your mind to a crazy solution in order for the more realistic solution to become available to you.

Ambitions

Ambitions are really long-term goals that you are willing to invest time and energy in achieving. If you want to run a private practice in Harley Street, London, then going to medical school, becoming a doctor and then putting in several years of hard graft are going to be necessary preliminaries.

So think of your ambition as somewhere you want to be at some point in the future. The good news about an ambition is that there is no rush and so no emotional pressure. That doesn't mean to say that an ambition has to be years off in the future – just be realistic about the time scale involved.

Before you start with your self hypnosis session some preparation is necessary.

Pen and paper time again.

Arrange your sheet of paper in landscape format and draw a horizontal line from one side to the other. At the left hand end write NOW and at the right hand end write your ambition. Then think of all the steps that are essential for this to happen. Be aware that you don't have to be too specific here or fill in too many gaps. The idea is to get you motivated, not to scare you with the complexity or enormity of the task you have set yourself. The idea also is to allow for the Universe to step in and assist you – so there may be shortcuts. So only add essential steps. In the example above, qualifying as a doctor is an essential step that you cannot get around – unless you want to run a practice in a non-medical discipline.

Here's a light-hearted example for you to get the idea.

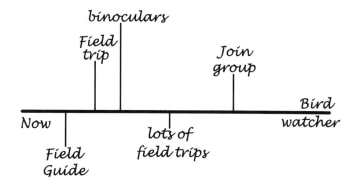

Imagine that your ambition is to be a birdwatcher. You have seen people who are birdwatchers and you like that they have a reason to get out into the countryside, or the local park. So between now and you being a birdwatcher there are things you have to do. The first thing is to get hold of some means of identifying the birds you see. This is a Field Guide here, but there are phone apps that do the same thing, or may want to get on the internet and just print out your own information sheets.

So after doing some research into how to identify what you see, you need to go and find some birds to identify. This is the first field trip. After that you will need some binoculars so that you can see identification details more clearly and watch birds from a greater distance. Binoculars are also one of the status symbols of the birdwatcher.

Then you need to go on a lot of field trips to get some experience and move yourself away from novice and into amateur territory. At this point you may wish to join a bird group where you can go on trips with like-minded people and shorten your learning curve by tapping into the expertise and knowledge of others. Finally you can award yourself your bird watching badge.

Now, what I'd like you to consider is that each of those items along the line is a mini-goal – a target in its own right for which you can create another timeline sheet. Here is the one for the binoculars mini-goal.

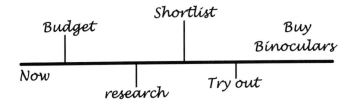

Now for the self hypnosis.

Take yourself into trance and see yourself as if you had already achieved your ambition. Make it as real as you can. Fill it with the sights, sounds, smells and sensations that you would expect. If you do not know quite how it might feel like because it is a long way from where you are, then imagine it as you would like it to be for you. Include in this picture all of the things that surround your achievement. The life style changes you would need, your car, clothes, home, family – whatever it is that surrounds this and makes it special for you. With my birdwatching example it may be that you imagine yourself somewhere like the Galapagos Islands with a high quality telescope and binoculars watching thousands of blue-footed boobies at their nesting site, hearing the noise, smelling the ammonia and being amazed watching them dive and fish. Enjoy the whole thing. Create a beautiful, enjoyable fantasy for yourself with all the trimmings.

Now while you are enjoying this fantasy just notice if any negative emotions come up – anything saying why you cannot have this, any doubts or concerns you have about your right to this dream. Notice that this doubt is just a thought, picture, or feeling and let it go. If you are watching boobies you might turn the negative sensation into a fish and feed it to one of the chicks. If you can use your fantasy to incorporate and destroy the negativity then do so. If not then tie it to a big bunch of helium-filled balloons and watch them carry it off into the distance. Or place this negativity or doubt into a rocket and fire it at the sun and imagine it being consumed and turned into life-giving heat and light.

These negative sensations will come up, and the same ones may even come up again and again. Your only task is to let them go. Turn them into an object or symbol, if you wish, and destroy it. Do this again and again until you feel lighter. Even in the same session keep doing it until you feel the release. If it takes a long time to let go of the negativity then finish the exercise there and recommence where you left off on the next occasion. Though I would strongly encourage you to persist until you feel at least a little lighter.

Once your ambition is clear and free of negative influence then you can come back to the next step on your timeline. In the birdwatching example this would be the *Join Group* step. Repeat the process of imagining having already achieved this and release any negativity that comes up.

Work your way down the line in this way to the present moment.

Then go back up the list, from Now towards the final goal, but this time use your mini-goal timelines. For my example I have used the purchase of a pair of binoculars. At one level binoculars are two identical tubes with a lens at each end. At another level they are incredibly complex and delicate pieces of optical equipment that can make the difference between an enjoyable hobby and a disappointing one. You can pay less than £10, or more than £2,500 and everything in between. Make the wrong choice here and you will suffer. But you need to know how much you have to spend, then you have to do whatever level of research is necessary for you, then make a shortlist, try them out and finally make the purchase.

Repeat the main process with this mini-goal. Start at the end, work backwards and then forwards if any of these items – like budget – are also mini-goals. If you don't have the money then explore ways of getting it using this process.

Initially this is not a quick process, but as you repeat the exercise you will move more quickly and you will find it easier and easier to release any negativity associated with your ambition. As long as it is important to you, as long as you desire it, then it is worth going through this process.

What happens with this is that as you repeat and repeat and repeat you cause a restructuring of your subconscious that switches its understanding of this from a dream to a reality – an inevitability. Once your subconscious regards this outcome as inevitable then it will happen. It will happen because your subconscious will be much more aware of opportunities and will draw your attention to them. The Universe will know that you are serious about what you want (because you keep thinking about it with passion and pleasure in your heart) and so will move mountains to assist you in achieving your desires.

You do not have to identify all of the steps. You may even jump across some of them as long as you hold the picture of the result in your mind. This picture though, must be as if it is now and not at some point in the future.

To recap.

1. Draw the timeline of the major steps to your goal.
2. Draw timelines of each step that needs more details.
3. Go into trance.
4. Place yourself at the far end of the timeline.
5. Make it real.
6. Release negativity about success
7. Come back one step towards the present.
8. Go to 5 unless you have reached NOW.
9. When you reach NOW go forward in time one step.

10. Use mini-goal timelines and repeat this whole process with the mini goal timeline.

11. Move up to the next mini goal.

12. When you reach your ambition rest and look back at all that you achieved on your journey towards this success.

13. Give yourself a pat on the back.

14. Come back to waking consciousness

15. Take one action that will move you towards your ambition before 24 hours has passed.

Likes

Likes are those things that would be nice to have. Those fleeting thoughts that drift into the mind from time to time. These are the thoughts and ideas that float into the mind either out of the blue or triggered by something we see or hear. I find that quite often these will manifest quite quickly and what seems to be important is a complete lack of attachment to any outcome. It is just an "Oh! That would be nice", followed by a quick daydream, followed by letting it go and not forming any emotional bond with it.

So I want you to consider that the things that fall into this category are just fun things. These are things that will not cause any lasting change in your circumstances but will give you anything from a few minutes to a few hours to a few weeks of pleasure and enjoyment.

Pencil and paper.

Make a list of at least 10 fun things you would like to experience, 10 fun things you would like to own, and 10 incredible places you would like to visit.

Regard this as your daydream list.

Now if you don't know anything about what you want then look it up on your computer and do a little research. You need to have enough information to create a realistic daydream.

Select what you consider to be the most outrageous item and the most insignificant.

Take yourself into trance.

Play with the most outrageous item. Have fun with it. Use your imagination to have it. Then, when you have had fun with that, move forward a little in time so that this outrageous thing is now a memory in your recent past. Then imagine telling all your friends about how wonderful an experience it was. Tell them the stories, tell them about the fun you had, and how empty life felt when it was over. Then let it go.

Now repeat this exercise with the other item you selected.

Then bring yourself back to waking consciousness and forget about it.

You can do this exercise daily or weekly until you have worked with all of the items on your list, but make a point of doing it regularly. When you have completed your list make a new one.

Working with Resistance

From time to time you will encounter resistance. I have already incorporated one resistance removing method into the self hypnosis session on ambitions. There is absolutely no reason why you should not use this technique whenever you encounter that voice of negativity that is always so keen on showing us why we cannot succeed.

Consider this idea:

If you do not already have it,

and you want it,

then there is resistance to having it.

This turns the whole wealth acquisition problem on its head.

What this would mean is that when you find yourself with a Need, Ambition, or Like, all you have to do in order to manifest it is to locate and release any resistance to having it.

Pen and paper time.

Head the paper with whatever it is that you wish to manifest.

Two columns one headed *What I like* about this, and one headed *What I dislike* about this.

Then make at least ten entries under each column. Also do one like and then one dislike, one like, one dislike.

Birdwatcher

Like

- Give me something to do
- Learn a new skill
- I enjoy the countryside

- I like solitary activities
- Give me a reason to get some exercise
- I'll be able to shop for some new boots and outdoor clothing
- There are probably people on-line I can chat to about this
- It will be good knowing the names of things I see
- It will add a new dimension to being outdoors
- I do enjoy wildlife

Dislike

- Probably have to go out when the weather is bad.
- Have to meet people who know lots more than I do
- I don't know anything about binoculars
- I don't like being a beginner
- When people see me with binoculars they might think I am spying on them.
- I might drop my binoculars
- There are so many birds, I'll never learn them all
- It will cost too much
- I'll spend all that money and then find out I don't like it
- I always give up because I am no good at new things

The list of dislikes is your resistance. Give each of them a priority number from 1 to 10. 1 will be an item that will have the least power to stop you, and 10 will be the item that will have the most power to stop you or prevent your success.

Focus on the lowest item on the list.

Take yourself into trance. While focusing on that item, notice any negative feelings or thoughts that come up and then let them go in the way I showed you earlier. Or just surround that situation with light and see it dissolve. Notice also any physical tension in your body and release that too by allowing that area of your body to consciously relax. Now think about the rewards or benefits you may receive by engaging in this activity (one of the items from the like list, perhaps). Allow your imagination to roam freely, and fully feel the pleasure and enjoyment that is yours.

Return to normal waking awareness.

Each day tackle the next item on the list. Once you have processed all ten items then create another list of likes and dislikes. You will find that more come up, or the same ones come up again. Do not be concerned if you have to process the same item several times. You will know when to stop because you will either have what you want or be thoroughly enjoying getting there.

The Child in You

Another way to process resistance is to take yourself into trance and imagine yourself in a pleasant outdoor location. Allow your subconscious to present to you that part of you that resists having what you want. This part may appear in human form, usually as a much younger version of you, or it may be an animal, or spirit. Explain what it is you want and ask this aspect of you what is the reason that it is holding you back. Listen for an answer. Usually this aspect of self is protecting you from some real or imagined problem.

For instance, if you feel uncomfortable in social situations, but are seeking to do something that requires socialising, then this aspect of you may resist that because it knows that deep down you feel uncomfortable. All it knows is your discomfort. It is unaware that you wish to change this and learn how to be more comfortable by exposing yourself gently to more social situations. Explain what you are trying to achieve and how it will ultimately bring you happiness. Then surround this aspect of you with light, allow the light to penetrate it thoroughly, take it by the hand and show it your goal, show it how much better your life is now that you have this thing and then allow this part of you to be absorbed into your body.

Bring yourself back to normal waking consciousness.

Again this may need to be repeated. You will feel an internal shift once the resistance is lifted.

Symbolic Resistance Shifting

For this you take yourself into trance and imagine your resistance to success as a physical barrier blocking your way. This could be a wall made of bricks or stone; an electric fence, a fence that is impossibly high to climb; or a shark filled moat. The barrier, or obstacle, can be anything your imagination can create. Go with whatever crazy image appears for you.

Then come up with a creative solution to breach the barrier. You could build a bridge across the shark-filled moat or use an armour plated submarine. A fence could be cut through, blown up, or driven over in a tank. The wall could be smashed with a crane and wrecking ball. It doesn't matter how you do it. Just come up with some way that you can destroy or get past the barrier. Have fun with this and do not take it too seriously.

After you have demolished your barrier then continue on your path until you reach your reward. See yourself enjoying all the good things that you expect to have once you reach your goal. Appreciate your achievement as if it were already in your life and then just let it go and bring yourself back into full waking consciousness.

Then take one small step, do one small thing that is a movement in the direction of what you want. Even just tidying up is an action that demonstrates a decision to take control and start to direct your own destiny. You need to act on your intentions. You need to demonstrate to the Universe that you are ready and willing to receive all that you want.

For your convenience I have created template sheets for the processes in this chapter. You can download them for free here

www.self-hypnosis-mastery.com/html/self-hypnosis-download.htm

A Little More On Relationships

"Loneliness doesn't come from having no one
around you, but from being unable to communicate the things that are important to you."

Carl Jung

A good relationship is one that nurtures your growth and development. A good relationship allows you to reach your fullest potential and realise your dreams.

This is the territory of Spirit.

Most people want to be in a good relationship. Many want to be in a different relationship from the one they are in. There are also a lot of people who are alone and want someone to share their life and their dreams with.

Not many people achieve this. Very few of the patients who come to see me are in a healthy relationship. Some know the truth but, for one reason or another – usually financial – they make the best of it. Mind you, that makes sense because people in healthy relationships already have emotional support, encouragement, and someone who believes in them – so they don't often need to seek help for emotional issues outside of their relationship.

I highly encourage you to read some of John Gray's work like Men Are From Mars, Women Are From Venus, or Why Men Don't Listen and Women Can't Read Maps by Allan and Barbara Pease. These books introduce you to the idea that men and women have different thinking styles because men and women evolved for quite different societal roles. Understanding how your partner thinks allows you to understand why their behaviour sometimes seems annoying and hurtful when it is nothing of the sort. I also encourage reading of Miguel Rees' The Four Agreements for this will introduce you to some new ideas about interpersonal communication.

Communication is really what relationships are about.

If there is no communication then there is no relationship.

If you cannot share your deepest thoughts and feelings with your partner without ridicule or put down then there is no relationship. However, that doesn't mean that any time is the right time for sharing. Clearly if your partner is showing signs of being pre-occupied, anxious, or worried then your words are unlikely to be even heard, never mind taken seriously.

In order to begin the process of change I want you to imagine that you have exactly the relationship (even if that is no relationship) that you desire. In other words you and you alone are the creator of your relationship experience. This is a necessary first step if you wish to bring about change. If you see your partner as being the reason for your unhappiness, or the reason that there are problems in your relationship, then nothing that you can do with self hypnosis will create any change for you, for you are denying responsibility for your life and your circumstances.

We have to play the game that we create our own reality in order to bring about any change, for it is only by accepting responsibility that we can change anything.

Pen and paper time

Divide the paper into two columns. Head one of them **Want** and the other **Give**. Then write the numbers 1 to 10 underneath each heading. Now make a list of all the items that would be present in your perfect relationship. List what you want in, and from, a partner. Then do the same thing in the other column only this time write down what qualities you bring to a relationship. You can have more than ten items in each list, but make sure you have at least ten.

Select one item from each column to work with. If you are in a relationship work with your current partner in your imagination.

If you are not in a relationship then create a fantasy partner to work with.

Take yourself into trance.

Create an imaginary situation where you live out the first item from your *Want* column. Make this as real as you can. Incorporate information from all of your senses. While you do this be very tuned in to your emotional state and notice if you feel any resistance or emotional discomfort. This may come as negative thoughts, or a slight emotional disturbance. If that happens then focus on the discomfort and, as best you can, let it go using one of the techniques you have already learned. Repeat this until you can experience your *Want* with only pleasurable thoughts and feelings. If negative thoughts or feelings resist your attempts to release them then imagine them transformed into an individual and ask this individual what they want and what they are trying to do for you. Continue this conversation until you understand why you have this resistance. Once you understand you can choose to let it go if you wish. If there is some gain for you in resisting what you want then explore alternative ways of receiving that gain.

Once you are at peace with this *Want* then move on to your *Give*.

Repeat the process with the first item from your *Give* list. Imagine yourself living it out in an interaction with your partner, but be sensitive to negative thoughts, feelings and pictures that arrive as you imagine this scene. Work through the negativity in the same way as you did earlier.

Do not expect that because these are things that you have to give that there will be no resistance to giving. There will.

Once you have finished processing the emotional content around both items then bring yourself back to full waking awareness. Arrange a time with yourself to process the next two items on your list. Continue with this (I would suggest daily) until you have completed your list. Then make another list. If some of the same things come up, that is ok. Work through this list in the same way.

If you are in a relationship then after each session of processing do something for your partner that lets them know that you value and appreciate something specific about them.

If you are not in a relationship then just say something nice to someone you know.

The problem, you see, is not your partner it is you. Your partner simply responds or reacts to how you are with them. They are especially sensitive to how you perceive them within your own private thoughts. Once you have made peace with who you are you will find either that your relationship improves until it is exactly what you desire, or that your partner will leave and create space for your perfect partner to move into your life.

That doesn't seem to be very much about one of the most important aspects of our existence. It certainly doesn't seem to be very much at all when a relationship gets so bad that it needs fixing. But if you do these things, and also the exercises in the earlier chapter on relationships then, as long as you are genuine and you persist – miracles will happen. Things will change.

The problem is that we always see the fault as lying with our partner and not with our own thoughts, feelings and past experiences. All that you can change is you. The world out there, and that includes your intimate relationships, just reacts to you. As you move to a greater sense of peace and harmony within; as you move towards a greater sense of acceptance and allowing of others to be just the way they are without censure; so you will find that your world, and your relationships, will reconfigure themselves around you to exactly the extent that you change your thoughts, feelings, attitudes and beliefs. You can change other people – but you can only do it by changing you.

Forgiveness

"When you judge another, you do not define them,
you define yourself"

Wayne Dyer

Although this is not the last chapter in the book, it is the last one that I am writing. I thought I had finished and was in the process of proof-reading the last chapter on Freedom when I realised that I had left something out, something really important. What I had left out was Forgiveness. Forgiveness is essential if you are to experience freedom, but it is so important I decided to give it a chapter of its own rather than shoehorn it into the Freedom chapter. I feel it needs separating out from freedom purely because if you hold any hatred in your heart you are forever chained to the object of your hatred and can never experience freedom. So it needs to come first.

Of course if nothing has ever happened to you and you hold no hate, dislike, or even buried anger, within your heart then feel free to skip ahead to the next chapter.

Many, many people seek help from me because events in their past caused a pain that makes it difficult to function in their world. Others just didn't get the love, support, and encouragement that they needed in order to create a safe world for them to play in. Either way, the past, or individuals from the past, may be problematic in your moving forward and enjoying freedom in life.

I noticed one of those little things that stroll around facebook the other day. It said "say something about your ex" I read the ten comments that this had so far attracted. One of them was neutral. The other nine were negative.

Any negative emotion that you experience is felt only by you.

I was talking to a prospective patient the other day. She was telling me about the breakup of her marriage and how long dreamt of plans for rapidly approaching retirement were now in the gutter. She had lost everything and was starting life from scratch all because her husband could not keep his hands off a twenty-something year old. The anger was consuming her and disrupting her life and her sleep.

While she was explaining her problem to me I noticed that the focus, of her story was the *badness* of her husband. I said that unless she was prepared to forgive him, something which I would guide her through, I would be unable to help.

It seemed that was an unacceptable solution.

You see, while you hold on to the hatred, or the anger, or however you describe your negative feelings, no healing is possible. No healing is possible because this negative emotion is damaging you and will continue to damage you and pollute your mind as long as you hold on to it.

In the initial discovery that someone has betrayed you (and I know from personal experience that feelings of betrayal are extremely difficult to shift), it is quite reasonable to experience powerful negative emotions. This is part of a quite natural grieving process. This process takes time and you need to allow it to simply run its course – unpleasant though that course is. But when that is over, many people do not want to let it go. With bereavement it is like letting go of a loved one as though they never existed. With a relationship it can be as though you are letting them off the hook for what they did to you.

People behave the way people behave. Their behaviour is not always our behaviour. Quite often the problem is that someone behaves in a way that we would not countenance. If you believe that fidelity in marriage is an automatic responsibility and would never even consider entertaining thoughts of being with someone other than your spouse then you will have a tough time if your spouse is unfaithful.

In fact, I once had a patient who needed some help dealing with a partner's unfaithfulness even though they themselves had been unfaithful in the recent past. So we can, within our own minds, have rules for the behaviour of others even though those rules don't apply to us.

If we can stay with relationships for a little while longer I will give you an idea of the scale of the problem with infidelity. These figures relate to the US but I have no reason to suspect they are significantly different in other western societies.

60% of people will be unfaithful at some time during their marriage. This may cause a break up or it may be that it happens because a relationship is failing and the partner has already started *shopping around* for a replacement. Around half of marriages end in divorce. 3% of children are raised by a man who thinks they are their own offspring, when they have actually been fathered by someone else. In the town where I did most of my growing up, Liverpool, this number is 1 in 6 children.

No matter how much in love you think you are, no matter how much you believe you have met your soul mate, the chances are only around even that your first spouse will be your only spouse.

Relationships end. People grow apart. Smile. Thank them for the time you spent together. Move on.

To fill your heart with hatred and anger, or to fill your soul with longing for what was, is the road to Hell. Take some time to heal and when you are ready then forgive.

Forgiveness is not saying that what happened was ok.

Forgiveness is not inviting in more of the same treatment.

Forgiveness is letting go of the emotional baggage that is causing you to suffer.

Forgiveness is recognition that the only one hurting is you and you deserve better.

What happened happened. There is no way around that one. All you can do is to make peace with it. You do this by letting go of the emotions that tie you to the past.

One of the crazy ideas that most of us carry around in our heads is that people can somehow do something different from what they actually did.

"You shouldn't have done that"

As though that somehow helps.

A time machine that could take you into the past to whisper into your own ear that what you are about to do is a really bad idea might help. But then who would believe themselves whispering in their ear that what they really want to do is not sensible? Would you?

"I would never do that"

As though that somehow changes what was.

"You should have had more sense"

As though that statement immediately impregnates the sense that was apparently lacking in the past.

Smokers smoke even though it is most likely going to kill them. Immediate pleasure invariably wins out over future pain.

I need to stress that I am not saying that what happened to you was ok. I am not saying that dangerous people who harm, rob, or cheat others should be immune from the consequences of their actions. What I am saying is that you cannot change the past. You cannot unhappen whatever happened.

What you need to decide is whether or not you have suffered enough – even if you are the guilty party and your pain is the result of regret. If you have suffered enough then you are ready to forgive. If you haven't then you will need to choose to continue to suffer and then return when you decide you have suffered enough. Are you guilty of something? If so is your pain the pain of regret for having done something you wish were otherwise? Or is the pain because of the suffering you inadvertently caused others? Quite often we do things we later regret because we get caught up in the moment and are unable to foresee the consequences of our actions.

We don't do bad things because we are bad people we do bad things because we are not gods and cannot see the impact of all the ripples in time that spread out wider and wider as a result of every action we take and every thought we think.

If you have not suffered enough then you need to decide on an appropriate sentence for yourself, so that you know when you have served your time. I have had forty and fifty year olds come to see me still plagued by something they did that upset their parents when they were fifteen or sixteen. I tell them that they have given themselves a life sentence with no chance of parole. Murderers get off with less. I ask them if their crime was as bad as murder. This usually results in a sheepish smile and they are off the hook when they realise they have been punishing themselves for decades for a minor transgression.

People make mistakes.

Sometimes those mistakes cause anguish to be felt by others or by themselves.

It is time to let it all go and move on towards freedom.

Pencil and Paper time.

Sit down somewhere quiet where you will not be disturbed for at least an hour. It is really important that you finish this task in one session so make sure you have privacy for it.

If you are working with something you did that you feel bad about then write a letter addressed to everyone you feel you have harmed.

I need to stress that this letter will never be seen by any eyes other than your own so you can say whatever you wish quite safely.

Then write about the experience. Think about why you behaved the way you did and what drove you to do it. Write about all of the things that were going on for you at that time. What else was happening that may have affected your judgement.

In other words make a clean breast of everything – but, under no circumstances, apologise for what you did.

Just explore in writing what led you to do what you did.

As you write get into the emotions, good or bad, that you were feeling at the time.

Bear in mind that what you knew then is not what you know now.

When you have finished emptying out everything inside of you relating to that event then write "I forgive myself for this".

Sign and date it.

If this is about something that someone else did then your letter is addressed to them.

I want you to write down how what they did adversely affected your life. Write about your suffering, lost opportunities, how your life hasn't worked. They will never see this letter. So forget about what other eyes might think should they see it. Use whatever language seems appropriate.

Get everything down on paper. All the little angry thoughts that pop up from time to time. The revenge you fantasise about. Everything that relates to this incident, so that nothing is left inside you.

When you have finished end it with "I do not approve of what you did. I forgive you. I release myself from this now and forever."

Sign and date it.

If you wish to read through it you may, but it is not necessary. If you felt no emotion while writing it then you have not written what is in your heart. You must keep writing until you feel the emotion rising up within you. I only stop writing after the tears have flowed even though, on occasion, my letter has taken eight pages to reach that point.

If you have somewhere safe to do this outside then burn the letter and as the smoke rises say to yourself "God/Universe it is yours now. I have done with it."

If there is nowhere safe to burn it then tear it up into tiny pieces and flush it down the toilet. As it goes say to yourself. Goodbye forever.

Take yourself into trance.

Go to your favourite place and relax as fully and deeply as you can.

Go to your Healing Room.

Create a new Safe Place accessed by a new door off your Healing Room..

This is somewhere that you will feel comfortable, relaxed, safe – and most importantly – in control.

This could be a warm room, maybe with an open fire, comfy armchairs and so on.

It could be a sacred space on a hillside or mountain top.

The centre of your favourite stone circle, a beach, in the countryside...

It needs to be somewhere that you feel at home and in control – but not your home or any of the places you may have already used in your self-hypnosis. This Safe Place is your Forgiveness Space.

Once you have created this space in your imagination be there as fully as you are able.

Be comfortable and *own* this space knowing that you are master here.

Invite into this space a wise supporter. I would strongly advise using someone like a Spirit Guide or Guardian Angel, but if you have no beliefs that would support this then simply choose someone whose wisdom you admire, whether they are living or dead, and invite them to be present with you.

Now invite the person you are working with from your past. It is most important that you understand that a person's behaviour is not who they are. People behave in inappropriate ways because of the circumstances they find themselves in and the life experiences they have had. So while this person is in your presence be aware that what they did and who they are are quite different.

Now, if you have anything left to say to this one then say it.

Give them an opportunity to respond.

Ask your wise friend for their input.

You can continue this for as long as it feels beneficial to you but beware of just spending the time proving yourself right and them wrong. Rather use this space to share the impact it had on your life and how it made you feel.

This is your opportunity to empty out all of the negativity within you, not to reinforce it. So focus on you and how you feel/felt.

Once you have finished then say to them "I forgive you for what you did. That does not mean that what you did was ok. That does not mean that I now approve of what you did. What it means is that I honour myself and love myself sufficiently now to be free of you forever. You no longer have any power over me. I am free. Goodbye."

Then allow the image of them to dissolve.

Ask your wise friend if they have anything more they would like to share with you.

Thank them and allow them to disappear.

Now, if, and only if, you wish.

Take your mind back to the incident and play it through just the way you would have liked it to have happened. In other words, in your imagination, I want you to fix whatever went wrong.

Allow good feelings to fill you.

Rest in the knowledge that you are perfect and now free of the chains of the past.

Bring peace back into your body and mind. If necessary leave your forgiveness space and drift off to your Favourite Place.

When you are ready return to full waking awareness.

> "We do not heal the past by dwelling there; we
> heal the past by living fully in the present."
>
> Marianne Williamson

So now we are ready to experience Freedom and all that means
to us.

Freedom

*"Everything in your life is
a reflection of a choice you have made.
If you want a different result, make a different choice."*

A sense of freedom is key to experiencing happiness. I've already mentioned that happiness is to be found inside and is not a consequence of the accumulation of material goods or even the money to buy them.

But, just in case you are still hanging on to the idea that "If only I had enough money then..." be mindful of the findings of an MIT study that found that 1,900 Florida Lottery winners were bankrupt in less than 5 years after their win. These individuals received anything from $50,000 to $150,000. Now you might think that those are hardly life-changing sums of money, but the interesting thing is that the bigger winners just took longer to go broke and exactly the same thing also happens with multi-million dollar winners. Another study, by the American Psychological Association, which looked at the lives of 22 major lottery winners, found that they were no happier than people who were just getting on with their lives. In fact the lottery winners were actually less happy than the control group.

Why were they less happy? They were less happy because they discovered that money didn't make any difference to their level of happiness and that made them unhappy.

You can be wealthy and miserable because when you get used to the lifestyle that wealth brings then that becomes just another normal and the money then becomes irrelevant – only your bills will be correspondingly bigger.

Happiness comes from within and to seek it anywhere other than within is insane.

Yes, I know it's nice to have money and it's nice to have enough money to pay the bills and treat yourself to a few luxuries and if that happens by way of a windfall then I have no doubt that life will improve. If you are careful then life may well improve forever. I'm not saying you need to have no money in order to be happy.

What I am saying is that money is irrelevant to happiness.

The pleasure that comes from being able to spend freely is a transient experience. Pleasure is always transient and should never be confused with happiness. Pleasure is good and a life that contains many pleasurable experiences will be much more fun than one that does not, but pleasure is always fleeting. If you've ever bought a brand new car you will know that within three or four weeks driving it is very little different from driving the car you traded it in for. It is just a comfortable vehicle that gets you where you want to go. It doesn't make the traffic jams go away. It still needs filling up (or plugging in). It still needs washing and maintaining with new tyres now and then.

What sufficient money does is to enable a sense of freedom. A reliable car does create a sense of freedom. You see, freedom is about your ability to be, do, and have whatever you want. It is also about your ability to go where you want when you want. If you live in San Francisco and want to go to New York then money can mean the difference between walking and flying. It can mean the difference between first class travel or less comfortable travel. It can mean the difference between the bus and the train or even the adventure of driving yourself. So money doesn't stop you if you are really determined, but it can make the journey more comfortable.

The reason I mention money here is that there is a lot of spiritual tosh around money. Money is great and it's nice to have. It makes life easier – but the minute you think money and happiness are the same thing, or that poverty and spirituality are the same thing then you are off-track.

Freedom, though, just like happiness, is an internal thing. It is a feeling-sense that you have or don't have. If you have a boring humdrum job; it is a real struggle to get out of bed each work day; and all you have to look forward to are coffee breaks and home time, then you probably feel trapped. If you do feel like this, your only taste of freedom may come if you can manage to get away for an annual holiday. The strangest thing, of course, is that your annual holiday seems like an illusion the minute you return to work because it feels as if you have never been away.

Yet others love their jobs and awaken excited and looking forward to whatever the day may bring. They also enjoy their annual holiday and enjoy it all the more because when they return to work they will have so much more energy.

I know this to be true because I've had both of those experiences.

So being employed is no bar to feeling a sense of freedom in your life.

While you blame your circumstances for the way you feel then nothing can change.

Once you start to look within for ways to feel better – freer, then things really do start to change.

Freedom is the deep inner knowing that you can do whatever you want – should you choose to do so. That does not mean you have to. It does not mean that you should drop everything and follow every whim. What it does mean is never feeling trapped. You can never feel trapped if you know that should your job consistently fail to excite or inspire you that you can move on without regret. You can never feel trapped if you know that your intimate relationship with your current partner will only continue while they support, encourage and respect you. You, equally, have to grant them the right to be who they are. That doesn't mean you have to show them the door the minute they get angry about something you have done. It does mean that on balance you get those things much more often than not and that your relationship is generally experienced as a harmonious one.

Freedom is really about you trusting you. It is about you trusting your own intuition, your feelings and your sense of what is most appropriate and then being able to follow through on those things. You don't *have* to follow through but you have to know that you can if you choose to.

You may well prefer the illusion that employment gives you financial security and so are freest when employed and knowing that you have a regular income arriving in your bank account once a month. You may feel free when no one is pulling your strings and you make all your income generating decisions for yourself. Again the picture/illusion/story that you surround yourself with doesn't matter. After all it is not for me to say what is right for you and what is wrong for you. Those choices are yours to make. All that I wish to draw your attention to is that if your life and what you do with it rewards you, then great, do more of that. But if it doesn't, then make some small changes. Start with little things and then move on to bigger things.

I have mentioned specifically two areas of life – work and intimate partners. That is because most of your waking time is spent at work and most of the rest of your time is quite likely to be spent with your family. Get these sorted and life takes on a rosy glow. I have already covered relationships in earlier chapters so here I will deal with how to change your dissatisfying work into satisfying work using self hypnosis.

The trick is to find nuggets of good in the drudgery.

Pen and paper time.

Mentally go through the whole of a work day and write down all of your activities.

Then score each of them from 1 to 10 where 10 is I like this a lot and 1 is I hate this.

Pick the one with the highest score..

Take yourself into trance

Go to your Healing Room

Then remember doing something you really enjoy.

Allow the pleasurable feelings to grow and intensify.

Holding on to those pleasurable feelings imagine the higher score work situation that you selected.

Run through it in your mind while focusing on the pleasurable feelings you kept hold of.

Run through it twice more while holding on to those pleasurable feelings.

If the good feelings start to slip away then return to the memory of something enjoyable to refresh them.

Now, while still retaining those pleasurable sensations, run through the work situation again, but this time make whatever changes you need to make in order to make it even more enjoyable for you. So mentally adjust your work situation so that it is just as you would have it if you were designing your own job.

Repeat this twice and savour it each time.

Now return to your original pleasant memory and feel those feelings fully once more.

Bring yourself back to full waking awareness.

Do this each day selecting the next highest scoring item from your list each time. When you have processed all of the items on your list then create a new list. It is ok if this new list has the same, some of the same, or completely different items. Just pretend that you are creating this list for the first time and be genuine. Then repeat the whole exercise with your new list.

The purpose of this exercise is to encourage you to focus on the positive aspects of your work so that you enjoy them more. When you start to focus on the small changes you would like to incorporate in your job then you invite the Universe to step in and give you a hand.

What will happen after performing this exercise for several days is that you will find, without effort, that you will start to look forward to those small pleasures in your day and as you learn to savour and enjoy what may actually only be a few moments they will seem much bigger to you and the balance of pleasure vs drudgery will start to shift. As this balance starts to shift your inner resistance will also shift to a state of acceptance and appreciation of the job you have. Once this happens then you will find that either you are enjoying this job so much you want to stay, or that you will find another, better job without effort.

So while what you resist persists, what you focus on increases.

Also use the journey to and from your place of work to expand your mind. Listen to audio books, or inspiring recordings while on your journey. I highly recommend Michael Neill's Effortless Success as an entertaining and freeing way to lighten your journey to work. Bob Proctor is another speaker who many find quite inspirational. If you are interested in Law of Attraction you might enjoy Esther & Jerry Hicks Master Course CD Program, which is an audio CD set I frequently listen to while driving.

It is essential that you find small things to look forward to in your day, even if these are your breaks. But if your breaks are the only aspect of your day that you look forward to you must learn to look forward to the positive aspects of the breaks rather than simply that they are an escape from work you hate. So, in your self hypnosis, think about the tastes and textures of your beverages, your snacks, the conversations with colleagues and focus your pleasurable feelings on these. Far better, of course, if you find some aspect of your job to look forward to, but there will be some small thing in your day that you can use. As you continue with this practice what you will find is that you become aware of more things to appreciate and look forward to.

This exercise shifts your point of focus from all the negatives in your day to the positives. Once you start to seek out the positives you will find more and more.

I need to stress that what I am suggesting here is not designed to help you to tolerate the intolerable. But, if you accept for a moment that you create your own reality (even though you don't understand quite how that works) then you have to accept that you somehow attracted your current circumstances. That means that you are currently a magnet for circumstances that are not what you would freely choose. If you just look for a new job, without doing the inner work, then on the first day of your new job you will find that you have to take you with you. Within a very short space of time your new job will be as intolerable as your previous job – because you didn't change you first.

You have to do the inner work. You have to change you; change your outlook; change your expectations; and change what you perceive your value is, in order to create a real shift in your external world circumstances.

The self hypnosis exercise I have described above can be used with anything you want to change in your life. First look for the small things about it that you like. Use self hypnosis to enhance and increase your positive feelings around these things.

Remember acceptance is not saying it is ok forever. Acceptance is recognition of what *is* right now. You cannot fight what is. It is a waste of energy. But you can acknowledge a desire for change. You can focus your attention on those things you would like to change by imagining them the way you would like them to be.

Here is another self hypnosis exercise that you can use when things did not go the way you wanted them to. This can be used for any circumstance in your life where you are unhappy with the outcome.

Take yourself into trance.

Go to your Healing Room.

Bring to mind a pleasurable experience from the past.

Allow the good feelings to fill mind and body.

Allow those good feelings to intensify and deepen even more.

Now take yourself back to the beginning of the event you were unhappy with.

Run through the event again in your imagination, but this time allow it to play out in the best way possible for you.

Run through it again but this time allow only a small improvement to take place. Make the improvement sufficient that you are satisfied with the outcome, but it isn't necessarily great.

Now run through it again and make it the most ridiculously magnificent outcome you can imagine.

Go back to the pleasurable experience you began the session with and once more feel all the good feelings you had back then.

Now move forward in time, a month, a year, ten years, and see how your life is playing out differently because the event you are working on turned out just the way you wanted it to.

Go back to the pleasurable experience you began the session with.

Bring yourself back into full waking awareness.

Should the memory of the original event intrude into your thoughts at any time during your day then just remember one of your imagined outcomes. If the outlandish one makes you smile then I strongly suggest that you use that one. Persist with this and it will bear fruit.

Sometimes when things don't work out they can have a powerful negative effect. You may find that the memory keeps on playing over and over again and just turns into a worry that, like a tape loop, keeps going on and on in your head.

The technique I have just described is an excellent way to stop the loop from playing, especially if you can imagine a ridiculously outlandish outcome that makes you smile whenever you bring it to the forefront of your mind.

It is so good you can even use it to change the future.

If you have an event coming up that you are not expecting to go well. Maybe an interview, a *chat* with your kids or your partner, a performance... then use this technique to work on this future event. See a good outcome, an ok outcome, and an outcome that's so ridiculously improbable that it makes you laugh. Then as you go about your day, when the worrying thoughts pop up just replay the outcome that made you smile. Persist with this and what you will discover is that when this future event eventually becomes a *now* event it will proceed so much better than you expected when you first began to worry about it.

You will have demonstrated to yourself a method for creating your own reality. Not precisely but you will have made a positive shift in *what was to be*. This will empower you and you will begin to see how all the negative stuff that you experience in your life is drawn to you **by you**.

Your Mind is powerful. Use it to your benefit.

What's Next

"The way to get started is to quit talking and begin doing."

Walt Disney

I hope you have enjoyed reading this and if you have already completed any of the exercises then I hope you found them of value. Self hypnosis, like any other skill, gets better the more you do it. So don't worry if it wasn't amazing the first time, or the second time, or the third time... Self hypnosis is experienced differently by everyone. What is important is that you engage with this on a daily basis at least until you begin to notice that your life is changing.

From that point onwards you will feel as if you have a tool to help you with any problems that you encounter. This is a truly powerful position to be in because from that moment onwards you have control of your life. You can make the choices you want to make rather than simply accept that which is imposed upon you. You will experience true freedom as you feel the power of your mind coursing through your body and your life.

I have come to the subject of appreciation frequently in this book. I make no apologies for repeating myself. In my own experience, moving to a state of appreciation is the key to well-being. Without this nothing else you do will have any lasting impact. You may consider appreciation to be the glue that holds well-being together. If you take nothing else from this book, take away my thoughts and ideas about the Art of Appreciation and put them into practise in your life every single day.

What you need to do now is go back to the chapter Self Hypnosis. Read through the steps and then have a go. If you have already done this then do it again. If you can't remember all of the steps then it's perfectly ok to open your eyes and read the next step. Do it until you get the hang of it. It is straightforward and simple to learn but keep doing it until you can follow the steps without having to read the instructions. If you have any problems with that, remember my special offer for the Self Hypnosis training

CD that will give you a short cut to start enjoying the benefits of self hypnosis.

Then think back through all of the exercises and if any one of them jumped out at you and you wanted to do it, then do that exercise. You make faster progress doing fun stuff than when working on serious issues so save them for later. If nothing grabbed you then select the chapter that represents the least troubling problem you have and go through the exercises in that chapter. This is just so you can develop comfort and familiarity with the process of taking yourself into trance and doing the necessary work while you are there.

Now go back to the chapter Confidence and work your way through all of the chapters in sequence and practise the exercises that relate to your specific problems or challenges.

I have been working with myself for so long now that all I have to do is close my eyes, with the intention of doing some inner work, and I immediately shift into that altered state we call trance. I deal with my challenges in my mind before I face them in the real world. Since I have been doing this regularly my life has become more peaceful. Good things happen frequently too and I work at what I love to do. But the best bit is that every now and again I experience a little magic that makes me take a step back and go ooooh! That was nice. This reminds me that the world truly is a magical place and although life can be a struggle from time to time, there are always things we can do to reach out and connect with that magic.

Self hypnosis is the most enjoyable way I know to make that magical connection and live life from the heart rather than the head.

~~~~

Also, don't forget to visit the book's web page and leave a comment to let your friends know about how it might benefit them too. The book's website will give you access to all of the downloads mentioned in the book, and if you visit the *Shop* I have compiled a list of books that I think will help you on your journey. The *Shop* also has all of the items mentioned in the book listed in one place for your convenience. Just click on *Mentioned in the Book* over on the right hand side of the *Shop* page.

Finally I would love to hear about your successes using the techniques in this book, so please leave me a message there, or email me.

You can email me at enquiry@self-hypnosis-mastery.com

Many thanks for spending your valuable time with me, & good luck.

###

Connect with me online

You can find out a little bit more about me here.

Websites:

www.HypnosisIsEasy.com

www.self-hypnosis-mastery.com

www.chakras-for-health.com

Twitter: @m_hadfield

Give me a Like on **Facebook:** Hypnosis is Easy

If you have enjoyed this book then please let me know on my facebook page.

My blog: http://HypnosisIsEasy.com/wordpress/

email: enquiry@self-hypnosis-mastery.com

More Books by the Author

How to Lose Weight Easily - and Free Yourself from Diets Forever

The big question is how *can* you lose weight without dieting?

The big problem is trusting that something new will work.

But consider this: there is a multi-billion dollar diet industry that depends on diets failing in order for that industry to survive. Diets can temporarily help you to lose weight, but they mess up your metabolism and create such a strong sense of social isolation and craving for denied foods that most people give up long before they hit their target weight. Study after study shows that diets cause long-term harm and weight gain.

How to Lose Weight Easily does not ask you to deny anything, so craving cannot be experienced. It does ask that you make some changes, but, of course, you realise that unless you do something different then your weight will remain unchanged.

You are guided gently through the process of understanding your relationship with food and how to make the small changes that accumulate into a large weight loss. These small changes are easy and sustainable so that you can maintain them forever without any hardship or denial.

It does sound too good to be true, but it works if you follow the guidelines laid out in the book. *How to Lose Weight Easily* has a simple 10-step action plan for you to follow.

When you follow this action plan you will lose weight.

Free Chapter:

The following is a free chapter for you from How to Lose Weight – and Free Yourself from Diets Forever.

Here's What I Can Do For You.

I've written this book to help you lose weight. So if you are serious about losing weight and prepared to make some small, easy changes, then I am certain that this book will help you to get what you want. But you need to want it enough, and you need to believe that it is possible for you to lose the weight you want to lose.

I had a call the other evening from a potential client wanting some information about the weight loss program I offer. As I was talking to her and mentioning some of the things I touched on above, I could hear her enthusiasm growing as I spoke to her. She recognised that she was finally talking to someone who truly understood the problems she had encountered in the past when trying to lose weight.

I explained to her that the key to success is determination.

That caused a little reticence, and I could *feel* her withdrawing from the conversation, so I explained what I meant by determination. Determination isn't the same as failing and then trying again; then failing again and trying again, and still failing. Determination is knowing that success is inevitable because you are going to keep going until you arrive. It's just making a decision that you know you are going to stick to. In the story about my current episode of weight loss I said I wasn't sure how long I'd been doing this for. The duration wasn't important because I was determined to lose the excess. For me determination is just an inner knowing that I will reach the target. With that, I don't need a timescale. In fact I believe a timescale is counter-productive. Once you accept that success is inevitable, you cannot fail. Once you keep a goal permanently in mind, the past is irrelevant.

All that matters is whether or not what you are doing right now is consistent with your goal. If it isn't you have the choice to change it. And, in a nutshell, that's exactly what I'm going to teach you how to do.

If losing weight the old way was easy you'd surely have done it already. But you keep on doing it and failing. You might lose weight and keep it off for a while, but sooner or later it returns and you find yourself back on the hamster wheel. And of course there's all that food you really, really enjoy but is so fattening and so delicious and it would be just a horrible life sentence never to be able to eat that stuff again.

And you always want to eat. And you've failed so many times you have almost no expectation of success. You want someone to wave a magic wand and make it all go away. I know it's easier to believe in magic than to believe in yourself, and a lot of people who come to me for help really want magic. Sometimes the results are *like* magic, but most of the time it's the two of us working together to achieve the desired results.

So, knowing that I usually achieve the desired result, what if I told you that you *can* lose weight? What if I told you that you *can* keep it off? What if I told you that you can not only do this, but also eat what you want when you want?

If you are as sceptical as I am then you probably think that's too good to be true and would be very wary. I don't blame you - it certainly sounds like some sort of scam.

You know what they say… if it's too good to be true - it probably isn't.

It only sounds too good to be true because the difficulty is not where you think it is. What would be too good to be true would be if I were telling you that you can carry on exactly as you always have done and I will still help you to lose weight. But that isn't what I'm saying. I'm saying I know how to make the necessary changes you need to make in order to lose weight and those changes will not only be changes in your eating patterns, but also changes in your thought patterns about food.

But, and this is most important, those changes do not need you to ban any particular foods. And because there is no ban on any particular foods we banish cravings completely. We completely eliminate the battleground, so there is no battle. You will not suffer. You can eat what you want, but you will eat less of it and still feel satisfied if you follow my guidance. I need to stress that the 'eating less' isn't any kind of a trick, or a way to turn this into a calorie-reduced diet. The eating less is discovering that most of the food you eat is eaten unconsciously and not enjoyed - or even noticed most of the time. I encourage you to eat consciously, enjoying and savouring every mouthful until your body tells you that it has eaten sufficiently - for now. I encourage you to eat when you are hungry. I certainly do. While I was losing those 12lbs I mentioned earlier, I enjoyed cake, chocolate biscuits, chips, apple pie, crisps and other forbidden foods. There was no deprivation and so no craving. In fact I'm finding, as I continue with this process, that I'm experiencing a loss of interest in food. Life isn't about food. Life isn't about all the food you will miss if you attain and sustain a healthy weight. If food is your only pleasure, then you really need to start exploring other sources of creative stimulation and entertainment, because if that really is what your life revolves around then you may find it difficult (not impossible though) to release your attachment to it. If you've dragged a ball and chain around all your life, then freedom may make you feel uncomfortable and strangely light for a while.

That reminds me of a story I read about how they train elephants in India. If you want to picture in your mind something big and heavy, an elephant is a pretty good candidate. A full grown elephant, as I'm sure you realise, is a beast to be reckoned with and not an animal that a puny human could tell what to do. After all, when elephants get mad, they can pick up a person and dash them to the ground as though they were a rag doll. But elephants are animals that are trained for forestry work and their mahouts have little difficulty getting them to haul heavy logs, or anything else they want them to do. And do you know how they stop them from wandering off at night? They fasten a stake to the ground and tie the elephant's leg to it with a bit of rope. The interesting thing is that if the elephant just walked away, the rope would snap, or the stake would pull out of the ground. The stake and rope do not actually secure the elephant, because they are nowhere near strong enough. What makes the rope and stake work is an idea in the elephant's mind.

The mahout starts with the elephant when it is very young, and ties it to a stake. The stake and rope are sufficiently strong to prevent a baby elephant from getting away. But the baby elephant pulls and struggles against the restraint until it eventually learns that it is a waste of time. Then the elephant gives up. It knows that it is pointless pulling against the rope - so it stops. And it *never* pulls against the rope again. The elephant grows up, but doesn't realise that rope and stake don't. It doesn't continue to test them as it gets bigger. It believes it is not free and behaves accordingly. As soon as the rope is placed around its leg when work is finished for the day, the elephant just stays put.

This is a demonstration of the power of conditioning. You can experience something in childhood and believe it to be true for the rest of your life. You can feel overwhelmed, or believe that something is impossible, and that belief can be so powerful that you never bother to test it out and see if it is still true for you. How much of your inability to control your eating is down to you constantly telling yourself that you can't? If this is true for you, you might consider changing that message slightly and just start telling yourself 'I don't know how to control my eating yet?'

When you approach losing weight the right way – the way I'm teaching you – you may discover that it can be even easier than you thought. I believe it is possible for you to have what you want. I say this because, over the years, I have helped many people to have what they wanted. There is one thing I need to stress though. If you are in your 30's or 40's or 50's and very overweight it is unlikely that you will return to being the sylph-like 16 year old you once were. So be realistic in your aims. If you are realistic you can do it and you can succeed. If you are unrealistic with your target weight then all you do is set yourself up for failure and disappointment. So, aim initially to lose 10lbs or 20lbs (or to drop one clothes size) - even if you want to eventually lose much more than that. That way you can enjoy success when you hit your target and you can enjoy *that* success and all it brings with it. Then, knowing that you now know how to achieve a target weight, or clothes size, you can set another target of 5lbs or 10lbs and succeed at that. When you break this process into manageable chunks you enjoy success after success after success and the whole weight loss process just becomes an enjoyable game. A game where you win every single time you play.

Sound good?

Are you ready to succeed?

Okay, so now we get down to the nitty gritty - what exactly do you have to do that's different from everything you've tried in the past and how will it help you to lose those excess pounds?

###

Chakra Balancing - 7 Easy Steps to Improved Health & Well Being

There are seven major energy centres in the body. They act like valves controlling the flow of energy throughout the body. Life experiences can pinch off this flow in some areas, causing others to overcompensate. Too much, or too little, energy flowing through the chakras leads to physical and emotional problems – anything from a headache, to severe pain, or even life-threatening disease.

Chakra Balancing explains what the chakras are and how, by following seven simple steps you can take back control of your life and, possibly for the first time, start to feel that you have control. The author shows you two different ways to assess your chakra health and three different methods of restoring balance and then moving towards optimal chakra functioning.

Free Chapter:

The following is a free chapter from Chakra Balancing.

Symptom Treatment or Healing?

Undoubtedly there is a lot of information out there about chakras, healing, balancing, and energy systems. But when I started to look I found it was all a bit of a mishmash. I even found contradictory information. So, especially if you are new to this, it is very difficult for you to discover what you need to know. This difficulty becomes critical if you have a specific problem that you are seeking help for.

Help is something that so many seek from our Health Professionals and discover that the help they expect is just not available. They also discover that Western Medicine cannot solve what, quite often, appear to be simple problems. In fact, I was watching a TV programme a couple of evenings ago that was all about the antibiotic problem. You are probably aware that antibiotics have been over-prescribed for decades. They are frequently prescribed for non-bacterial problems and fed routinely to farm animals - so you even consume them in the meat you eat. This over-use has resulted in the evolution of highly resistant strains of bacteria that kill. These strains developed purely as the result of the over-use of antibiotics.

What was suggested in this programme is that in as little as five, or maybe ten, years, routine operations – such as hip replacements – will no longer be offered because it will be impossible to protect you from bacterial infections in the surgical wound and you will die as a result of your pain-relieving operation.

Surgery is finished.

So as each year passes it becomes clearer that Western Medicine can no longer maintain the pretence that it has all the answers. Consequently there is a very real need to begin to take alternative viewpoints seriously. It is now obvious that to treat the body as a series of unconnected bits – any one of which could go *wrong* – is no longer acceptable.

Another problem, when you seek alternative solutions, is the information overload. There is so much of it readily available that it is difficult to know where to start. Then, when you do an internet search, what usually comes up first are ten pages of people trying to sell you stuff you don't want before you even begin to find the occasional source of helpful information.

Western Medicine is failing to provide what is needed. I know many people who suffer from chronic, disabling pain and all the doctors are able to do is supply medication that takes the edge off the pain but does nothing to heal the problem at the source. People go into hospital and come out with problems they didn't have when they went in.

I live in a town of 60,000 people. We have 17 pharmacies and 40 doctors in general practice. I had occasion to take a friend to see a doctor recently. The waiting room was so full there were patients standing in the corridors waiting to see a doctor. This is in a practice where you need an appointment to get in!!!

Western Medicine is *not* able to stem the tide of disease. But then, with 17 pharmacies and 40 doctors to support in a comfortable lifestyle (and I haven't counted the doctors in the town's hospital), where is the interest in healing? Good health puts them all out of work!

I remember when I was growing up back in the 60's the news and TV programmes would be full of all the amazing things that medicine would cure by the end of the century – along with the promise of free electricity, courtesy of nuclear power, and free gas, courtesy of the newly discovered North Sea Gas fields. It has eradicated just two diseases in the past 50 years - smallpox and rinderpest. But we still have cancer, tuberculosis, flu, common cold, arthritis... the list is a long one.

It is time for a new approach, one that incorporates the best of everything yet is not driven by the need to finance the hungry maw of the billion dollar pharmaceutical industry.

There is a need for simplification; for someone who knows, and can explain, how to begin that process of moving towards what you want. Someone who is willing to show you just how to get to where you want to be.

The people who win out and get what they want are the people who embrace a broader outlook on health and well-being. It is not a newer outlook though, for these ideas about the body's energy system predate Western Medicine by several thousand years. But it *is* new to us in the West.

Embracing these ideas and working with chakras is not an all or nothing choice. The winners take the best of both worlds and use what works for them. I remember when I broke my wrist about 12 years ago, I was very grateful for the Western medics who x-rayed my wrist, diagnosed the problem, and provided plaster and later a wrist support. But in all that I never took any medication for pain. I used my mind to deal with that.

I have spent the last 20 years exploring the world of complementary and alternative medicine. There are undoubtedly quacks out there. There are systems that work largely through suggestion while pretending to work some other magic. Yet there are some that consistently produce results without needing to believe in them. Hypnosis is one of these. Working with Chakras is another.

I write from personal experience.

My starting point was that I became aware that science did not have explanations for some of the experiences I was having. I became aware that my mind, and everyone else's mind too, was not confined, nor constrained, by the bone walls of the skull. I enjoyed some success healing others with nothing more than my hands held a few inches away from their body and my mind focusing on their wellness. While I was doing this I became aware that, with my hands, I could feel something of them a few inches away from their body. I can best describe this as a cushion of energy. In people who were struggling emotionally this did not extend very far – barely an inch – in people who were well it extended much further out.

I also discovered that within this cushion of energy I could sense temperature differences. There were hot spots and cold spots. When I worked on these areas to restore the temperature to normality, I found the problem they had eased.

This was my introduction to working with the Human Energy Field.

That was when I became seriously curious about chakras.

That was also when I began using a pendulum to assess chakra condition. What I found was that it related very closely to the state of physical health and well-being. After identifying problem chakras I found that working directly with them brought about immediate health benefits.

But that left me with a problem. The problem was to find a way for everyone to be able to assess and change their own chakra health without any need to involve anyone else – unless of course they wanted to. So I started to work on that and in the next chapter I will tell you how I discovered the solution.

###

Audio recordings

Chakra Meditation CD

In this visualisation, you are guided on a deeply relaxing journey into the heart of your own energy system. Hypnotic music drifting quietly in the background eases you into a receptive state where you can connect with and remove blockages to the free flow of the energy within you. Each chakra is visited in turn as you fill yourself with a rainbow of colour.

Spirit Guide Meditation CD

This is my most popular download, and my biggest seller (in CD form) at health fairs and shows. I receive a great deal of positive feedback about the pleasure that this recording brings to those who listen to it. The visualisation facilitates connection with your Spirit Guide by creating a peaceful and relaxed mind state followed by a meeting with your Guide.

A selection of Hypnosis & Meditation audio MP3 downloads are available at http://www.hypnosisiseasy.com/downloads.htm

Resources

The Power of Now *Eckhardt Tolle*

Will Power Rediscovering our Greatest Strength *Roy F Baumeister & John Tierney*

The Journey *Brandon Bays*

Getting Well Again & The Healing Journey *O. Carl Simonton* M.D.

Peace, Love and Healing *Bernie Siegal*

Quantum Healing *Deepak Chopra* M.D.

Toxic Psychiatry *Peter Breggin* M. D.

What Doctors Don't Tell You *Lynne McTaggart*

The Secret *Rhonda Byrne*

Ask & It Is Given *Esther and Jerry Hicks*

Men are from Mars, Women Are From Venus *John Gray*

Why Men Don't Listen and Women Can't Read Maps *Allan and Barbara Pease*

Free recording software:

http://audacity.sourceforge.net/

SELF HYPNOSIS MASTERY
HYPNOSIS FOR PERSONAL
DEVELOPMENT

SELF HYPNOSIS TO REPROGRAM
YOUR SUBCONSCIOUS MIND

Appendix 1

This is a sample script to show you the sort of thing you might want to create for yourself as a recording to help you drift into self hypnosis. You can simply read this into a recording device and then play it back to yourself whenever you want to do some self-hypnosis work. If you have no idea how to go about making your own recording email me at :

enquiry@self-hypnosis-mastery.com

and I will send you some information.

But to make it really easy I have made an MP3 recording of this script for you so that you can hear an example of how to deliver it. The pacing is important. After listening to this example you can feel much more confident about making your own recordings. However, in order that you are able to gain the maximum benefit from this download, I have added some relaxing music in the background. The music continues for 10 minutes after I have finished reading the script. Because of this you can listen to this to take yourself into a trance and then, while the music plays quietly in the background you can do your self-hypnosis trance work. When the music stops you will know that you have been working for ten minutes and that maybe it is time to bring yourself back into full waking awareness. I make just a nominal charge for this recording to help cover the costs of my download service.

You will find the download at:

http://www.self-hypnosis-mastery.com/html/script-sample-audio-mp3.htm

where you will find details of how to obtain your copy.

Instructions about how to deliver the script are in italics and are not meant to be read aloud.

Pauses are indicated by ... the pause should be long enough to mentally re-read the preceding phrase. This gives the mind sufficient time to process the instruction.

Speak in a relaxed, calm, unhurried manner.

Make yourself comfortable... Place your feet flat on the floor... Rest the palms of your hands on your thighs as you sit comfortably relaxed... Gently allow your eyelids to close... as you continue to listen to the sound of this voice... Just focus on the sound of this voice... as you continue to listen... Just imagine the words floating softly into your ears... Other sounds drift away into the background of your mind... Other sensations become only a distant awareness... as you continue to listen to the sound of this voice... As you continue to listen... as you continue to focus... on that one sound... you may be aware of a softening of your muscles... a softening of the muscles around your eyes... a softening of the muscles in your cheeks... a softening of the muscles around your mouth... And as your neck muscles start to soften and release their burden of tension... you may find... that your head begins to drop gently backwards against the chair... or forwards onto your chest... and that's fine... don't fight it... just allow it to happen... at its own pace... and in its own time... You may even find that... as the muscles of your face and neck start to soften... your mind begins to drift and wander... and that's fine too... just continue to focus on the sound of this voice... and as you continue to focus on the sound of this voice... just let go of all that tension in the muscles of your arms... allow the muscles of your arms to soften... you may even be aware of a lightness developing in your arms... or even a loss of awareness of your arms... and that's fine... just fine... it really doesn't matter... this is for you... and about you... and whatever you experience is yours... and is special to you... so just allow it to happen... don't fight... just float... just float... and perhaps imagine yourself as a leaf on a gentle stream... floating along... no concerns... no cares... no worries... just enjoying the beautiful countryside as you float gently by... and as you continue to float gently by... become aware of the softening of the muscles of your chest and back... just let it all go... let go of that tension... it's so nice just to be free for a while... and you begin to feel this wonderful softness... starting to spread down into your abdominal muscles... and your abdominal muscles start to soften... start to release all that tension they carry around so often... softer... softer... softening... like a burden being placed on the ground... let go... and that floaty feeling spreads downwards now into your thighs and then on down into your calves and feet... as you continue to be aware of the softening that is taking place...effortlessly...

And now as you continue to relax, breathing freely and easily... drifting... dreaming... wondering... curious... aware of sensations of lightness... floatiness... I'd like you to imagine, as best you are able... that you are standing at the top of a set of stairs... the stairs can be anywhere you like... as long as you feel safe and secure... a grand hall... a garden... an exotic destination... you feel safe and comfortable... and in a few moments I am going to count down from ten to one... and each time I count down... you are going to take a step... and with each step you take you are going to become even more deeply relaxed... and then even more deeply relaxed than that... and when we reach step one and I ask you to step off you will find yourself in a wonderful safe place... so ready now... take that first step... ten...(*count these down at the same pace as your normal breathing so that each number naturally matches an out breath – slower is better than faster*)... nine...eight...seven...six...five...four...three...two...one... feeling deeply relaxed and step off now and find yourself on a wonderful tropical beach (*you can substitute here any place that has positive memories for you – I am simply describing this so that you have an idea of how to word it*) the sun is shining... warm... just the right temperature for you... the sky is a deep blue with a few fluffy white clouds... feel the gentle touch of that warm breeze comfortably refreshing your skin... notice the sand between your toes... and the clothing you are wearing... if you wish... walk down to the water's edge... have a paddle... or a swim if you

like... there is no one here... so you can please yourself... ... ...
hear the sound of sea birds calling... and the gentle sound of palm
leaves in the breeze... you notice a hammock slung between two
palm trees... and a lounger a little further along the beach... take
your pick... and make yourself comfortable as you rest freely and
easily... and your mind drifts and wanders as you...

Appendix 2

Releasing Resistance to Change

Relax as best you can.

Imagine your life as it would be if you were free of this problem.

Live that life fully in your imagination.

Use all of your senses as best you can – in just the same way that you create a fantasy in your mind.

Incorporate whatever lifestyle changes you expect to occur. Greater income, better job, more (or less) time with family, more (or less) socialising, better (or worse) holidays...

Explore all aspects of how you expect your life to be if your problem is released totally and completely and you are free forever.

While you are engaged in this fantasy pay particular attention to your emotional state. Notice when negative emotion (anxiety, stress, worry, concern, anger, sadness etc.,) arises. When it does, open your eyes, make a note on the appropriate page and then return to the fantasy. Also notice if any negative thoughts arise (I can't have that, I don't deserve that, that will never happen, it's all just a fantasy...). Make a note of them also and then return to the fantasy.

So write down the date, what it was you were imagining and what you felt or thought about it. You may have several entries for one session. Do this daily and keep a record of each session.

If you miss a day then make an entry for that day anyway and record the reason you chose not to do the exercise.

All of this is valuable information (even not doing it) that will help you to overcome your resistance to living the life you desire.

Spirit

Appendix 3

Just How Ill Are You?

(Remember this is just a game to play in your mind).

If you were guaranteed a cure what would you be prepared to do in order to have it?

For this Thought Experiment each of these questions guarantees a cure.

So, in order to become completely well, would you be prepared to:

(Answer each question yes or no.)

Change your job?

Move house?

Move to another town where you have no friends or relatives?

Move to another country?

Change your diet?

Live on a seriously restricted diet e.g. no Dairy products, or no Wheat products?

Go on a retreat for a month?

Go on a retreat for six months?

Spend two hours each day in meditation?

Spend four hours each day in meditation?

Leave your partner?

Leave your children?

Change most of your attitudes to yourself?

Change most of your attitudes to others?

Stop judging others completely?

Stop judging yourself completely?

Stop feeling guilty – no matter what you have done?

Change your religion? (if you have one) *or* Take up a religion? (if you don't have one)

Give 5% of your earnings to a charity of your choice – for life?

Give 50% of your earnings to a charity of your choice – for life?

Spend two hours each day in rigorous exercise?

Experience a prolonged physical illness in order that you can confront and be free of your fears?

Become homeless and live on the streets?

If you have missed out any answers, then go back and complete all the questions.

I will not be asking you to do any of these things. All I will be asking you to do is to look at the way you think. But consider this, if you have ticked many more 'no's' than 'yes's' in the above table – *are you really ready to change the way you are and become well?*

You will notice that there are no easy questions in this table. There are no questions that can be given a 'yes' without a moment's thought. This is quite deliberate. But the questions are simply an opportunity for you to look at those things that might be keeping you where you are, an opportunity to consider some things that might be maintaining your 'unwell-ness'. The questions are designed to invoke a 'fear' response.

You have come to me for help and you immediately find yourself being asked questions that, if you take them seriously (*and I seriously suggest that you should at least seriously consider them*) are quite threatening. Leaving your job, moving to a place where you don't have any friends, sitting cross-legged on the floor for hours each day... but the important point to remember is that, in this Thought Experiment, doing what the question asks makes you better. So the questions simply provide an opportunity to see how much you value your **unwellness**. If you have answered 'no' to every question then it would seem almost as if you would rather be unwell than to make any effort at all to become better.

But I will leave you to ponder on that one for now.

~~~

Printed in Great Britain
by Amazon